ADVANCES IN
COLLECTION DEVELOPMENT AND
RESOURCE MANAGEMENT

Volume 2 • 1996

ADVANCES IN COLLECTION DEVELOPMENT AND RESOURCE MANAGEMENT

Editor: THOMAS W. LEONHARDT
University of Oklahoma

VOLUME 2 • 1996

JAI PRESS INC.

Greenwich, Connecticut   London, England

Copyright © 1996 JAI PRESS INC.
55 Old Post Road No. 2
Greenwich, Connecticut 06836

JAI PRESS LTD.
38 Tavistock Street
Covent Garden
London WC2E 7PB
England

All rights reserved. No part of this publication may be reproduced, stored on a retrieval system, or transmitted in any form or by any means, electronic, mechanical, photocopying, recording, filming or otherwise without prior permission in writing from the publisher.

ISBN: 0-7623-0097-3

Manufactured in the United States of America

CONTENTS

LIST OF CONTRIBUTORS   vii

INTRODUCTION   ix

A PREREVOLUTIONARY COLLEGE ENTERS
THE COMPUTER AGE: HISTORIC BUILDINGS,
FIBER OPTICS, AND FACULTY ATTITUDES TOWARD
ONLINE LIBRARY RESOURCES
   Caroline Hunt and Katina Strauch   1

PROMISES AND PERILS FOR TRADITIONAL
INTERLIBRARY LOAN SERVICES
   Sue O. Medina and William C. Highfill   27

COLLECTION DEVELOPMENT AND
DOCUMENT DELIVERY: BUDGETING FOR ACCESS
   Millie L. Syring and Milton Wolf   49

INCLUDING ACCESS IN CONSPECTUS METHODOLOGY
   Rebecca C. Drummond and Mary H. Munroe   63

USING THE WLN CONSPECTUS TO ASSESS
A LAW LIBRARY COLLECTION
   Elizabeth Thweatt   81

A COLLECTION ASSESSMENT MODEL:
A CASE STUDY AT THE GANSER LIBRARY
   Sarojini Lotlikar   93

USING THE WORLD WIDE WEB FOR ELECTRONIC
SERIALS COLLECTION DEVELOPMENT
   Brian Quinn   105

COLLECTION DEVELOPMENT AND
MANAGEMENT IN THE DIGITAL LIBRARY
    Sally Jo Cunningham   127

THE TEAM APPROACH TO THE MANAGEMENT OF
A GOVERNMENT DOCUMENTS COLLECTION
    Eileen Theodore-Shusta and Ray Wang   139

TOTAL QUALITY MANAGEMENT, CULTURE, SYSTEMS, AND
CUSTOMER SERVICE: APPLICATIONS
FOR COLLECTION DEVELOPMENT
    Theresa C. Trawick and Rhae M. Swisher, Jr.   147

COLLECTION DEVELOPMENT: A COLLABORATIVE EFFORT
    Cynthia H. Shabb and Judith L. Rieke   181

DUPLICATES EXCHANGE UNION: FROM
WORLD WAR II TO THE WORLD WIDE WEB
    Rebecca House Stankowski   197

NATIVE AMERICAN AND CHICANO VIDEO AND FILM:
TOWARD A NEW MODEL FOR COLLECTION
DEVELOPMENT IN ACADEMIC LIBRARIES
    Ann M. Massmann   207

PROMPTCAT: AN EARLY ASSESSMENT
    Claire-Lise Bénaud and Sever Bordeianu   223

EVALUATING APPROVAL PLAN PROCESSING:
IS PROMPTCAT AN OPTION?
    Barbara Albee and Robin Rohrkaste Crumrin   239

LIST OF CONTRIBUTORS

Barbara Albee	Acquisitions
	Indiana University Purdue
	    University, Indianapolis

Claire-Lise Benaud	Catalog Department
	General Library
	University of New Mexico,
	    Albuquerque

Sever Bordeianu	Serials Cataloging
	General Library
	University of New Mexico,
	    Albuquerque

Robin Rohrkaste Crumrin	Cataloging
	Indiana University Purdue University,
	    Indianapolis

Sally Jo Cunningham	Department of Computer Science
	University of Waikato
	Hamilton, New Zealand

Rebecca C. Drummond	William Russell Pullen Library
	Georgia State University

William C. Highfill	Auburn University

Caroline C. Hunt	College of Charleston

Sarojini Lotlikar	Cataloging Department
	Helen Gansen Library
	Millersville University of
	    Pennsylvania

Ann M. Massmann	Center for Southwest Research
	Central Library
	University of New Mexico

LIST OF CONTRIBUTORS

Sue O. Medina	Network of Alabama Academic Libraries
Mary H. Munroe	Collection Development William Russell Pullen Library Georgia State University
Brian Quinn	Information Services Texas Tech University Library, Lubbock
Judith L. Rieke	Collection Development Health Sciences Library University of North Dakota, Grand Forks
Cynthia H. Shabb	Collection Development Chester Fritz Library University of North Dakota, Grand Forks
Rhae M. Swisher, Jr.	Troy State University
Rebecca House Stankowski	Technical Services Purdue University Calumet, Hammond
Katina Strauch	Collection Development College of Charleston
Millie L. Syring	Document Delivery University of Nevada, Reno
Eileen Theodore-Shusta	Human Resources Coordinator Ohio University Libraries
Theresa C. Trawick	Electronic Services Troy State University
Elizabeth Thweatt	Collection Development Gonzaga University School of Law Library, Spokane
Ray Wang	Government Documents Binghamton University Libraries
Milton Wolf	Collection Development University of Nevada Libraries, Reno

INTRODUCTION:
Thomas W. Leonhardt

The intent in beginning this series was to document current trends in collection development and resource management in their broadest terms with an emphasis on electronic information technology.

We also hoped that we would discover new voices who would share with us their ideas and experiments in the workplace. The authors in this volume provide evidence that we have succeeded in our intent.

Information technology is a theme common to all of the chapters in this volume. Information technology offers challenges and opportunities in collection development and resource management that we could only dream about a few years ago. Thanks to the opportunities and challenges afforded in this electronic age, we can offer new approaches to old problems. Despite the standardization necessary for real progress, the personalities of ourselves, our states and regions, and our institutions dictate that we find our own ways of doing things. Information technology allows more creativity not less, and it is probably going to get better.

Caroline Hunt and Katina Strauch survey the current literature on information technology and higher education and let us know the prevailing attitudes and trends at a historic, prerevolutionary municipal college.

Sue O. Medina and William C. Highfill remind us of the need for standards, protocols, and infrastructure in the world of interlibrary lending and borrowing, especially as unmediated borrowing by patrons becomes more common and necessary.

Millie L. Syring and Milton Wolf look at the other side of document delivery, access on a broad and futuristic scale. They argue that we must begin to budget remote access along with the traditional budgeting for books and serials.

Rebecca C. Drummond and Mary H. Munroe also recognize access to materials outside one's own library as commonplace and suggest that a conspectus approach to access should be as much a part of collection development as the traditional approach to assessing collections.

Elizabeth Thweatt and Sarojini Lotlikar, in separate papers, present case studies of collection assessment using the conspectus approach. Each suggests that within this one tool there is much room for creativity and adaptability.

Brian Quinn suggests some possible selection criteria for electronic serials while explaining some of the problems inherent in this format.

Sally Jo Cunningham is concerned with the subject-specific digital library. As such libraries grow, maintenance and development issues will become critical.

Total quality management (TQM) has not taken the library world by storm despite a great deal of interest several years ago. Even so, Eileen Theodore-Shusta and Ray Wang used TQM's team approach to bring a government documents program into compliance with depository guidelines.

Theresa C. Trawick and Rhae M. Swisher, Jr. describe a TQM team approach to collection development, internal and external cooperation, and improved spirit, pride, and quality.

Cynthia H. Shabb and Judith L. Rieke do not invoke TQM, but they stress the need for campus-wide collaboration if a university is to have a successful collection development program. They rethink some of the things that we tend to take for granted.

Another thing we tend to take for granted is the value of our duplicates, discards, and unwanted gifts. Rebecca House Stankowski presents a brief history of the Duplicates Exchange Union and reminds us that exchanging duplicates, another form of document delivery, is an important way to share resources.

Ann M. Massmann urges us to recognize the inherent value of film and video in representing the strong oral traditions of Native Americans and Chicanos and argues that we need to reflect this value in collection development, cataloging, and teaching.

Finally, Claire-Lise Bénaud and Sever Bordeianu, and Barbara Albee and Robin Rohrkaste Crumrin, in separate papers, describe and evaluate the PromptCat approach to acquiring and cataloging new books. These two chapters should be of interest and help to those considering PromptCat for their institutions.

Thomas W. Leonhardt
Editor

A PREREVOLUTIONARY COLLEGE ENTERS THE COMPUTER AGE:
HISTORIC BUILDINGS, FIBER OPTICS, AND FACULTY ATTITUDES TOWARD ONLINE LIBRARY RESOURCES

Caroline Hunt and Katina Strauch

ABSTRACT

Numerous articles in the professional literature over the last decade have addressed faculty use of computers. Some issues, such as budgeting and training, appear consistent from one institution to another. Faculty attitudes, however, may be less easily categorized than has been thought; surveys at the College of Charleston showed very little correlation between computer usage and seniority, professional field, or background. Institutions should carefully ascertain the attitudes and needs of their own faculty rather than making assumptions based on national norms.

OVERVIEW: THE COLLEGE, THE LIBRARY, THE TECHNOLOGY

Founded in 1770 and chartered in 1785, the College of Charleston is the oldest municipal college in the United States and one of only 13 U.S. colleges to predate the Revolution. "The College," as it is always called, has long combined tradition with innovation. Thus, the College preserved a classical languages requirement until well into this century and has recently revived a special diploma, the *Artium Baccalaureatus*, which may be earned (in any major) by fulfilling a rigorous additional program of classical languages and history. The College has also shown a remarkable ability to adapt to changing times: admitting women (1918), joining the state college system (1970), and initiating a series of master's level programs (1980s and 1990s). The College's entire student population was less than 100 until this century and still under 500 upon entering the state system in 1970. The rate of growth may be demonstrated by the increasing size of graduating classes: 62 in 1963-1964, 125 in 1973-1974, 627 in 1973-1974, and 1,530 in 1993-1994. Keeping pace, the number of roster faculty increased from 28 in 1963-1964 to 112 in 1973-1974, 256 in 1983-1984, and 339 in 1993-1994.

The Robert Scott Small Library houses books, periodicals, government documents, microtexts, and special collections in all subject areas which support the curriculum. The library, with holdings of approximately 466,114 volumes, receives over 2,588 periodicals and is a complete depository for South Carolina state publications and a selective federal depository. The College of Charleston Library was the first academic library in the state to computerize its catalog completely (1986) and has led the way in statewide automation initiatives through CoastNet (a regional electronic network). The libraries emphasize electronic research methods and resources including the Internet, FirstSearch, InfoTrac, the Wilson Indexes, CARL UnCover, and a variety of CD-ROM databases. Despite space problems caused by the institution's rapid growth, the library has consistently offered state-of-the-art research assistance to students and faculty. Inevitably, success in bringing faculty up to date on the new library technologies has been somewhat uneven. We believe that our problems and our solutions differ significantly from those we have read about in other institutions. After an overview of the changing technology climate on campus, we briefly survey the existing literature, then summarize two faculty surveys which we administered a year apart. A concluding section shows how we believe the College of Charleston differs from institutions previously reporting on issues of online resources and makes recommendations for continued progress.[1]

A faculty member who has been at the College for 20 or more years—and there are 50 of these, nearly one-seventh of all faculty—sees today not only a vastly increased student body and faculty roster but a strikingly different campus. The three "original" buildings date back to the antebellum period: Randolph Hall (1828), the Porter's Lodge (1850), and the original library (1857). In addition to building much-needed large facilities—a new library, classroom buildings, a gymnasium, and residence halls—the College bought numerous old houses, moved or reoriented them, and renovated them for faculty offices and other uses during its major expansion in the late 1960s. Today, the main campus consists of nearly 100 buildings, of which nearly three-fourths are old houses. With such a large number of small historic buildings, computer networking is both more essential than at more centralized campuses and far more difficult to accomplish. In 1990, the College installed a fiber optic network between buildings and twisted pair connections within buildings; each academic department and administrative office has at least one connection. Individual faculty and staff members have direct access in some buildings but elsewhere must resort to modems (if cables have not yet been extended from the building's hub to their offices).[2]

While access has expanded gradually, computer resources have grown more rapidly. Three fully computerized classrooms are in constant use. The oldest of these, originally an Apple lab (IIe and IIgs), has been upgraded with Macintosh LCs; it is located in the computer building and serves the School of Education, particularly its Computers for Teachers course. Software available in this classroom includes ClarisWorks, HyperCard, and HyperStudio; the individual computers are also linked through a router to the Academic Computing VAX, Ashley, providing full Internet access. Dr. Robert Perkins, who directs this Demonstration Lab for Assistive Technology, has released time to superintend its use and maintenance. He pointed out to us the necessity for such supervision to maximize effective use of such facilities. (Perkins is also responsible for the new WWW home page for the School of Education. In recent months, an innovative pilot project has paired Perkins's students, who create HyperStudio-generated lessons, with local teachers, who access these computer-aided instructional materials through a dedicated web server.)

Another computer classroom, located in a regular classroom building, is used primarily by the Department of English and Communication and is furnished with Macintosh units and with a variety of instructional software including Daedalus, an interactive aid for composition courses introduced to this campus by Dr. Joseph Kelly, assistant professor of English. A third classroom, with IBM compatibles, is managed by Academic Computing and used mainly by the Department of Computer Science. Beginning in January 1996, a classroom in the library itself became available both for scheduled library instruction and for occasional use by other faculty.

Students have been generally responsive to the computerization of the campus; faculty response, predictably, has been more mixed. (We exclude from these considerations the Computer Science faculty, who are necessarily heavy users and who also have made efforts to help improve computer literacy campus-wide. We particularly admired their home page, which contains a great deal of information in easily accessible form and includes subpages for students. Although their responses to our surveys have been tabulated like those of other faculty, we felt it unnecessary to do any follow-up interviews about departmental attitudes. The reader should bear in mind that "except for Computer Science" applies to many, if not most, of our remarks.)

As an example of uneven faculty response, instructors who teach in the computer classrooms often report little interest in the concept on the part of their colleagues. There are two consistent users of the computer classroom facilities in the School of Education and usually about four in English and Communication. (Neither department has a Local Area Network, which as we explain later may contribute to uneven computer usage by departmental faculty.) In all three areas—education, English, and communication—there is considerable variation in usage within the group of faculty teaching in the computer classrooms. One English professor makes extensive use of the interactive software in teaching freshman composition but does not specifically teach the use of online library resources; two others, however, promote online library services in classes at several levels. In other words, there does not seem to be as direct a connection as we expected between computer literacy (or even computer-aided instruction) on the part of individual faculty members and their promotion of *online library resources* with students.

In 1994-1995, the average roster faculty member was 44.5 years old and had been at the college slightly over 10 years. Newer faculty members come from a wider range of graduate schools than those who have been here 20 years or more, and some have international credentials. Over two academic years (1993-1994 and 1994-1995), we surveyed the faculty to ascertain their attitudes toward, and use of, electronic technologies for teaching and research.[3] (Each year's results were printed in the inhouse computer newsletter, *Cougar Bytes*.) We expected to find the usual correlations between computer usage and age/seniority, as well as between usage and academic discipline. What we actually found was considerably more complicated. One striking aspect of both surveys was the reluctance of many faculty to encourage their students to use electronic resources; also of interest was the tendency of many faculty to prefer print resources even when the same data were available electronically.

REVIEW OF LITERATURE

In reviewing recent literature about the use by university faculty of electronic resources, we observed that libraries were often omitted from discussions of computer-related higher education issues; we also found that, when faculty usage and attitudes were examined, libraries (as opposed to word processing, etc.) rarely appeared as a significant element in that examination. The articles we surveyed fell into three broad groups, dealing respectively with the general impact of computer technology on higher education, with technological literacy and classroom applications, and with faculty usage and attitudes.[4] We also found, unexpectedly, that most other surveys which overlapped ours in their subject matter did not coincide with ours in their results. These discrepancies are discussed in our final section, "Conclusions, Recommendations, and Applications to Other Colleges."

The Impact of Computer Technology on Higher Education

The first group of articles is the most general and, generally, offers the greatest possibilities for differences of opinion. Two provocative examples demonstrate the possible extremes in the discourse. Heterick and Gehl, in "Information Technology and the Year 2020," trace the information age from its beginnings and project the "futuribility" and the anxieties of information technology in society as well as in higher education. Citing as one major trend the methodical digitization of information, Heterick and Gehl predict that "by the year 2020 higher education will be well past the point of seeing information technology as an accretion to the historical way of doing business and will be using the technology to radically change the way society learns."[5] Challenging this kind of optimism is Wisner's "Back Toward People: A Symposium," outlining the communication breakdowns experienced by librarians and faculty in the wake of the information revolution. Wisner argues, "the profession's current focus on technology has compromised academic librarianship's scholarly values, eroded the quality of rhetoric between librarians and patrons, and contributed to the ascendancy of information over knowledge."[6] In contrast to most of the literature, Wisner's article illuminates the dangers to scholarship, and indeed to basic interpersonal communication, of a preoccupation with keeping abreast of new technological developments.

"The New Computing in Higher Education," by Gilbert and Green, discusses embracing the computer age as essentially a competitive initiative. The academic institution functions by presenting its use of technology as inevitably contributing to the workplace and the economy. Considering the growing pains universities experience in implementing new technology, Gilbert and Green validate higher education's impetus toward keeping abreast of new developments as an inescapable consequence of the current "electricity revolution." Ward's "Technology and the Changing Boundaries of Higher Education" explores breaking down boundaries within academe, using technology which allows knowledge to become more accessible to formerly divided factions. Ward considers many of the existing boundaries obsolete and observes that information technology has contributed to this obsolescence. Billington, in "What Is Liberal Education in a Technological Era?" discusses the interdisciplinary propensities of information science across fields as diverse as technology, science, politics, and art. Technology serves as a unifying tool in modern education, linking fields which became isolated by conceptual, geographical disparities in the past and by effecting a broader consciousness among students and faculty.[7]

Financial realities are addressed in "Paying the Digital Piper," by Green, showing the problems colleges and universities face in creating an adjustable budget for the rapidly changing developments in information technology. As Green emphasizes, "colleges and universities have long needed a financial model that adequately addresses short-term (i.e., 3-5 year) capital costs for science labs, computing and technology, and other important, often expensive resources that have a short half-life."[8] Oberlin, also concerned with the lack of appropriate models, admonishes planners not to fall into a "black hole" of unrealistic and inflexible planning but rather to adopt a "life-cycle" approach in "Departmental Budgeting for Information Technology: A Life-Cycle Approach."[9]

Other articles concern the attitudinal impacts of technology in higher education. Hackman's "What Is Going On in Higher Education? Is It Time for a Change?" highlights several turbulent and divisive revolutions currently taking place, especially the gap in communication and cooperation among different groups in academia (resulting both from poor use of information technology and from recalcitrant attitudes toward modernizing antiquated teaching methods and outdated technology). Hackman maintains that the "force of expanding technology" figures as critically in adding breadth to academic reformation as the forces of "increasing gender equality, increasing globalism, and increasing multiculturalism."[10] Gilbert's "If It Takes 40 or 50 Years, Can We Still Call It a Revolution?" suggests that "the transformation of education through the integration of information technology into teaching and learning ... will not happen overnight; it will not be a revolution." Gilbert takes a comprehensive approach to technology integration, drawing from a wide knowledge of common problems and anxieties surrounding effective implementation of technology in institutions of higher education. Despite his observations of typical faculty anxieties over learning and using new technological advancements, Gilbert hopefully observes, "now, many faculty members are thinking of the knowledge base in their fields as dynamic and dependent upon the interaction of scholars, teachers, and learners, not as a fixed 'canon.'"[11]

Another category of articles deals not only with the abstract impact of technology but with specific strategies for implementation. One of the most useful articles concerned a single institution, the California Polytechnic State University at San Luis Obispo: "Moving

Toward the Virtual University: A Vision of Technology in Higher Education," by Baker and Gloster. This article describes Cal Poly's progress toward more effective use of information technology to ensure learning productivity, reduce labor overload, deliver higher quality education and services to students, and amplify the quality of instruction.[12] The authors' methodical approach to effectively and economically integrating complex technology in a way specifically tailored to the needs of Cal Poly provides a model both for reformation in attitudes and for cost-effective use of information technology at other developing institutions (such as the College of Charleston). A parallel article is "A Strategy for Educational Technology in Higher Education," by Adman and Warren, which describes the institutional strategies for integration of educational technology several U.K. universities, requiring "high-level political commitment, varying degrees of financial investment," yielding "significant quantifiable gains in efficiency over relatively short time periods." As Adman and Warren assert, these strategies can be implemented to ensure "that such gains are made without compromising either teaching quality, or the research base."[13] An article discussing implementation in libraries is "The People Speak: The Dispersion and Impact of Technology in American Libraries," by Hauptman and Anderson, relating the results of recent surveys to assess the progress of implementing information technology in American libraries (including college and university libraries). What emerges from these surveys is that "few information workers believe that their facilities contain state-of-the-art equipment as availability of funding tightens throughout the nineties." "Minor reallocations" of funds, Hauptman and Anderson point out, indicate a trend away from those costs which "traditionally ... have eaten up virtually all allocated monies"—that is, personnel, monographs, and serials. While calling for a more careful balance of antiquated materials with new advances, Hauptman and Anderson emphasize that "technologies must be viewed as capital investments with monies raised, allocated, and expended within a short depreciation cycle."[14]

Technological Literacy and Classroom Applications

One group of articles in this category discusses the use of computer-assisted learning in the various disciplines. Green and Gilbert's insightful article, "Great Expectations: Content, Communications,

Productivity, and the Role of Information Technology in Higher Education," takes a pragmatic view. Using the model of the replacement of the slide rule by the calculator, they detail the factors needed to bring about change in instructional productivity, pointing out the differences among disciplines and examining whether technology benefits the instructional environment of a specific discipline. "The Technological Revolution Comes to the Classroom," by Kozma and Johnston, addresses the theories of Herbert Simon and Derek Bok about the effective integration of computer technologies in academia. Kozma and Johnston challenge Bok's predictions that computer technology can be of little use to the fields of moral philosophy, religion, historical interpretation, or literary criticism. Kozma and Johnston are concerned with the ramifications of implementing progressive technology into the academic system, taking into account which educational problems respond best to technological innovation, what role the faculty plays in the process, which organizational arrangements better facilitate integration, and the overall costs of all of these considerations.[15]

Some articles deal more specifically with classroom applications in higher education. DeLoughry's "Expanding Technology Use in the Classroom," in *The Chronicle of Higher Education*, delineates the efforts of the American Association for Higher Education in focusing on how computers can improve teaching and learning. The same author's "Spreading the Use of Technology," also in *The Chronicle*, discusses the AAHE's role in encouraging more active discussion among administrators and faculty about the use of technology at the collegiate level. Luna's "'Technology' and 'Technology Education'—College Students' Definitions" exposes the boundaries unwittingly created by the ambiguous terminology of students, administrators, and faculty attempting to verbalize both concepts and specific machinery within the confusing realm of technological information. Luna explicates the results of a survey which exposes these boundaries and proposes solutions to bridge the gap in communication among those attempting to teach and learn using technological innovations.[16]

A related group of articles examines the importance of computers in secondary education, with implications for colleges and universities. Wright's "Technology Education—The New Basic for the Twenty-First Century" emphasizes the implementation of electronic technology in secondary schools as fundamental to institutions' goals of education. That the use of such technology is so elemental to the success of education at this level strongly suggests the direction universities and colleges should consider in creating a base of resources and technology for a newly computer-literate student body. "Wanted: A New Literacy for the Information Age," by Ross and Bailey, sounds a call to arms for those in charge of determining the future of education (especially secondary schools). Appealing with an urgency which applies also to colleges, Ross and Bailey admonish educators that a failure to address the new literacy could condemn U.S. students to a future dominated by outmoded teaching at every level.[17]

Faculty Usage and Attitudes

Schwieso's "Staff Usage of Information Technology in a Faculty of Higher Education" explicates a survey conducted at the University of Reading (U.K.) to assess the use of information technology by academics. Schwieso lists the questions, analyzes the results, and concludes that many faculty owned their own machines, that most were unable to accomplish original programming, and that faculty attitudes toward information technology tended to be essentially pragmatic.[18] The article provides insight into common anxieties and misconceptions of faculty in American, as well as British, colleges and universities. Another comparative account was "Attitudes Toward Computers and Information Technology at Three Universities in Germany, Belgium, and the U.S." by Leutner and Weinsier, who conducted a survey to "search for intercultural differences or cross-cultural consistency of attitudes in this field."[19] They found that European students tend to prefer non-computer over computer-based subjects, while American students displayed no such preference.

"Electronic Information Technologies and Resources: Use by University Faculty and Faculty Preferences for Related Library Services," by Adams and Bonk, was the most relevant to our specific situation. Their extensive survey, conducted at the four graduate University Centers of the State University of New York, dates from the fall of 1992 and was "designed to assess faculty needs for access to computer equipment, databases, electronic information resources, and materials not in the library collections." A priority was "to determine the present state of readiness of faculty to utilize electronic/

networked information resources." The response rate was 27 percent (out of 3,713 surveys distributed). Adams and Bonk found that over half their respondents used e-mail and online library catalog resources from office or home; other uses (electronic journals, abstracts, catalogs of other libraries) were less often used. Obstacles to faculty usage included lack of hardware, of software, of training, of information on databases, of operating funds, of interest or need, and of time; from this array, "lack information on databases" emerged as the major obstacle, followed by "lack training." These problems, as well as the difficulty of promoting usage among faculty who were not networked, corresponded to our findings. Although there are parallels between the findings of the SUNY survey and ours, there are also significant differences. First, the correlation between discipline and online usage did not match our results; in the SUNY survey, only 55.4 percent of humanities faculty had computers versus 85 percent in the social sciences and 90 percent in sciences; similarly, only 34.3 percent of humanities faculty were networked versus 63.3 percent in the social sciences and 84 percent in sciences (123). At the College of Charleston, these differences between disciplines barely existed. (Professional schools were included in the SUNY survey, a category which did not apply to us.) Further, Adams and Bonk found that frequent use of online resources was "in inverse correlation to rank ... the percentage of assistant professors who frequently use [these resources] ... is between 10 and 15 percentage points higher than their full professor colleagues."[20] We expected, but did not find, a similar ratio.

A different kind of faculty survey, conducted by Bane and Milheim, measured rates of Internet use by computer-literate faculty. In their article, "Internet Insights: How Academics Are Using the Net," Bane and Milheim conclude that the net is popular among computer-literate faculty for "doing business": maintaining quick communications among individuals and groups, conducting research through Internet database access, and transferring material from sites such as NASA. As the authors emphasize, the advantages voiced by those who actively use the Internet include its capacity to "overcome barriers of time and distance for distribution of highly specialized resources.... It is democratic, breaking down barriers of status and gender."[21] Noted as disadvantages of using the net are the necessity of specialized knowledge for proper use of the system (which inhibits those already anxious about beginning the process), the lack of security for network communications, "heavy traffic" in connecting with frequently used sites, costs of connectivity, under-utilization of Internet capacities, and a lack of central directory to network resources. Despite such disadvantages, the authors project the popularity of the Internet will continue to increase as more academics come to consider the Internet as ultimately essential to their jobs.

A faculty-usage article concentrating on the humanities is "The Humanist and the Library: Promoting New Scholarship Through Collaborative Interaction Between Humanist and Librarians" by Burnette, Gillis, and Cochran. The authors differentiate humanities scholars as inherently more private in their research habits, making it more difficult to keep them current in developments in information technology. Because humanists tend to work alone (without assistants), to develop their own means of finding information (not always effective), and to hesitate to seek assistance, they face unique difficulties. Another analysis of problems in faculty attitudes was "Faculty Uses of Computers: Fears, Facts, and Perceptions" by Hirschbuhl and Faseyitan, which explores faculty lack of confidence and motivation in an increasingly technical age and recommends appropriate training for faculty to compensate for anxiety and for the pressures associated with becoming computer literate.[22]

FIRST COLLEGE OF CHARLESTON SURVEY (1993-1994)

During December and January 1993-1994, we surveyed faculty to determine their use of computer hardware and software, both on and off campus. We distributed over 300 copies of the survey to academic departments just before the Christmas vacation. By February, we had received 116 replies: 108 from roster faculty, a respectable proportion of the 285 who received the questionnaire, and eight from adjuncts.

Hardware

The results indicated a wide range of equipment, knowledge, and uses. The first set of questions brought 48 different answers for the workplace machine and 45 for home equipment (plus 14 that we could not classify). It was apparent from the nature of the answers that many users did not know what they had in their offices: replies like "IBM WordPerfect" abounded. Slightly over 50 persons reported the use of IBM-compatibles at work, while slightly over 40 had some kind of Macintosh; two claimed Unix workstations, and a few were unclassifiable. Proportions at home and "other" (e.g., machines used while traveling) were similar.

Network Access

The second set of questions involved networks and the machines (e.g., VAXes) that give access to them. For on-campus computers, the largest number of faculty cited access to Ashley (88), followed by Wando (36), Cooper (23), Stono (17), and Sun (2). (Ashley, Wando, and Cooper are VAXes named after local rivers; since our survey, two more rivers are represented by new VAXes primarily serving students, Edisto and Folly.) One respondent apiece cited Jove, Zeus, Novell Teaching Network, and Wizzard Zone (CSCI) Mac Network. External networks cited were CompuServe (4), Prodigy (1), America Online (6), and of course Internet (10), the last one presumably omitted by many respondents who had already cited Ashley, the usual Internet gateway; subsequent answers showed far more than 10 people using Internet. Single users also reported Psychology Network, Fred Mail, SERVE, and AppleLink. So far, there were few surprises. The last question, however, revealed a ratio of 53 users with network connections compared to 50 with dial access, while 17 respondents said they had no access at all. We had expected a higher percentage of faculty to be "wired" into networks.

Usage

Moving to "What do you use these for?" we found that e-mail users outnumbered library resource users almost 2 to 1 (64 to 34), while only 21 people cited Internet usage. No other use was in (and most did not approach) double digits. Uses included generic activities like "teaching courses" (9), "administration" (6), "work" (2), and "professional work" (1), as well as "research" (6), "scholarly discussions" (1), and "databases" (3); somewhat more specifically, users mentioned "tests" (1), "math programs" (1), and "scientific computations" (1); "SIS" (6), "student records" (4), "advising" (4), "enrollments" (1), and "monitoring class roles [sic]" (1); "statistical analysis" (1), "run SPSS," (2) and "data analysis" (2). Single users reported other applications ranging from "Chit-Chat" and "USA

Today headlines" to "letters," "bulletin boards," and simply "personal." Of those responding affirmatively to the network question, 64 said that they used these resources in their own research; 20 said they did not. Surprisingly, the highest numbers were for "e-mail to keep in touch with other researchers" (8) and "communicate with other researchers" (7), with lower numbers going to the actual research, such as "bibliographic resources" (2), "data analysis" (4), "mathematical modeling" (1). However, seven people reported "library research," six used FirstSearch, and there were citations of "search holdings at other institutions" (2), "check database elsewhere," and "literature searches" (1). One person reported simply "background research," and one liked to "send drafts of papers."

The most disheartening responses came in the next section, to the question "Do you encourage your students to use these resources in their coursework?" Only 54 replied in the affirmative, while 61 said no. Of these, many actively *discouraged* students from using network resources, for reasons ranging from assumptions that only advanced students need these skills to "it would clog up Ashley." We were surprised by these answers, particularly since many of them came from faculty who were themselves quite computer-literate. As a group, the computer science, mathematics, and business faculty who responded showed the greatest willingness to introduce students to these resources; these were followed by psychology, education, philosophy, and biology.

Network Applications

Network uses, the next section, provided more predictable answers. Internet had 81 positives, matched by e-mail, both inside (81) and outside (82) the college. Library resources in general netted 61 users, with specific applications showing that FirstSearch (42) far outstripped CARL (4). (We suspected that many people are unaware of the instant ordering capabilities, by fax, available through CARL.) Bitnet Discussion groups were mentioned by 28 respondents, a figure which we believe is in fact much higher.

Only 27 people reported that they had a LAN in their department; of these, two seemed unsure of what this meant. Of the remaining respondents, 39 said they had no LAN, and 34 answered, "do not know what it is." Since so few have a LAN, it was not surprising that 37 respondents replied "none" when asked about specific databases on the LAN, while another 24 said "don't know." The only databases mentioned were D-base (2), Sigma plot (1), and Systat (1).

Print Versus Non-Print

We then surveyed print resources. Respondents named 48 separate professional indexes, most highly field-specific. The availability of online reference sources seems not to have affected faculty usage of paper sources as much as one might expect; 31 people said they had been affected "not at all," and only 10 replied "very much." To the question of which format they preferred, responses were clearer: 13 for paper, 31 for electronic, and 58 between, representing people who, according to their comments, cheerfully used both.

Visions of the Future

The final section concerned future resources. A wide range of users included proprietary services (America Online, Prodigy, CompuServe) which would not normally be found on a campus, and many requested databases which we already had: FirstSearch, ERIC, MLA, PsycLit, and National Trade Data Bank, among others. Some, because they were submitted by several different people, overlapped (e.g., Philosopher's Index and WESTLAW). Some excellent suggestions were made, many of which we followed up subsequently.

Conclusions From the First Survey

In the 1993-1994 survey, we found that general computer usage by faculty was uneven. Inevitably, knowledge and usage of online library resources was equally uneven. Some faculty appeared knowledgeable and helpful to others, both students and faculty, who knew less than they did. (Among heavy users, there was some tendency to criticize the institution's organization of its computer networks, equipment, and personnel.) The majority of faculty, those with a moderate amount of knowledge and average usage, seemed unaware of the resources already available and/or hesitant to "share" them with students. Several requested seminars or classes to instruct faculty—a good idea, we thought, as a faculty which does not understand electronic resources can hardly encourage students to use them. Second, we found that the prevalence of modems (and corresponding lack of networked units) was a major problem; faculty members with modems must either restrict their availability to students by telephone or restrict their modem use to hours when students know they cannot dial in—a pedagogically impossible choice. Third, we noted that a comprehensive plan for equipment upgrading and replacement should be developed, as much of the equipment reported to us verged on the antique.

When we concluded our first survey, we believed that the relative seniority (and age) of much of the College of Charleston faculty, as well as the institution's culture of conservatism, contributed heavily to uneven computer usage by faculty. Follow-up interviews with some respondents seemed to confirm this view, though we did discover among the senior faculty some individual heavy users who for various reasons had not responded to the questionnaire. Even at this stage, we noted far less correlation between discipline and attitudes toward computer resources than seemed to be the case at other institutions.

INTERIM: RAISING TECHNOLITERACY VIA THE INFO-FAIR AND RELATED ACTIVITIES

As part of its ongoing effort to familiarize the college community with available resources, the Robert Scott Small Library hosted two Info-Fairs, one in January 1994 and one in September 1994.[23] These events were co-sponsored by the library, the Office of Media and Technology, Academic Computing, and Administrative Computing, all sponsoring separate informational booths. (The first Info-Fair occurred while we were tabulating our 1993-1994 responses, the second between our two surveys.) During the two-day January event, booths in the library promoted information access via online and CD-ROM databases and demonstrated Internet access. Internet overview classes were offered by Academic Computing; the library staff taught a seminar on library online searching and one on accessing the Internet via Gopher. During the September Info-Fair, the library again offered space for booths (sponsored again by a variety of campus offices) promoting information access on new library databases and the significance of the Internet, specifically access via Gopher and Mosaic; multimedia attractions; and new hardware and software options. The September Info-Fair seminars were on library online searching (a repeat) and on World Wide Web access via Mosaic and Netscape (a new seminar). Turnout was good for both fairs, and the Internet classes were always packed—sometimes standing room only. There seemed to be a hunger for information about the Internet. Most classes on library searches, however, were considerably smaller.

Our impression on both occasions was that the Info-Fairs succeeded better with students and staff than with faculty, though faculty were present from most academic departments, these faculty attendees seemed to be either (1) people already familiar with the computer environment and its library applications or (2) people with a moderate amount of exposure who wanted to learn more. The group about whom we had been most concerned—those faculty who appeared to be largely ignorant of online library resources—attended in smaller numbers.

THE SECOND COLLEGE OF CHARLESTON SURVEY (1994-1995)

In November 1994, we sent to new (first-year) faculty the same survey that we had administered the previous year to all faculty. An encouraging number of the new faculty responded; from slightly over 50 copies distributed, we received 22 replies.

Hardware

Again, we found a variety of equipment and a wide range of knowledge about it. The first set of questions produced 17 different answers for the workplace and 17 for the home. Some users seemed not to know what they were using: vague replies like "word processor" and "PC" occurred. Five new faculty reported IBM-compatibles at work, and the same number reported Macs; proportions at home were similar. About two-thirds of respondents said they had access to the campus network, most through modems (10 at the office and 2 at home).

Network Access

The second set of questions involved networks and access to them. For on-campus computers, the largest number of new faculty cited access to Ashley (15), followed by Wando (8), Cooper (4), and Stono (2). One respondent cited Jove. Two external networks were mentioned: Prodigy (3) and America Online (1).

Usage

When we asked, "What do you use these for?" we found that e-mail users, the only category in double figures (12), outnumbered all others. Generic activities such as "research" (2) and "management" (1) were cited, though some respondents were more specific, with "statistical analysis" (2), SIS (1), and "advising" (2). Single users reported applications ranging from "budget" to "news service" and "administrative information." Contrary to our expectations (and last year's results), only two mentioned "library search." This figure went up when we asked directly, "Do you use these network resources in your own research?" To this, three said "no" and another "indirectly"; three said that they "use library catalog to locate books and articles," while one used online resources "only for ILL requests." Other activities mentioned included "acquire basic biological data" (1), "sending/receiving data and papers" (again, surprisingly, only 1), and "contacting grant agencies and colleagues" (2). The most surprising answers came when the respondents were asked, "Do you encourage your students to use these resources in their coursework?" The greatest number (5) again replied in the negative—though two qualified that as "not yet." Only two respondents encouraged their students to use the resources, in both cases for specialized situations; one found the resources a "major component of herpetology class," and the other noted that "grad school applicants can search WWW for info."

Network Uses

The next section on network use produced no surprises. Despite their negative bias toward encouraging students, 11 said that they themselves used Internet, and e-mail was popular both inside (11) and outside (14) the college. Eight cited FirstSearch, and 10 others "library resources." Bitnet had two users, and CARL four. Asked about a network in the department, seven said "no," and three did not know. One each in theater, geology, and psychology replied in the affirmative. In response to the question, "What specific databases if any do you have access to internally on your departmental network?" one did not know, and two said "none."

Print Versus Non-Print

As to print resources, respondents named 18 professional indexes, ranging from "Agricola" to "Oceanic abstracts." In only one case, "biological abstracts," with two users, did more than one respondent use the same field-specific source. The availability of online databases seems not to have affected usage of paper sources among new faculty members; six said they had been affected "not at all," and only two replied "very much." Most (11) were indifferent, with three preferring paper and four electronic. Two-thirds of the respondents (14) seemed happy with either.

Conclusions From the Second Survey

In the final section of our survey concerned with future resources, eight different suggestions were made; nearly half requested databases which, in fact, we already had. In studying the range of responses to the entire questionnaire, we noted with surprise that they virtually echoed the previous year's findings. We had expected new faculty, who as a group are younger than those already here and many of whom came from large university graduate programs, to show more knowledge of computer resources, heavier use, and—most important to us—a greater willingness to encourage students to use those resources. This was not the case.

We also, however, noted several significant differences from the 1993-1994 results. First, the new faculty members were more critical of the limited access available on our campus; presumably, they come from places where this is less of a problem. Second, results were more closely tied to field than in the previous year; the disciplines that traditionally score higher in computer use in nationwide surveys (laboratory sciences, education, computer science, and psychology) scored higher on ours also. In 1993-1994, there had been less correlation between field and usage (except in computer science). Finally, the presence of LANs (e.g., in psychology and business) and/or the existence of a departmental commitment to teaching with computers (e.g., in education, which requires a computer course) apparently increased computer awareness and usage among faculty;

departments which had *both* a LAN *and* a departmental commitment to computer usage (physics, geology) had much higher rates than other departments.

In follow-up interviews in physics and geology, we found department-wide agreement about the use of computers with students—including the use of library resources online. Dr. Jeff Wragg, who oversees the physics LAN, told us that his department covers both computer use in general and library searching in particular in its new Research Seminar for senior majors. The physics LAN has QuickMail, a departmental fileserver, and Internet access; unlike some other departmental LANs, physics includes access for students via computers in the departmental student study room. Physics undergraduates concurred with Wragg's assessment of department-wide usage, as did the department chair, Dr. Robert Dukes, and several other faculty members. Dukes and everyone else who spoke to us spoke with enthusiasm of the resources available on the World Wide Web, particularly access to abstracts and full-text articles in the field. (Interestingly, this usage was not reflected in the survey results from the sciences, apparently because faculty did not connect the web with library-style searching.) A home page for the department was under construction at the time of our interviews.

The Department of Geology also encourages computer-related learning at every level--a commitment of long standing, according to department chair Dr. Michael Katuna. The departmental fileserver (which, like the one in physics, is available to students) has Photoshop, graphing programs, SISTAT and other statistical programs, and spreadsheets. Students and faculty use the SUN/JOVE network, featuring the impressive ERDAS image processing system. Prof. Mitch Colgan of the Remote Sensing Lab described to us both the SUN/JOVE first-generation, IBM-based network and the subsequent Mac-based LAN. The Department of Geology has arranged for an undergraduate to receive bibliographical training through the library's Technical Services division, a project which has improved library research strategies for both students and faculty in the department. Geology also had a home page under construction.

ADDITIONAL LIBRARY EFFORTS

Meanwhile, the library continued its efforts to spread information and create a more favorable climate for computer usage, especially of library resources. Over a three-week period in March and April 1995, the library offered Internet/library searching classes each week. "Snake Handling on the Net: Easy, Valuable, and Fun Internet Searching," a post-beginner class, introduced the variety of Internet resources available via Gopher and, especially, Netscape. "What Is the Internet Anyway?" was designed for complete beginners. It gave a historical overview and explained e-mail, Telnet, FTP, basic Gopher, and the World Wide Web in simple terms. "Finding a Needle in a Haystack: Advanced Library Searching" described keyword and Boolean searching and other advanced techniques. Not surprisingly, "What Is the Internet Anyway" was the most heavily attended offering, and "Finding a Needle in a Haystack" the least. Attendance at all seminars was lower than hoped, probably because they occurred at the end of term when both students and faculty face numerous deadlines. However, a heartening fact was that many seminars had up to 50 percent faculty in attendance, up from previous efforts.

A parallel library effort is a pilot project to put course reserve materials on the college's Gopher. According to Sheila Seaman, Assistant Dean for Public Services, this could simultaneously increase computer usage (and literacy) among undergraduates and help with the ever-present space shortage in circulation, where reserve materials are now housed. A grant proposal is in progress, titled "Planning for the CoastNet Electronic Reserve Room." As a participant in developing regional inter-university networks (such as CoastNet), the institution's graduate school, the University of Charleston, has applied for funding for a "regional electronic reserve room" which could "provide material in a variety of electronic formats" and make use of World Wide Web and related graphical technologies. The project also has the purpose of "addressing unique intellectual property issues inherent in electronic reserve library development," according to the grant proposal sent to the Telecommunications and Information Infrastructure Assistance Program of the National Telecommunications and Information Administration by Dr. Wayne Patterson, Vice President for Research. Meanwhile several documents have been put on the Gopher: for example, previous years' examinations for two courses taught by one of this article's authors (Hunt)—these materials were accessible on disk and posed no issues of copyright.

The College of Charleston page (http://www.cofc.edu) includes an extensive listing for the library, and this library page currently offers links to web sites in the various disciplines as well as giving information specific to the College's library facilities. Plans called for considerable expansion of the library's web offerings for 1995-1996; this has occurred.

Outside of the library other activities were in progress. Prof. John Newell of history was preparing an Internet-oriented course in the Middle Ages for the 1996 Governor's School, a program based at the College which attracts gifted and talented high school students from across the state. The English Department now has a graduate course in research methods, stressing online databases in addition to the traditional material. Several departments have home pages in full operation: those in physics and geology, under construction at the time of our second survey, are now accessible. Computer science has already been mentioned. The Department of Mathematics has a particularly well-developed home page, in which many faculty members offer links to preprints, useful sites, and opportunities for comment and interaction. More surprisingly perhaps, home pages are now available in education (mentioned earlier), political science, languages, and music; the home page for English and communication became accessible in August 1996. Individual faculty members and students also have home pages, in some cases without departmental links as yet. Clearly, the advent of widely available web technology is affecting faculty (and general) attitudes more decisively than any other recent development. Fittingly, the library's exposition for the fall semester 1995 was a WebFest, sponsored by the same group of offices as the earlier Info-Fairs.

CONCLUSIONS, RECOMMENDATIONS, AND APPLICATIONS TO OTHER COLLEGES

At the College of Charleston, although access will continue to be a problem as long as faculty are scattered in numerous small buildings that are not fully "wired," much could be done at little or no additional cost to expand usage of what we already have. The challenge of maximizing resources will probably grow more, not less acute as the College enters a new phase of geographical expansion with the purchase of several new properties: Bishop England school (adjoining to the west), the Southern Bell property (across the street to the north), and a large building a few blocks away on King Street.

Our concern, however, is only indirectly with access. We are interested in expanding the comfort zone for faculty and students to *use* computer resources—particularly online library resources. It now seems likely that this expansion *of usage*—particularly of *usage with students*—occurs most effectively in our institution when an entire department is committed, particularly when pedagogical applications are discussed within the departmental setting. We have therefore recommended at the school level that departments without LANs be encouraged to consider the potential benefits of installing them as funds permit and that departments with LANs assess their use with a view toward expanded effectiveness. We are also encouraging department chairs to initiate discussion of computer instruction (particularly library searching) in department meetings. Finally, we have suggested to the administration that new faculty receive as part of their orientation a more extensive introduction to computer resources.

In terms of the more general application of our findings, we would recommend that other institutions avoid the unquestioning extension of published data of a general nature to their particular institution. For example, most published surveys suggest a correlation between discipline and usage, with the sciences ranking at the top and the humanities at the bottom. We did not find any such correlation; each discipline had some very frequent (and competent) users, and nearly all had some virtual nonusers. At least three humanities/social sciences departments had quite high rates of literacy/usage, while two science departments ranked relatively low. We also, even more surprisingly, did not find the usual inverse correlation between rank/seniority and computer usage, either in general areas or use of library resources. (The sole exception to this lack of correlation appeared to be the Department of Mathematics, in which we observed that the most highly-developed web home pages belonged to relatively young and/or junior faculty. However, computer usage and computer teaching in general appeared to be as evenly distributed in mathematics as everywhere else—certainly not anywhere near an inverse correlation.)

Individual follow-up interviews—possible only in institutions with a fairly small number of faculty—revealed further complexities. We found, for instance, faculty members in several departments who were computer-literate themselves but did not extensively promote use of online resources by their students; in most cases, this was because they felt that other skills were more significant, particularly at the freshman level, and they could not adequately cover everything in a single course. We also found that anomalous individual faculty members isolated in departments of nonusers or light users, like the very senior sociologist who was his department's hardware expert, the professionally-published computer expert in a humanities department, and the two software consultants in another humanities department, were likely to be used as resources by colleagues but less likely to influence others significantly toward increased computer usage. (Interestingly, all but one of these "anomalous" computer enthusiasts were at least 45 years old, and most had been at the College for many years.) Thus, although most of these individuals promoted online resources with their own students, their example did not seem to raise awareness of these resources among their peers. Perhaps coincidentally, many of the anomalous faculty failed to return our survey and were located through follow-up interviews; many years of working in isolation had made them pessimistic about spreading computer literacy, we decided.

Finally, we found that global strategies for increasing usage—the Info-Fairs, for instance—were largely reaching those who were already converts; in contrast, the greatest change in attitudes and usage came from peer influence, either in small groups within departments or at the departmental level. (We also suspect that departments which encourage input from students have an advantage, as nearly every department turned out to have one or more resident student computer experts. Several departments told us that they had made extensive use of student expertise in computer areas.) Thus, departments or subgroups within departments appeared to be the most effective way of spreading knowledge and computer culture, particularly with regard to the use of online resources with graduate and undergraduate students. We conclude that, although decisions about what needs to be done must still perhaps be "top-down," nevertheless faculty training is far more likely to be effective if implemented through smaller units.

NOTES AND REFERENCES

1. Many members of the college community helped with this project; some are mentioned in our paper, while others appear only in these notes. Margaret Ehrhardt, Director of Academic Computing, advised and encouraged us throughout. The College's president, Alex Sanders, read drafts of the individual surveys and the paper, providing helpful feedback.

2. Michelle Smith of Institutional Research provided statistics, and Monica Scott of Facilities Planning helped with architectural information. As of the winter 1995-1996, network expansion is scheduled to furnish virtually every faculty member with a fiber-optic connection.

3. For assistance in collating replies to both surveys, we wish to thank Chris Hendrix, an undergraduate at the College. Seabrook Wilkinson helped to turn the second survey into a report. Both surveys are reprinted here in substantially the form in which they appeared in the College's newsletter from Academic Computing, *Cougar Bytes*, except for the conclusions. Since *Cougar Bytes* is not available outside the College, we have not included these articles in our bibliography.

4. Julie Gates and Seabrook Wilkinson, graduate students in English, assisted in compiling the bibliography of existing literature.

5. Robert C. Heterick and John Gehl, "Information Technology and the Year 2020, *Educom Review* 30 (January/February 1995): 25.

6. William H. Wisner, "Back Toward People: A Symposium," *Journal of Academic Librarianship* 20 (July 1994): 131.

7. Steven W. Gilbert and Kenneth C. Green, "The New Computing in Higher Education," *Change* 26 (May/June 1994): 91-95; David Ward, "Technology and the Changing Boundaries of Higher Education," *Educom Review* 29 (January/February 1994): 23-27; David Billington, "What Is Liberal Education in a Technological Era?" *New Directions for Higher Education* 85 (Spring 1994): 37-49.

8. Kenneth C. Green, "Paying the Digital Piper," *Change* 27 (March/April 1995): 54.

9. John Oberlin, "Departmental Budgeting for Information Technology: A Life-Cycle Approach," *Cause/Effect* 17 (Summer 1994): 22.

10. Judith Dozier Hackman, "What Is Going On in Higher Education? Is It Time for a Change?" *Review of Higher Education: A Bulletin for the Association for the Study of Higher Education* 16 (Fall 1992): 7.

11. Steven W. Gilbert, "If It Takes 40 or 50 Years, Can We Still Call It a Revolution?" *Educational Recor* 75 (Summer 1994): 23, 25.

12. Warren J. Baker and Arthur S. Gloster II. "Moving Toward the Virtual University: A Vision of Technology in Higher Education," *Cause/Effect* 17 (Summer 1994): 4-11.

13. P. Adman and L. Warren, "A Strategy for Educational Technology in Higher Education," *Journal of Computer Assisted Learning* 10 (March 1994): 50.

14. Robert Hauptman and Carol A. Anderson, "The People Speak: The Dispersion and Impact of Technology in American Libraries," *Information Technology & Libraries* 13 (December 1994): 255.

15. Kenneth C. Green and Steven W. Gilbert, "Great Expectations: Content, Communications, Productivity, and the Role of Information Technology in Higher Education," *Change* 27 (March/April 1995): 8-18; Robert Kozma and Jerome Johnston, "The Technological Revolution Comes to the Classroom," *Change* 23 (January/February 1991): 10-31.

16. Thomas J. DeLoughrey, "Expanding Technology Use in the Classroom," *The Chronicle of Higher Education* 40 (May 11, 1994): A16, A20; DeLoughrey, "Spreading the Use of Technology," *The Chronicle of Higher Education* 41 (March 31, 1995): A20; Gaye Luna, "'Technology' and 'Technology Education'—College Students' Definitions." *Tech Directions* 53 (April 1994): 22-24.

17. Thomas Wright, "Technology Education—The New Basic for the Twenty-First Century," *NASSP Bulletin* 78 (September 1994): 24-30; Tweed Ross and Gerald D. Bailey, "Wanted: A New Literacy for the Information Age," *NASSP Bulletin* 78 (September 1994): 31-35.

18. Joshua Schwieso, "Staff Usage of Information Technology in a Faculty of Higher Education," *Educational & Training Technology International: ETTI* 30 (February 1993): 88-94.

19. Detlev Leutner and Philip D. Weinsier, "Attitudes Toward Computers and Information Technology at Three Universities in Germany, Belgium, and the U.S," *Computers in Human Behavior* 10 (Winter 1994): 569.

20. Judith A. Adams and Sharon C. Bonk, "Electronic Information Technologies and Resources: Use by University Faculty and Faculty Preferences for Related Library Services," *College and Research Libraries* 56 (March 1995): 121, 123.

21. Dr. Adele F. Bane and Dr. William D. Milheim, "Internet Insights: How Academics Are Using the Net," *Computers in Libraries* 15 (February 1995): 34.

22. Michaelyn Burnette, Christina Gillis, and Myrtis Cochran, "The Humanist and the Library: Promoting New Scholarship Through Collaborative Interaction Between Humanists and Librarians," *The Reference Librarian* 47 (1994): 181-191; Dr. John J. Hirschbuhl and Dr. Sunday O. Faseyitan, "Faculty Uses of Computers: Fears, Facts, and Perceptions," *T.H.E. Journal* 21 (April 1994): 64-65.

23. Jerry Seay of the Robert Scott Small Library assisted us with drafting both this and a later section on the Info-Fairs and related activities. We have also consulted several other library staffers: Sheila Seaman, Michael Phillips, and Alis Whitt.

PROMISES AND PERILS FOR TRADITIONAL INTERLIBRARY LOAN SERVICES

Sue O. Medina and William C. Highfill

ABSTRACT

Highly structured interlibrary loan practices used to obtain information not available within a library's own resources are changing with increasing volume of requests, application of technology to library functions, widespread availability of information in electronic formats, and the emergence of commercial services marketing information and document delivery to end users. Factors affecting traditional interlibrary loan services and trends forcing libraries to change how information is delivered to users are examined. Formal reciprocal borrowing agreement within library cooperatives is proposed as one solution to strengthen interlibrary loan programs and overcome some perils threatening successful information delivery services in today's libraries. The Network of Alabama Academic Libraries, a statewide consortium, is described as an example of how changes in traditional library practices can improve service.

INTRODUCTION

The commitment of librarians to serve users by retrieving information regardless of where it is housed has fueled rapid growth in interlibrary loan transactions. Theoretically, staff of any library can obtain needed information from any of the libraries and other repositories throughout the world which hold the needed material. Today's librarians rely increasingly on access to remote resources to overcome limited local resources.

As volume and complexity of interlibrary loan activity have increased, so too have the protocols and infrastructure necessary to ensure successful interactions. A basic protocol, the *National Interlibrary Loan Code*,[1] guides transactions for all types of libraries. The electronic messaging systems of OCLC, RLIN, and DOCLine, each framed by protocols for system members, facilitate the efficient placing of requests and the responses they elicit. Members of the regional Southeastern Library Network (SOLINET) have agreed on a protocol for their interactions (SOLINE). Many state library associations maintain their own codes covering lending and borrowing among all types of libraries within the state. Local agreements frequently supplement national, regional, and state codes. For example, transactions among Alabama public libraries are directed by guidelines issued by the Alabama Public Library Service (APLS), lending activity among members of the Network of Alabama Academic Libraries (NAAL) is governed by policies of its Resource Sharing Program, and transactions between public libraries and NAAL members follow procedures specified in an agreement between NAAL and APLS.

Protocols and communication systems improve the likelihood that borrowing requests will result in locating and retrieving information needed by users. Libraries adhering to formal protocols or participating in electronic systems such as that provided by OCLC commit to actions that markedly enhance the success rate of all participants. This paper identifies issues affecting future success and recommends cooperation to improve success in obtaining items via interlibrary lending.

Current trends in interlibrary loan services portend an escalating number of requests. In the future, this greater volume will be accompanied by increased costs for borrowing, fewer libraries offering free or low-cost lending, and the prospect of users sending their own borrowing requests to remote libraries. To help manage the increased demand for interlibrary lending and borrowing, librarians will increasingly rely on electronic systems to place and manage interlibrary loan requests. Librarians will have available and will make greater use of commercial document services, shifting reliance for the provision of information not available locally to the commercial sector from traditional library-to-library transactions. The growing availability of indexing and abstracting databases will increase demand for a greater variety of resources. The nascent full-text and full-image databases, while they have yet to prove their reliability as acceptable substitutes for traditional print publications, may blunt the effect of growing demand somewhat. Finally, increasing financial constraints on libraries of all types will result in libraries that have traditionally lent large numbers of items being unable to cope with the increasing demands placed upon their staffs and resources. They will be unable to acquire current information resources at a level consistent with that of the past. As a result of shrinking collections in individual libraries, library cooperatives will grow more important as libraries must share resources to a much greater extent in their efforts to offer effective information services for users.

ESCALATING NUMBER OF REQUESTS

Relaxed policies governing acceptable interlibrary borrowing requests and the ease with which users can identify a myriad of possible information sources are important factors contributing to the increase in interlibrary borrowing requests. One way librarians have dealt with this increase is to limit the volume of requests they receive by restricting lending to only those libraries with which they have reached formal reciprocal agreements. Thus, a growing number of requests mitigates against an increasing rate of success in obtaining materials via traditional interlibrary loan. Alternatives for library-to-library lending, such as those provided by full-image or full-text databases and commercial document suppliers, may meet demand for many current and selected retrospective serial materials. However, it is unlikely that either will meet the need for most historical items because few materials of this type have been converted to electronic format nor are they likely to be.

The revised *National Interlibrary Loan Code* adopted in 1993 formally relaxed the criteria for acceptable requests by removing restrictions on the types of materials which could be sought and by eliminating restrictions against borrowing for purposes other than support of serious research and study. Concerns have been expressed that the revised code will add to the difficulties already overwhelming willing lenders.[2] In reality, this more lenient policy merely codifies what has become regular practice in many libraries. Nonetheless, librarians who once relied on the *Code* to reduce the volume of borrowing by restricting interlibrary lending to materials used for research purposes will lack the reinforcement and security of an externally-imposed reason for limiting user requests. Staffs of lending libraries, especially those of larger academic and research libraries, can anticipate an even greater number of requests to reach them because they will no longer be filtered to remove requests for items that are not "serious" research materials. An expected response of these librarians already in evidence will be to establish priorities to serve their own lending and borrowing partners and to reject requests from others. Also, some are implementing new fees or raising existing charges in a deliberate effort to encourage borrowers to choose other potential lenders.

If unmediated interlibrary borrowing, or requests placed directly to remote libraries by users, culminates in widespread use, it will certainly influence the volume of interlibrary loan requests. New technology and protocols permitting users to place interlibrary loan requests directly to potential lenders are currently being tested in a number of libraries. Software and advanced telecommunications enable users to browse the bibliographic records of remote collections and initiate lending requests without the intervention of a librarian at the local library.

In Switzerland, users may browse holdings records for collections of remote libraries and purchase coupons allowing them to order photocopies directly from any library in the system. Photocopies are sent directly to users, completely bypassing the local library.

Users of libraries in the Ohio Library and Information Network (OhioLink) can also request items directly from any of the network's 18 members.[3] The Committee on Institutional Cooperation (CIC), representing some of the nation's largest academic libraries, includes a similar initiative in its plans to create a "Virtual Library." OCLC allows end users to request items cited in FirstSearch as well.[4]

Librarians planning unmediated interlibrary loan services anticipate that it will offer faster and easier service to patrons. Patrons will no longer have to locate an interlibrary loan office or fill out printed forms to place a request. Savings are anticipated because library staff will not conduct an initial interview of the patron and will not have to rekey information about the item being sought. As data are collected and experience gained in unmediated interlibrary loan projects, librarians are seeking patron-initiated interlibrary loan software that will verify user eligibility and prohibit sending simultaneous requests for the same item to several different libraries. In addition, they are requesting software capability to permit them to block certain requests, for example, those for articles from periodical issues owned by that local library.

The decision to install software supporting unmediated interlibrary loan activity among the members of a consortium must be supported through carefully negotiated resource-sharing agreements. These transactions have the potential to shift interlibrary loan department workload from borrowing, the primary justification for having the department, to lending. This will make it even more difficult to defend extending interlibrary lending beyond reciprocal partnerships. Consequently, librarians participating in arrangements in which they are expected to respond to direct borrowing requests from remote users may be forced to narrow lending priorities even further.

GROWING MIGRATION TO ELECTRONIC MESSAGING SYSTEMS

More and more, librarians grappling with the enormous growth in interlibrary loan activity can manage it only with the assistance of automation. Librarians can look forward to relying primarily on one or more electronic messaging systems because use of the traditional printed interlibrary loan forms hinders efficiency. Several national and international shared bibliographic database organizations such as OCLC, RLIN, or DOCLine support electronic messaging systems for interlibrary loan. These systems offer substantial advantages over manual methods; for example, locations for needed materials can be identified almost immediately. Messaging systems, because of their links to large online union catalogs, aid in ensuring accurate bibliographic verification and identifying holding libraries. Extensive staff time need not be spent on either of these matters.

Some statewide resource sharing programs are enhanced through electronic messaging for interlibrary lending. These programs primarily involve public libraries but may include other types as well. Procedures vary according to the vendor providing the messaging system, but most include a backup library, or "library of last resort," that mediates requests to libraries external to the group. OCLC enables non-members to participate in electronic interlibrary lending by creating a category of selective users through "Group Access Consortia." Several such statewide consortia have been formed. Libraries in this category may use the OCLC ILL subsystem for interlibrary lending within their group and may arrange for a full OCLC member to mediate their requests to external libraries. As a result, even very small libraries have access to international resources via electronic interlibrary loan systems.

Library automation systems and other computer software that interface with the national electronic messaging systems also facilitate the management of interlibrary loan transactions and eliminate manual handling of administrative details. Most local systems improve efficiency in responding to requests by making it easier to verify circulation status or identify lending restrictions on an item-by-item basis. Other computer software such as PC-based SAVEIT,[5] supports data collection for routine statistics and copyright compliance, easing the burden of cumbersome management requirements.

Overall, these technologies have contributed to greater efficiency in interlibrary loan departments by enabling the processing of a greater number of requests without additional staffing. Librarians cannot manage the large volume of lending and borrowing requests without aid of such automation. Difficulties demonstrated in handling cumbersome paper forms have made use of an electronic messaging system essential if requests are to be filled in an efficient and timely manner. In the future, it is likely that libraries without access to automation may be excluded from borrowing from libraries except those with which they have reciprocal agreements permitting use of printed request forms in lieu of electronic communications.

INCREASING FINANCIAL CONSTRAINTS

The cost of interlibrary lending, too often ignored or overlooked by borrowing libraries, is a highly relevant factor in successful interlibrary loan service. A 1991 national study by the Association of Research Libraries and the Research Libraries Group found an average cost of $10.93 for a research library to lend a document to another library.[6] This cost was echoed in a study of two New Jersey libraries contracting to provide interlibrary lending services, primarily to public libraries. The costs for these two libraries to lend items or provide photocopies averaged $18.70 for one library and $16.21 for the other.[7]

Borrowing libraries also incur interlibrary loan expenses. Although the New Jersey study did not examine the costs for borrowing libraries, the ARL/RLG study indicated that research libraries spent an average of $18.62 to borrow a research document or article or to purchase a photocopy of an item for a patron.

Staffing accounts for the largest expense. The ARL/RLG study reported that staff costs represented 77 percent of the expense incurred in both lending and borrowing. Many lending libraries attempt to recover this cost by charging a handling fee in addition to charges assessed for photocopies, postage, telefacsimile communications, and insurance. Librarians struggling to cope with a surfeit of borrowing requests may likewise seek to discourage requests by setting high fees for borrowers outside their reciprocal borrowing groups.

Academic libraries, historically large volume consumers of interlibrary loan services, face increasing economic pressures. University support for libraries, as a percent of total expenditures, has been decreasing steadily over the last 20 years.[8] Many administrators of libraries with generous policies which have permitted free or subsidized lending are beginning to weigh critically the value of any service not directly benefiting their own students and faculty. Academic librarians will have to recover real, not token, costs for lending requests that are not offset by filled borrowing requests made for their own users. They cannot process a greater volume of requests with existing staff, and institutional funds are not available for adding more. Growth in staffing to support lending services may well have to be obtained through cost recovery for those services.

For the past several years, librarians in large academic libraries have expressed dismay over the growing number of borrowing requests they receive via OCLC. Many of these requests could be directed to other holding libraries noted in the OCLC database but are sent to the largest libraries without apparent concern for the high volume of lending requests those libraries receive. In response to this situation, OCLC initiated the ILL Fee Management program (IFM) to record interlibrary lending transactions and to assist with billing for charges set by the lender. The monthly OCLC bill for this program reconciles credits and debits, recording credits for lenders and billing borrowers.[9] Development of this program has been encouraged by the administrators of large net lender libraries who see it as a means of recovering costs and of discouraging or rerouting requests.[10] The program is also welcomed by those librarians who would like to recover costs but have been unable to invoice for payment or to receive funds. It is highly probable that a large number of OCLC libraries will participate in the IFM program for all interlibrary loan transactions except those covered by formal reciprocal agreements. Thus, it will become easier for libraries to charge for lending services, and given that facility, it is less likely that charges will be waived as they have been in the past. In addition, participating libraries may set two tiers of charges, one for libraries participating in IFM and a second higher charge for those not using that system. The higher charges reflect the need for libraries to recoup the extra costs associated with the local administration of fees not managed through the IFM billing via OCLC.

An alternative to dealing with interlibrary loan fees may be seen in the current practice of SOLINET libraries participating in SOLINE.[11] To remove the financial barrier for library users in the Southeast, these libraries waive handling fees for lending *original* materials among SOLINE participants. A subset of the initial SOLINE group called SO6, currently composed of 80 libraries, waives charges for *photocopies* as well. Participants in the program cite the elimination of expensive accounting procedures and paperwork along with the need to recognize the historical poverty of the region as important reasons to support no-fee lending. This goodwill is only as strong as the efforts of borrowing libraries to abide by the protocols of SOLINE in attempting to eliminate disparity in lending to borrowing ratios.[12]

Economic pressures faced by all libraries and growth of reciprocal lending consortia will make it increasingly difficult for those not participating in formal agreements to identify other libraries willing to lend to them without compensation, either in the form of materials borrowed on a reciprocal basis or reimbursment for the actual cost of the service. Successful borrowing via interlibrary loan will depend upon the ability of the borrowing library to pay other libraries for expenses incurred on its behalf.

INCREASING AVAILABILITY OF NEW AND USER-FRIENDLY TECHNOLOGY

Librarians have embraced technology in their efforts to offer all information available that might meet the real or perceived information needs of their users. The availability and growing affordability of indexing and abstracting databases online and in CD-ROM format afford users sophisticated search strategies applicable to a previously unimagined wealth of information. This is occurring, paradoxically, at a time when libraries are experiencing a serious erosion in their ability to maintain current information resources locally at a level equal to that of the past.

The easier it becomes for users to identify materials that might be helpful, the greater the demands on the library to provide those materials. Today, it is common for users to present several pages of citations from an electronic index and state. "I want to get these on interlibrary loan." As users obtain the ability to browse in remote online systems, especially those containing special indexing for materials not in the national shared bibliographic databases, demand for borrowing will escalate. Unmediated interlibrary loan will permit and even encourage users to initiate a greater number of requests. Unless the dynamics of the current situation change drastically, interlibrary loan librarians will respond in all likelihood by restricting their lending. In so doing, they will lend to fewer libraries, focus on finding materials needed by their own users, and decline requests from libraries not included in their reciprocal agreements.

GROWING USE OF FULL-IMAGE DATABASES AND COMMERCIAL DOCUMENT SUPPLIERS

From the limited perspective of the present, the library marketplace has become in a few short years a showcase for highly sophisticated computer databases. That sophistication will grow exponentially in the future. The storage capacity of CD-ROM technology allowed those in the information industry and others to convert many existing indexing and abstracting print tools into CD-ROM databases. These have been quickly followed by online databases which could be melded into local library information systems. The addition of user-friendly retrieval software places powerful information tools in the hands of users. Evolving databases now offer user-friendly retrieval software, indepth indexing usually with keyword search capability, and the full image of articles cited. This technology offers significant advantages over print indexes. These include speed of access, ability to construct complex search strategies, ability to modify strategies during the search process, and the coupling of retrieved citations with the content of the articles indexed. As vendors begin to offer competitively-priced databases, librarians may consider replacing print periodical subscriptions with full-image databases. Prices, however, will remain high enough to ensure that the publisher and vendor suffer no loss of revenue.

Permission to extract data from these sources is governed by licensing agreements negotiated with vendors. Most require payment either in advance as part of the purchase price or on a "per page" basis as surrogate documents are printed to compensate publishers for copyright compliance and anticipated loss of revenue previously derived from sale of paper issues of the journal. A number of vendors permit use of databases only by the library's principal users but prohibit use to provide copies for interlibrary lending. If such a prohibition is not in the contract, copying or distribution fees may be assessed which the lending library may not wish to pay. That expense probably will be passed on to the borrowing library in the same manner as photocopying charges.

Equally worrisome for resource sharing is the possibility that librarians relying on retrieving articles from titles available in full-image databases will no longer contribute local serials holdings records to union lists if print subscriptions are canceled. Even when librarians try to contribute records to a union list for titles accessed through a full-text database, a high level of uncertainty may exist about the exact contents these databases. Even though a database may be promoted as indexing from a certain date, entries for individual serial titles may have beginning dates which differ. Further, publishers may withdraw titles abruptly from a database and without notice to libraries, thus reducing coverage of the database.

The business sector has long viewed information as a commodity to be bought and sold but was unable to exploit its potential because it is difficult to distribute. With the coming of new technology, effective distribution is feasible and commercial service companies are seeking actively to market this resource. Commercial and other document delivery services now commonly offered to libraries are being directed increasingly toward the end user. Services are offered already to end users via the Internet (e.g., CARL UNCOVER and OCLC FirstSearch) and commercial e-mail systems.[13] Document delivery services directed to libraries are available from various vendors by dialing directly into the vendor's databases or through the Internet.

Prices charged for document delivery services must be high enough to recover costs incurred by the delivery company and the publishers and to afford a margin of profit for either or both. Despite these constraints, pricing will become more competitive and perhaps more affordable, especially for individual end users. End users are an increasingly important market, and vendors will encourage them to bypass libraries. Users will seek the most convenient sources, with convenience modified by the value placed by individual users on timely delivery, reliability, and cost. This may change the type of access to information service offered by libraries. Interlibrary lending and borrowing may become expensive luxuries that libraries will discontinue if document delivery can be obtained more cheaply from a commercial source. Availability of free lending will most certainly diminish and may well vanish altogether.

GROWING IMPORTANCE OF AFFINITY GROUPS FOR SUCCESSFUL INTERLIBRARY LOAN PROGRAMS

Affinity connotes the existence of an inherent similarity or a mutual relationship between entities. Libraries in the past have frequently formed affinity groups for dealing with common interests, activities, or problems. If libraries are to provide information needed by their users in the future, they will need to forge affinity groups bound by common, but to the individual library unobtainable, goals. The organization of such groups may be as formal as a consortium with its own staff or as informal as a few librarians agreeing to abide by a common policy for a single activity.

Sharing resources by facilitating the exchange of materials among its members is one of the most prevalent activities of a library affinity group. To succeed in its efforts, a group must minimize political, administrative, financial, or geographical barriers that impede the flow of information.

Interlibrary lending is an ideal shared program for affinity group emphasis even in the absence of more formal cooperative agreements. At a minimum, such a group must agree on the types of materials and information that will be shared, define the means for placing requests, minimize paperwork, and establish priorities for handling requests.[14]

OCLC: AN INTERNATIONAL AFFINITY GROUP

The largest interlibrary lending affinity group is OCLC. Its 18,000 participating libraries contribute their holdings to a shared bibliographic database representing nearly 30 million records with over 500 million location notations. Most OCLC members agree to lend, within their own policy limitations, to other OCLC members. The importance of contributing to OCLC, the prime example of a resource-sharing affinity group, can be seen in the dramatic improvements occurring in borrowing fill rate, response time, and interlibrary lending and borrowing efficiency. Mutual policies and procedures to which participants must adhere do not impinge on institutional integrity or autonomy, yet they provide a strong and proven foundation for more effective and efficient library services.

THE NETWORK OF ALABAMA ACADEMIC LIBRARIES: A STATE-BASED AFFINITY GROUP

One example of a state-based affinity group that has provided enhanced information services available to the users of its libraries is the Network of Alabama Academic Libraries (NAAL). The affinity that binds NAAL is the requirement that its academic members must be Alabama colleges and universities offering graduate education. These 20 publicly-and privately-supported academic institutions are joined by six other research libraries which cooperate in meeting the organization's goals but do not participate in its governance. Established in 1984, the network has developed programs that seek to improve the quality and number of information services available to graduate students, university faculty, and other researchers. Further, by cooperating with other groups such as public libraries, NAAL has expanded the information resources accessible to any resident of the state. Because of its success, NAAL may be recommended as a prototype to be studied closely in forming other affinity groups. It has been notable for its removal of political, financial, and geographical barriers to using library resources regardless of where those resources are held or where the researcher is located.

Acceptance of the concept that individual library resources are a component of a vastly larger statewide library resource to which all users have access was an early and critical philosophical step taken by the network. Focusing on improving information services and resources within the defined political entity of the state helped overcome resistance to sharing. That perspective helped forge an affinity where none had existed, such as that between publicly-and privately-supported schools and between institutions at the geographic extremes of the state. By agreeing to become components of this statewide collection, the Alabama Research Collection, the institutions overcame political resistance to cooperation. Another early initiative successfully implemented for the group was to make this larger collection accessible to all members. Accordingly, all NAAL members agreed to add records for their total print resources to the OCLC database. This online database has become the foundation upon which other cooperative activities have been built.

Another factor in the success of NAAL has been the formulation of a precise set of interlibrary loan guidelines and procedures. Interlibrary lending activities of NAAL members are affected by a variety of codes and agreements. Member institutions, as applicable, abide by the *National Interlibrary Loan Code*, the *Alabama Interlibrary Loan Code*, the SOLINET protocol for SOLINE, and the protocol for the National Library of Medicine network

(DOCLine). They also share partnerships that affect interlibrary loan with some or all of the following groups: Alabama Public Library Service (APLS) and Alabama public libraries, SOLINET, Association of Research Libraries (ARL), Association of Southeastern Research Libraries, Association of Law Libraries, and the Health Sciences Libraries Consortium.

In 1985, NAAL established its Resource Sharing Program to facilitate interlibrary loan transactions among its members. Although the policy for this program recognized already existing cooperative relationships among individual libraries, it sought primarily to strengthen resource sharing within the network. When political resistance to sharing all information resources in the state regardless of location was eliminated, the Resource Sharing Program then focused on removing financial hindrances to providing service and eliminating or markedly reducing delays in obtaining needed materials.

Several other NAAL programs have also helped to remove or reduce barriers to effective interlibrary loan service. Among the most commonly identified are a lack of knowledge of the holdings of other libraries, no quick means by which to place requests, reliance on the U.S. Postal Service as the only method for delivery, and insufficient financial resources to adequately support the interlibrary loan services needed at both borrowing and lending libraries. For NAAL, major increases in request volume can be attributed to a number of factors, including completion of a statewide retrospective conversion program[15] which added over 2 million holdings records to OCLC, implementation of a cooperative collection development program to acquire needed materials, elimination of financial barriers for users, and use of NAAL funds and recommended procedures to improve efficiency in member interlibrary loan departments.

Before the Resource Sharing Program was initiated, NAAL library users faced a number of obstacles to obtaining information not held by their local library. Critical among these was inadequate funding of academic libraries by their parent institutions. Not only did this limit local collection development, but it also hampered the ability of most institutions to staff adequately for interlibrary loan service or to absorb charges levied by lending libraries. Most could not lend without recovering some costs from borrowing libraries or their users. Charges by lenders often meant that many students could not afford the expense of an interlibrary loan transaction if the library could not absorb the charges associated with it. This is a significant issue because per capita income for Alabama's college students is less than the national average; they lack the financial resources to pay extra charges for interlibrary loan services.

Financial assistance by NAAL helps alleviate the financial burden for both library users and member institutions. Eliminating all handling fees and charges to borrowing students and faculty and to network members has to a great extent overcome this financial barrier to using the statewide resources. NAAL reimburses members for part of the expenses for borrowing and lending among NAAL libraries. NAAL also pays other costs such as basic telephone service charges for telefacsimile connections in each NAAL library and UPS fees for ground-based delivery among members.[16]

Using telefacsimile and UPS has facilitated document delivery demonstrably. Within NAAL, borrowed items are now received in an average of 4.5 days; the majority of items are received within two days. Prior to 1985, the average delivery time to a borrowing library was more than two weeks. Such long delays in receiving borrowed material frequently made the item irrelevant for students, especially at academic institutions on the quarter system.

Dramatic improvement in obtaining needed materials from within the collective resources of NAAL also illustrates clearly the importance of the existence of an affinity group in contributing to the effectiveness of the efforts of its members. NAAL members find over 60 percent of their filled requests from within their own membership, an increase over a fill rate of only 30 percent in 1985.

Improved interlibrary loan services and the means to achieve that improvement within the network has also had an impact on the participation of NAAL members in national resource sharing efforts. In OCLC, the number of requests made of Alabama OCLC members has escalated because Alabama libraries are often first in the OCLC queue,[17] have added records for retrospective materials to the online database, and have attained a reputation for excellent interlibrary loan service. Collectively, NAAL libraries lend 1.5 items for every item borrowed via OCLC.

Within NAAL, interlibrary loan volume has grown by 684 percent, from 9,401 transactions in 1985-1986 to 64,281 transactions in 1994-1995. Most NAAL members absorbed this tremendous growth in workload without substantial increases in personnel assigned to interlibrary loan tasks.

The collective importance of an affinity group can also be demonstrated in the efforts by NAAL members to improve the quality and quantity of information available to all Alabamians, not just users from the academic community. Their OCLC records are the foundation of the state's union catalog, ALICAT, maintained by the Alabama Public Library Service, the state library agency. The holdings of NAAL's academic members represent 72 percent of the total monograph holdings in the September 1994 edition. Most members contribute their serial holdings to the Alabama Union List of Serials (OCLC symbol, NAUL) which is also distributed off-line with ALICAT. To make academic library resources more widely available, NAAL encourages and facilitates interlibrary lending with public libraries by negotiating an annual agreement with APLS to lend to Alabama's public libraries without charge to the borrowing library. LSCA Title III funds are used to maintain the union catalog, ALICAT, and the Alabama Union List of Serials. These funds are used, too, for reimbursing NAAL libraries at a rate of $7.50 per net loan to public libraries. In 1986-1987, the first year of the agreement, public libraries borrowed 3,929 items; of these, 3,408 were net loans. In 1994-95, public libraries borrowed 7,200 items; 6,352 were net loans.

Other libraries, both within and outside Alabama, may access the state's union catalog either by connecting through OCLC or by purchasing a microfiche or CD-ROM version, but they face a myriad of locally-determined policies and charges in seeking to borrow from many of the libraries contributing to this catalog. In the absence of other groups of Alabama libraries which are able to negotiate reciprocal agreements, each NAAL library, in considering lending to those libraries, sets its own policies for lending and charges for that service. Those libraries may, in addition, encounter delays in service caused by lending libraries honoring the priorities and conditions set by their existing reciprocal agreements.

AFFINITY GROUPS AND SERVICE PRIORITIES

Librarians, when grappling with a growing number of interlibrary loan requests, typically respond by establishing policies and priorities for handling borrowing requests. All NAAL members honor the *National Interlibrary Loan Code* and accept requests on ALA ILL printed forms. While these requests are handled within the intent of the *National Code* to facilitate interlibrary lending nationwide, they are also subject to the handling policies established by each library. No library abiding by the *National Code* is expected to respond to any request that is not complete, legible, or submitted appropriately, for example, via OCLC, DOCLine, or on an ALA ILL printed form. Regardless of the reciprocal agreements in place or the format of the request, no lending library should be expected to assume the tasks of verifying a bibliographic citation, guessing at the requesting library's compliance with copyright law and guidelines, or deciphering illegible requests.

Accelerating interlibrary loan transaction volume has caused librarians in large lending libraries to analyze workflow and establish routines that insure efficient handling of requests. Many divide their workflow into borrowing (activities necessary to borrow items for the library's own users) and lending (activities necessary to lend items to other libraries) and set priorities for each activity. While these priorities are molded by the self-interest of the institution, the obvious first priority for any library is obtaining items needed by its own users. This self-interest justifies the existence of its interlibrary loan department. If a library did not need to borrow, it would have only marginal, if any, interest in unsubsidized lending. Consequently, it is not surprising that librarians, quid pro quo, return the favor by giving first lending priority to those libraries from which they borrow.

The affinity group to which a library belongs affects lending priorities. NAAL serves as one example of how lending priorities may be handled within a group. All intra-NAAL borrowing requests must be submitted via the OCLC ILL Subsystem or DOCLine because electronic systems contribute to more efficient handling of requests and reduce administrative record keeping. For all electronic requests, priority is given to other NAAL members and to partners in other reciprocal cooperatives such as the Association of Research Libraries, the Association of Southeastern Research Libraries, or SOLINE. Special libraries, for example, medical libraries and law libraries, also give a high priority to cooperating with other special libraries of the same type. When the volume of lending requests exceeds a level that can be handled reasonably by the interlibrary loan department staff, NAAL members perforce decline requests from lower priority libraries for which there are other holding libraries on OCLC or DOCLine. Electronic interlibrary loan systems automatically send these requests to other potential borrowers.

NAAL members also assign a high priority to borrowing requests from Alabama public libraries. These may be submitted electronically via OCLC or on ALA ILL or ALICAT CD-ROM printed forms. Requests submitted on printed forms must be verified in ALICAT to assure the lending library that the items have been cited with bibliographic accuracy and are known to be held by the library. By agreement with APLS, staffs of NAAL libraries do not attempt to verify items bibliographically, check ownership, guess copyright compliance by the library making the request, or decipher intentions. Incomplete or illegible forms are returned unfilled to the requesting library.

The dramatic increase in interlibrary loan transactions among NAAL members over the past 10 years has resulted in understaffed and overworked interlibrary loan departments. In coping with the burgeoning workload, priorities set for individual NAAL libraries may vary. An interlibrary loan librarian typically recognizes the following order of importance in departmental tasks: borrowing materials for local library users, responding to requests from members of its affinity groups, responding to electronic requests from libraries of the same type, and responding to electronic requests from other libraries. There is little time for handling electronic requests not covered by formal reciprocal agreements. When the number of daily requests exceeds the number that an interlibrary loan staff can handle, further requests are declined. It is unfair to hold a request for several days and then decide that it cannot be processed. Consequently, requests which cannot be handled soon after they are received are declined via the electronic messaging systems of OCLC or DOCLine. It is generally impossible for staff to ensure a timely response for requests submitted on printed ILL forms except for those submitted by Alabama public libraries. Most requests submitted on printed forms are almost always assigned a secondary processing priority. If they cannot be handled within 24 hours of receipt, they are usually returned to the requesting library marked "cannot fill."

It is imperative that librarians needing interlibrary loan service for patrons of their libraries form their own affinity group and attempt to fill as many requests as possible from within that group. Only then should affinity groups attempt to reach reciprocal agreements with similar groups to obtain materials that cannot be supplied from their own resources. To help insure success, every group formed to facilitate interlibrary lending should, before approaching other libraries, consider connecting to one of the widely-used electronic messaging systems for interlibrary loan purposes.

SUMMARY

The rapidly changing fiscal and technical environments for libraries will continue to alter traditional interlibrary loan service available to all libraries. Technology will change the way information is packaged, stored, retrieved, and delivered. End users will be able to select from a variety of providers as libraries and vendors vie to offer attractive information packages. Libraries not affiliated with others through formal resource sharing agreements will experience increasing difficulty in obtaining information via traditional interlibrary lending. The ranks of historical net lenders, especially those that in the past supplied materials for little or no charge, will be reduced as these libraries are increasingly unable or unwilling to lend outside of their own affinity groups. Free or almost free interlibrary lending will vanish. Full-image databases and commercial document suppliers will be able to meet selected information needs but only at a cost to the borrowing library and its users. Libraries that are not currently affiliated with a group supporting shared goals for information needs of their users should begin now to develop formal resource sharing agreements. These agreements should include plans to interface with national electronic messaging systems for interlibrary loan services, to initiate collaborative collection development, and to mediate reference assistance before initiating requests to borrow materials from other libraries.

NOTES AND REFERENCES

1. *National Interlibrary Loan Code* (Chicago: American Library Association, 1993).
2. For one example, see Peggy Jobe, "Loan Line: A New National Interlibrary Loan Code," *Colorado Libraries*, pp. 42-43 (Summer 1993).

3. "Ohio Patrons Can Initiate Academic Library Interloans," *Library Hotline*, March 21, 1994.

4. "Colorado State University Transfers File to OCLC PRISM ILL System," *OCLC Newsletter* No. 208 (March/April 1994), p. 34.

5. SAVEIT is a registered trademark of the Interlibrary Software and Services, Inc.

6. Marilyn M. Roche, *ARL/RLG Interlibrary Loan Cost Study* (Washington, DC: Association of Research Libraries, 1993).

7. *Costing Question Handling and ILL/Photocopying* (New Jersey State Library, 1989).

8. Frank W. Goudy, "Academic Libraries and the Six Percent Solution: A Twenty-Year Financial Overview." *Journal of Academic Librarianship* 19(September 1993): 212-215..

9. *OCLC Newsletter*, No. 298 (March/April 1994), p. 5.

10. The IFM program does not automatically reroute requests. Many ILL librarians seek free or inexpensive lenders. As more libraries enroll in the IFM program (especially those that did not charge previously because they weren't allowed to invoice and bill), they will not be included in the list of free lenders. Also, some IFM libraries are assessing a surcharge for lending to libraries that are not IFM participants. Borrowers will avoid these libraries except as a last resort—which is a more appropriate role for the largest libraries!

11. SOLINE also merges the various state and local Group Access Consortia (GAC) in the southeastern states into a regional resource sharing group. By agreeing to participate in SOLINE, full OCLC members that are not members of the local or regional GAC also allow the selective users who are members of a GAC to place ILL requests to them through the OCLC ILL Subsystem. Without this regional access, the selective users could place ILL requests only to the members of their own GAC.

12. Sadly, the issues discussed here are already affecting participation in SOLINE. A recent message sent to ILL-L, the Internet-based discussion list for interlibrary loan, noted that the University of Virginia Library "will no longer participate in SOLINE. In light of increasing costs and declining state support we must charge a book lending fee outside Virginia.... As early and active participants in SOLINE we do not make this decision lightly, and we will remain strong supporters of regional library cooperation. We will continue the few reciprocal agreements we have ... but we will enter into new reciprocal agreements only in rare instances.... We believe that economic and technological developments should lead to a new model of resource sharing.... We firmly believe that the OCLC Interlibrary Loan Fee Management (IFM) system is a firm foundation for this new resource sharing model, and we anticipate that using the system will reduce the costs associated with invoicing and fee collection." Douglas P. Hurd, Director of Interlibrary Services, "University of Virginia Lending," an e-mail message sent to ILL-L@usc.edu on September 16, 1995.

13. American Cybercasting Corporation, a for-profit company, electronically delivers 20 periodicals (mostly business publications and large newspapers) to local area networks on the day the periodical is published. If a college or company does not subscribe to the service for its network, individuals can subscribe and receive those periodicals via e-mail. *Chronicle of Higher Education*, January 12, 1994.

14. An excellent description of the basic elements of reciprocal borrowing agreements may be reviewed in Mary E. Jackson, "Interlibrary Loan, Document Delivery, and Resource Sharing," *Wilson Library Bulletin* (March 1994).

15. The initial retrospective conversion program is augmented as members continue to add records for their current acquisitions, separately-cataloged federal publications, analytics for individual items held in major microform sets, and holdings for serials.

16. Members of NAAL have begun to add ARIEL Document Delivery Workstations. NAAL provides five grants per year to fund ARIEL software and the scanner; members provide the rest of the elements needed to complete the installation.

17. Most Alabama libraries have OCLC three-character symbols that begin with the letter A and OCLC lists in-state holding libraries first and then other holding libraries alphabetically by OCLC symbol. For example, one library, Auburn University, has AAA as its OCLC holding symbol and receives nine times more requests to borrow than it initiates.

COLLECTION DEVELOPMENT AND DOCUMENT DELIVERY:
BUDGETING FOR ACCESS

Millie L. Syring and Milton Wolf

ABSTRACT

Extensive planning is now absolutely necessary if an academic library is to realize the maximum access to information for its users. A collection development policy, based on administrative documents that outline the mission and goals of the overall institution, is the starting point in this planning process. The policy should be the guide according to which materials are acquired and accessed. The Information Resources and Access budget (formerly the "book budget") is the key to providing access to information. Taking money off the top of the budget to fund document delivery is an access strategy academic librarians should consider.

INTRODUCTION

Technological change in an information world is almost as axiomatic as death and taxes. Whereas libraries used to be a long way down on the technological food chain, far behind the military and medicine, the Information Age has elevated the position of information providers much closer to the source of technological innovations. The introduction of the Internet alone has changed the way information is published, delivered, and consumed. With data, data, everywhere, there's almost too much to think.

Nevertheless, valiant efforts are being made to surf the tsunami of information and provide unparalleled access to the end user. For libraries, budgeting and staffing the access phenomenon has tested and found wanting many traditional principles of library operation. While it is quite clear that tomorrow will not be like today, there will be enough of a resemblance that all talk of a "paperless society" should be seen for the sensationalism that it is. As Abraham Lincoln once said, "The good thing about the future is that it comes one day at a time."

ASSUMPTIONS

But the times they are, indeed, a-changin', and new ways of budgeting and staffing for information access need to be addressed. Any extrapolation of this important area of collection development will call for numerous assumptions, some more tried and some more moot than others. Therefore, we have provided the reader with a list of our assumptions before we expand and elaborate our thesis. They are:

1. Electronic access to information will continue to increase as the rate of ownership continues to decrease.
2. From the standpoint of the total of the Information Resources and Access Budget, formerly the Book Budget, an increased percentage will be spent on access, and decreased percentage will be spent on serial subscriptions to paper copies. This budget will not grow significantly compared to the amount of information that will be available!

Budgeting for Access 51

3. Document Delivery, or Access Departments, will require increasingly more staff, equipment, and fiscal support.
4. Libraries will move away from the ARL concepts of quantitative measurements of quality and toward more user evaluations of quality. Wired libraries will surpass the research potential of many libraries with large collections that lack funds to both maintain their present holdings and emphasize, where appropriate, electronic access.
5. More scholarly materials, especially serials, will appear in electronic form. There are already over 500 electronic serials with numbers increasing yearly.
6. The scholar workstation will be the mainstay of higher learning's access to world information and the entrance to the virtual library. Online degrees and increased emphasis on distance education will be the engines that push for more online access to information.
7. The end user will become more accustomed to information self-service, from check-out to bibliographic inquiries to ordering.
8. Generally, librarians will be the most versatile, living information filters in higher education, and their services will be in high demand.
9. The imposition of moderate fees for new services will continue to grow. Interlending will be somewhat equalized by having net-borrowers pay modest fees to net-lenders.
10. Organizationally, the library will continue to flatten, roles will merge, and team-oriented goals with different leaders for different projects will become more commonplace. Information literacy (which includes computer literacy) will be the hallmark of future librarians, no matter what position they hold.
11. Increased digitalization of information will increase the use of materials already owned by providing more access to the contents.
12. Preservation for archival purposes will become a joint venture between research libraries and commercial suppliers of information. In some instances, the relationship between the commercial sector and the public sector will become as blurred as the one already operative between academic science faculty and the government/corporations.

PLANNING FOR ACCESS

Information collections of all stripes have never been able to provide their clients with all the information they need all the time. Throughout history, no one library has been able to amass all the stone tablets, papyri, or books to claim that it was self-sufficient unto itself. By judicious selection, however, some repositories have gained renown for the discriminating choices they have made in various subject areas. While unlimited wealth has always been a powerful ally in the search and acquisition of carefully thought out choices, even the very best of academic institutions have had to devise ways to procure information resources for their clientele which they did not own.

The recent advent of the Internet has offered academic libraries one more way to access information which they do not own. While many of the other methods, for example, interlibrary loan and cooperative purchases, extend local collections, the Internet has exponentially widened the potential choices to outside information resources significantly. Extensive planning is now absolutely necessary if an academic library is to realize the maximum access to information for its users. An integral element of access planning should be budgeting for document delivery. For the purpose of this paper, we will define document delivery as "any information which we purposefully acquire for our users that originates from outside our own information collections and which does not remain in our custody in perpetuity."

MISSIONS AND GOALS

The Information Resources and Access Budget is the key to leading the institution to its best place on the Information Highway. In most institutions, there are several aspects of the organization devoted to this goal, especially the computer center, and overall coordination of similar efforts should be sought whenever possible.

A Collection Development Policy, based on administrative documents which outline the mission and goals of the overall institution, is clearly a sine qua non. The collecting policy should address, among other things, what is to be acquired/accessed, the levels of acquisition, and the priorities of acquisition. Prioritizing

Budgeting for Access 53

acquisition is vital since it is highly unlikely that sufficient funds will be available for any extended period of time.

As the ways of delivering information to our users continue to proliferate, the manner in which we distribute the information budget needs constant scrutiny and revision. It is important to bear in mind that a "budget" is actually a planning document. The "real" budget is the list of expenditures paid for at the end of a fiscal period.

BABY HUEY

In acquiring information needs for most academic libraries, the behemoth that needs immediate attention is the cost of journal and serial subscriptions. Because these subscriptions tend to contain more timely information than books, especially scientific information, it is unlikely that not having any subscriptions would even be a consideration for any information-providing institution. Therefore, the Baby Huey of serials ownership must be controlled from the very outset if any reasonable budgeting is to occur. The yearly inflation increases alone affecting serials can easily wipe out an entire budget within a decade without ever having added one more subscription during that time! Thus, the cost of the serials an institution will own (note we did not say "should" own) must be decided before any other information purchases can be reasonably considered.

If you are already overburdened with serial expenditures (i.e., 70% or more of your overall budget), some difficult decisions are ahead of you. A close examination of your Mission And Goals statement and your Collection Development Policy, will facilitate your next steps. After determining what serial subscriptions will be maintained (utilizing use statistics, etc.), whatever remains of the overall budget should be used to move the institution closer to its goals and mission.

PROACTIVE

Assuming that your institution is wired for electronic access, you must lead the way in creating a climate that welcomes the opportunity for utilizing the tremendous information wealth of the Internet. As Machiavelli so long ago pointed out: "There is nothing more difficult to take in hand, more perilous to conduct, or more uncertain in its success, than to take the lead in the introduction of a new order of things."

In most institutions, it should be the role of the gatekeepers of information to lead the way to net surfing. For several hundred years now, it has been librarians who have been in the position to be information filters. Plenty of so-called "information" is out there on the Internet, and our job is to define what is reliable and accurate and to create organization out of the chaos. The Information Age has positioned us to be the agents of change to a multi-tiered information storehouse. No matter how user-friendly tomorrow's access to information becomes, there will always be a role for those persons who can teach information retrieval and who can stay reasonably current in what is likely to be a continuous white-water stream of technological information breakthroughs.

ACCESS HAPPENS

Beyond all the neat stuff and valuable information sites located on the Internet, we need to provide our users with access to information and materials that are not yet up on the net. More than just the slogan of the 1990s, "Access vs. Ownership" is a very real issue that all academic libraries are facing. Each library will come to grips with this issue, and the path chosen will not necessarily be the same for everyone. Some libraries may be forced by budget constraints to cancel serial subscriptions, others will draw the line on new subscriptions, both opting for other cost effective methods of supplying information to their users. What is clear is that access to information and materials, rather than physical ownership of them, must be part and parcel of collection development policies. Access, whether by supplying documents via document delivery departments, expedited or not, by subscribing to online or CD-ROM databases that contain full-text, or by providing Internet access to electronic journals, will happen. Gay Dannelly, Collection Development Librarian at Ohio State University Libraries, sees access as a form of ownership, analogous to paying rent on a short-term lease rather than paying a mortgage and attendant condominium fees![1] We should not, therefore, feel alienated from this new form of ownership but embrace it as one solution to providing the research materials needed by our students and faculty.

BUDGET STRATEGY

What you call your materials budget (other than "Insufficient!") may make the difference when you begin to allocate funds for support of document delivery. Referring to the budget as the "Information Resources and Access Budget" encompasses materials to be acquired and information to be accessed. There will be no question that access to information is vital to the institution and that access costs money! One strategy that lends itself to budgeting for access is to take money off the top of the budget before any other funding is disbursed, remembering, of course, that subscriptions begin the fiscal year as already expended funds. By taking money off the top for document delivery, for example, you promote a direction for information access without unduly penalizing any one funded unit and, at the same time, create a friendly competition to use those funds!

Depending on the size of your institution (and how much you have publicized and trained your users), a beginning Document Delivery budget of one-sixtieth of the budget or a minimum of $5,000 should be a good start for most academic libraries. These budget funds might be allocated for expedited delivery of articles, whether from traditional library sources or commercial document suppliers, document delivery department equipment and/or staff needs, Table of Contents Services, paying copyright/royalty fees, or pilot projects to offer new and better services.

DOCUMENT DELIVERY AS ACCESS STRATEGY

Academic libraries are clearly on the road to emphasizing access to materials through document delivery. Increased electronic access to information has created increased demand for the information contained in these resources, and many of these materials are not physically owned by the library. Full-text databases have whetted users' appetites for more "instant" information retrieval, and it had better be available as soon as possible!

Seeing this paradigm shift, the authors of the National Interlibrary Code made quite a radical adjustment to the 1993 updated version. Where the previous iteration cautioned, "Interlibrary loan is an adjunct to, not a substitute for, collection development,"[2] the 1993 version acknowledged increased use of interlibrary loan by stating, "Interlibrary borrowing is an *integral* element of collection development for all libraries, not an ancillary option" (emphasis added)[3].

Always a mainstay, traditional interlibrary loan functions well if the user is willing to wait for the materials. Increasing accessibility to information resources, such as online databases, online discussion groups, gopher, World Wide Web and e-mail connectivity with far flung colleagues, has set the stage for user demand for instantaneous delivery of information. Offering your users rush delivery or other expedited services is no longer an option but should be part and parcel of the standard menu of document delivery services. Academic libraries are responding to this demand by finding ways to speed up the interlibrary loan process, whether it be by sharing databases and resources within consortia and networks, by making it easier for users to request materials via imbedded mechanisms in OPACS or use of e-mail, by sending requested materials by courier, or by using expedited mail delivery services.

COMMERCIAL DOCUMENT SUPPLIERS

Probably the most significant change in the way academic libraries are providing document delivery has to be the use of commercial document suppliers. A 1994 survey of 90 Association of Research Libraries member libraries found that 87 percent were using document suppliers.[4] The benefits of using commercial document suppliers are quite attractive for many reasons, not the least of which is the cost of "doing" traditional interlibrary borrowing. According to the 1993 ARL interlibrary loan cost study, it costs $29.55 per completed interlibrary loan transaction containing both borrowing and lending components.[5] Not something to sneeze at when one considers the load you might be placing on libraries via your reciprocal agreements.

From a Collection Development standpoint, using commercial document suppliers' collections makes sense because their strengths are generally in science and business where the costs of ownership are often prohibitive. Per article costs delivered by commercial suppliers have become quite reasonable with incremental discounts given for higher levels of use. Additionally, commercial suppliers pay the copyright/royalty fees relieving document delivery departments

Budgeting for Access

from keeping track of copyright/royalty statistics on those items acquired from them. Many commercial providers will offer discounts to consortium users, and often a verbal agreement with other institutions to cooperate is sufficient to realize these discounts.

Some commercial suppliers with end-user databases (e.g., UnCover) allow the linking of library holdings with their databases, thus creating increased access to the library's collection and increased user satisfaction. On the flip side, your users will know that the library does not own the information sought, and they will know they can turn to their document delivery department to order it, or they can order it themselves.

SUPPORT OF DOCUMENT DELIVERY DEPARTMENTS

With increased emphasis on access, document delivery departments will need more resources, that is, more fiscal support, if they are to accomplish their tasks. Adequate staffing, equipment, and technology are essential. Fax transmission of photocopies and requests has become the norm in most departments requiring reliable fax equipment. Use of bibliographic utilities is nearly universal and demands that adequate, if not state of the art, microcomputer equipment be available along with capabilities for networking over the Internet. Software, such as ARIEL, that allows for scanned documents to be sent over the Internet to their destinations has increased the speed of delivery but has put additional pressure on budgets because of the startup costs. A scanner, a high-end microcomputer, and a laser printer are needed to implement this new technology.

What elements of this fiscal support can be allocated from the Information Resources and Access Budget? Answers to this question depend largely on available funding and the willingness to look for innovative approaches to fulfilling the goal of access to information.

PUBLIC RELATIONS AND TRAINING

In order to encourage the use of a Document Delivery Fund, adequate public relations must be generated and users must be continuously updated and educated about the various resources available. Subject bibliographers are in the best position to know the information proclivities of the faculty in their respective subject areas. And since a significant amount of research is highly interdisciplinary, it behooves the bibliographers to act as catalysts by introducing possibly related information to their constituents. A strategy of contacting individual faculty and academic departments with information on new databases and new document delivery services is a direct approach and should be a priority. This often can be achieved unobtrusively by e-mailing such information to the targeted persons or departments. "Advertising" in student and other campus publications is another strategy to make sure your users know what the library has to offer.

One way to promote document delivery services is by utilizing table of contents (TOC) services. Having TOC services available through the library's online system allows for browsing through many years worth of journals' contents if desired. Some services (e.g., UnCover's Reveal and EBSCO/doc) send pre-selected TOCs to users' e-mail boxes. TOC services can be excellent selling points to faculty when the time comes to cancel serial subscriptions. The library may not have the physical issues in the library to handle and browse through, but now the user does not even need to come to the library to see what's up with a favorite title. He/she can sit in the office and call up the online database, browse the TOCs, and select the articles needed. This approach will garner the most support if requesting items from document delivery departments is made easy and especially if the requesting process is automated (i.e., through e-mail, OPAC forms, etc.). Providing free access to TOCs by supporting a site license for campus users is a natural use of materials budget funds.

Users will need training to access new resources, too. Publicity can bring these resources and services to your users' attention, but make sure you have made plans to provide training in their use. Bibliographers and/or library instruction librarians should be poised and ready to offer training sessions on new resources. Document delivery staff should be up to speed on their new services and policies. Reference staff, too, should be ready to explain how to access any new resources and know what the document delivery policies are.

TO FEE OR NOT TO FEE

That is the question! Charging fees for services is a political football in libraryland. While our goal is to provide the highest level of service possible, our institutions are seldom funded to that extent. User charges for interlibrary loans have often been to recoup monies spent to procure the needed materials, that is, lender charges. Libraries, that can afford to, absorb those borrowing charges, but it is common for libraries to pass on charges to the user. When we opt to use commercial suppliers or institute rush services (which cost more in staff time and fees charged), the urge to charge our users something in return for the enhanced service seems justified. If we are cutting serial subscriptions and offering just in time document delivery, it may seem that we are penalizing our users for our collection development decisions, especially when we ding them for a per page charge or a flat fee *to wait* for their articles. But if we look at the reality of user behavior when it comes to accessing journal articles, we often see that users will be photocopying those articles from the paper issues we own *for a fee*! Few libraries can subsidize photocopying services. So, if you must charge a fee for new services, it would be a good idea to keep it around the cost of photocopying in your library.

Better user satisfaction and less abuse of a free service may be achieved if a small charge is added for document delivery anyway. Economists call this the fallacy of the commons, that is, when something is totally free to everyone, it is usually abused by everyone, and the final outcome becomes unsatisfactory. However, when a cost is assigned, most people act more responsibly and feel more satisfied.

INNOVATIONS

Academic libraries must be willing to experiment with new ways of supplying information to their users. Information Resources and Access Budget funds used for pilot projects can lead to increased funding. Experimentation with user-centered document delivery (i.e., non-mediated ordering from commercial suppliers) seems to be a strategy more academic libraries are leaning toward to provide for the information needs of faculty. Arizona State University's recent pilot project, called "Direct Doc," is not a return to the house call but might as well be! Materials budget funds were used to set up user-centered document delivery for faculty. Interested faculty were given passwords to several commercial document suppliers (UnCover, First Search, and Eureka/CitaDel) with instructions to order the journal articles directly from the suppliers. Articles were faxed by the suppliers to the users with no intervention by library staff. The project clarified the requesting behavior of the users and found that the majority of the articles requested using the commercial suppliers were contained in journals owned by the library. This behavior led to the decision to link the library's holdings to the most used database, UnCover. Now, faculty will be able to know which articles can be requested via the inhouse copying service and which ones they can order directly from the commercial supplier. The university's budget decision-making body decided to fund the holdings-linking project and future use of user-centered document delivery for faculty through separate monies![6]

User-centered document delivery is the wave of the future. Will it make for better service? It depends. Careful monitoring of use coupled with user training should make for successful outcomes. As more academic libraries take the plunge into this innovative method of supplying information, keep in mind one benefit to document delivery departments. Some document delivery traffic will be sent directly to the commercial document suppliers, which will take some of the load off document delivery staff. In times of increasing demands for service, any re-routing of document delivery traffic will be appreciated.

DOCUVERSE

Truly, the information world is becoming an electronic cyberspace without walls. With so much information in your face, it will require astute decisions about not only whether to own information, but whether it should be leased, licensed, rented, borrowed—or even downloaded. It is past time to acknowledge that academic libraries cannot physically own all the information needed to satisfy the research needs of our institutions and to plan in earnest for accessing what is needed. Collection development policies must focus on the access versus ownership issue and strive to make some sense of the amorphous "docuverse" gathering in the ether around us. Collection development must also be about "filtering" the grain from the chaff— an intellectual task that will command ever more respect by impatient, knowledge-hungry clients awash in information detritus.

Flexible experimentation with the Information Resources and Access Budget can be a key to locking the Pandora's box of increased serials expenditures, runaway inflation, and a decreasing ability to satisfy users' information needs. Ownership of information in a digital world is fast becoming an oxymoron, an anachronism created by the virtual library. Access the future!

SELECTED READINGS

Bluh, Pamela. 1993. "Document Delivery 2000: Will It Change the Nature of Librarianship." *Wilson Library Bulletin* 67(6): 49-51, 112.
Hewison, Nancy S., Vicki J. Killion, and Suzanne M. Ward. 1995. "Commercial Document Delivery: The Academic Library's Perspective." *Journal of Library Administration* 21(1/2): 133-143.
Jackson, Mary E. 1995. "Redesigning Interlibrary Loan and Document Delivery Services." *Wilson Library Bulletin* 69(5): 68-69, 113.
Mosher, Paul L. 1995. "*Real* Access as the Paradigm of the Nineties." *Journal of Library Administration* 21(1/2): 39-48.
Pederson, Wayne, and David Gregory. 1994. "Interlibrary Loan and Commercial Document Supply: Finding the Right Fit." *Journal of Academic Librarianship* 20: 263-272.
Saunders, Laverna M. 1995. "Transforming Acquisitions to Support Virtual Libraries." *Information Technology and Libraries* 14(1): 41-46.
Shapiro, Beth J., and Kevin Brook Long. 1994. "Just Say Yes: Reengineering Library User Services for the 21st Century." *Journal of Academic Librarianship* 20: 285-290.
Stix, Gary. 1994. "The Speed of Write." *Scientific American* 271(6): 106-111.
Stockton, Melissa, and Martha Whittaker. 1995. "The Future of Document Delivery: A Vendor's Perspective." *Journal of Library Administration* 21(1/2): 169-181.
Truesdell, Cheryl B. 1994. "Is Access a Viable Alternative to Ownership? A Review of Access Performance." *Journal of Academic Librarianship* 20: 200-206.
White, Herbert S. 1995. "The Cost of Knowledge and the Cost of Ignorance." *Library Journal* 120(11): 48-49.

NOTES AND REFERENCES

1. Gay N. Dannelly, "Resource Sharing in the Electronic Era," *Library* Trends 43 (1995): 665.
2. "National Interlibrary Loan Code, 1980" (adopted by Reference and Adult Services Division Board of Directors, New York, 1980), *RQ* 20 (1980): 29.
3. "National Interlibrary Loan Code for the United States, 1993" (approved by the RASD Board of Directors, February 8, 1994), *RQ* 33 (1994): 477.

4. Mary E. Jackson, "Uses of Document Delivery Services," *SPEC Flyer 204*, (Washington: Association of Research Libraries, Office of Management Services, November 1994), p. 1.

5. Marilyn M. Royce, *ARL/RLG Interlibrary Loan Cost Study: A Joint Effort by the Association of Research Libraries and the Research Libraries Group*, (Washington: ARL, 1993), p. 4.

6. Sheila Walters, "User Behavior in a Non-Mediated Document Delivery Environment: The Direct Doc Pilot Project at Arizona State," *Computers in Libraries* 15(9) (1995): 22-26.

INCLUDING ACCESS IN CONSPECTUS METHODOLOGY

Rebecca C. Drummond and Mary H. Munroe

ABSTRACT

Access to resources has become an important component in building library collections, in spite of resistance to giving up the idea of the "library as warehouse" concept of academic librarianship. However, access has been poorly represented in evaluations and assessments of collections, a fact that may well contribute to some of the misunderstandings, particularly administrative ones, surrounding the issue of access versus ownership. This paper argues for inclusion of access points as an integral part of evaluations and assessments, particularly conspectus methodology, and postulates some factors that will need to be added to conspectus guidelines and methodology to insure that access is adequately evaluated and recorded.

INTRODUCTION

Traditionally, using the conspectus methodology, collections have been measured in terms of ownership, not access. Levels are assigned to collections on the basis of what the library owns, not what it can obtain. As new technologies such as the Internet, rapid document delivery, and full-text products blur the distinctions between ownership and access, libraries need to be able to use the conspectus to describe access as well as ownership. This paper will discuss the traditional use of the conspectus to describe and assign levels to collections and argue that access as well as ownership should be reflected in the conspectus through the inclusion of access in the worksheets and in the guidelines. Standards for providing access to resources will also be discussed in the context of conspectus methodology.

ACCESS VERSUS OWNERSHIP—THE QUESTION

In the twentieth century, American university libraries sought to emulate the German academic precept that bigger collections were better. Libraries were advised to be self-sufficient and to meet patron needs, even if the material was requested only once in 10 years. Early methods of collection evaluation stressed quantity over quality by using quantitative methods, such as shelf list counts and volume comparisons, as the primary method for assigning conspectus levels. The ACRL Standards for College Libraries released in 1959 stressed quality, but Stielow and Tibbo observed that the standards "gave the general impression that collection adequacy could be measured in terms of collection size."[1] The Clapp-Jordan formula, which sought in 1965 to remedy the deficiencies of the ACRL standards, still used quantity to measure quality by using number of volumes as one factor in assessing library collections.[2]

Beginning in the 1970s, many libraries began to question the "bigger is better" credo. Rising book and serial costs, the publishing explosion, and inflation forced even the largest research libraries to begin to rethink this idea. Other factors such as space, budget constraints, and preservation concerns began to make it evident to many librarians that bigger was not even an achievable goal. However, old habits die hard, and the concept of bigger is better is still a prevalent philosophy. Johnson lists four beliefs that are still common in libraries today:

- The best libraries are those with the most physical volumes and the greatest number of monographs and active serials.
- Libraries must buy comprehensively across all disciplines to assure that some unknown title purchased today will be available when needed at some point in the future.
- Ownership is the ideal: reliance on resources off site is a poor second.
- It is more cost effective to own everything that might be needed than to expend resources only on what is needed when it is needed.[3]

Many librarians, administrators, and faculty act as though these assumptions still hold. Librarians and administrators use numbers to justify larger budgets and give numbers to accrediting agencies when programs are evaluated. Many faculty members are scandalized when they are required to go across town to another institution for the material they need. As a result, libraries still attempt to collect comprehensively. A university in a nearby state recently instituted a mammoth approval plan to buy everything published, prompting one bibliographer to call it "the big dumb university that buys everything" model of collection development, reflecting increasing doubts among librarians that comprehensiveness always equals quality. However, libraries applying to be an ARL (Association of Research Libraries) library are still required to hold a substantial minimum number of volumes.

Johnson recommends that "libraries should reduce their collecting scope by backing away from seeking to build multiple comprehensive collections."[4] Libraries should support major research interests and curtail collecting in areas that are no longer important to the institution. The implementation of this recommendation does not have to mean a complete overhaul of the entire collecting policy. It can be done at the subject level. One example could be a subject area like labor history. Suppose the library has expended time and resources to build a special collection of primary labor resources that supported an active program in the 1970s, but in the late 1990s only two professors are actively doing research in this field. In this hypothetical situation, suppose that the history department is now more interested in working class history, a broader emphasis and one not so focused on labor. The library could then move to match collecting levels to the change in emphasis and give up the necessity to continue comprehensive collecting in an area no longer relevant to curricular and research interests.

One powerful reason for libraries to continue older collecting models was the continuing difficulty and unreliability of methods of access. However, new technologies, such as fax transmission of documents in interlibrary loan, document delivery of journal articles, and electronic access to data bases via the Internet, make better access for patrons possible. Access to the World Wide Web expands the horizons even further, making some of the nation's premier special collections accessible remotely and using the graphical interface to provide on screen and downloadable art and photographs. Providing the full text of monographs is still a problem, but institutions such as the University of Virginia and Cornell are using scanning technology to make significant monographs available electronically and to provide the full text of manuscripts in digital form, a technology that is revolutionizing textual study of documents. More full-text databases of journals, newspapers, and complete works of authors are now available for patrons. When libraries commit to providing this access to patrons, libraries will have less need to have everything on site, and hopefully the urge to acquire everything will moderate.

The old "just in case" paradigm of collection development allowed users to see and touch physical volumes, but the patron had to travel from one library to another for access to discrete collections. The electronic revolution is beginning to change this paradigm. Patrons can gopher from one library catalog to the next and use the World Wide Web to access information not available before. For example, a project in Georgia is making finding aids from Georgia library special collections available electronically on the World Wide Web. Patrons know the material is available before making a special trip to the special collections department of a Georgia library. With the funding of the GALILEO Project in the University System of Georgia, many undergraduate resources will be available from individual computer terminals in libraries, faculty offices, dorm rooms, and homes across the state. Not everything will be available by computer, nor should it be. The virtual library of Star Trek episodes is not yet a reality. However, more and more basic resources are and will be accessible for patrons from home and all over college campuses.

Part of the problem that has encouraged the "bigger is better" philosophy is that access by traditional interlibrary loan has been the last resort for patrons or for scholars who have time to wait. Students who needed information quickly either had to go to another library, change their topic, or settle for what they could find in their home library. Johnson emphasizes that it is up to libraries to budget for access and service by making access a priority.[5] Libraries can make access a priority by evaluating and weeding little-used, expensive periodicals and services in order to provide free access through database searches, document delivery, or fax transmission. Interlibrary loan should be supported with more personnel and up-to-date machinery, and the emphasis should be placed on delivering information, not owning it. We need to develop guidelines for good access. We already know the definition of bad access—the patron not having the information in a timely fashion and not being able to browse the information before he gets it, assuming a library is willing to lend it. As libraries make a commitment to provide patrons good access to electronic materials, it will become more acceptable to administrators, accrediting agencies, and other libraries to include access when determining the level of a library's collections.

Futas, discussing microcomputers and reference, wrote: "In some libraries, the distinction between manual and online tools is perceived as a difference between having real materials and contracting for services from outside sources, not as having the same information in different formations.... Failing to come to grips with the issues of new technology will create an enormous disservice."[6] Indeed, failing to address the issues of evaluating access as part of library collections is a prime example of such a failure.

THE HISTORY OF THE CONSPECTUS SUPPORTS THE OLD PARADIGM

The conspectus method of collection evaluation is a technique developed by the Research Libraries Group in the early 1980s to describe collections owned by its member libraries. It had been preceded by the ALA *Guidelines for Collection Development* (1979) that classed collections by (a) comprehensive level, (b) research level, (c) study level, (d) basic level, and (e) minimal level to describe existing collections and current collecting activity.[7] The complex history of the RLG Conspectus is described by Blake and Tjoumas in "The Conspectus Approach to Collection Evaluation: Panacea or False Prophet?"[8] Using the LC classification scheme, collections are assessed by division (the broadest breakdown, such as history), the category (such as U.S. history), and the subject (the most specific breakdown, such as U.S. War of 1812). When collections are evaluated, levels are assigned from 0, out of scope, to 5, comprehensive, in which a library attempts to collect all published and unpublished materials in all formats. Language, collection strength, acquisition commitment, and collection goals are assigned for division, category, and subject. Methods can be quantitative, such as shelf list counts, or qualitative, such as list checking or citation analysis.

The conspectus was developed so that large academic libraries could share information on their areas of collecting strength. It was hoped that using the conspectus would foster cooperative collection development and make it unnecessary for libraries to attempt to collect everything. This methodology has been adopted and adapted by other academic libraries in the last decade. The RLG Conspectus has been used now by many libraries across the world and was modified by the Library and Information Resources for the Northwest Project (LIRN) to aid in assessing smaller and medium-sized library collections.[9] According to the *Pacific Northwest Collection Assessment Manual,* "the conspectus is a method which enables libraries to assess their collections on a subject-by-subject basis according to standardized criteria and to describe collection strengths and weaknesses."[10]

Even though the conspectus was initially developed to describe and evaluate large research collections, small and medium-sized academic libraries have attempted to use the conspectus methodology to describe their collections and have struggled with the concept that "the more we own, the better." The RLG version, designed for large research libraries, makes the assumption that large collections, which would fall easily into large and comprehensive levels, are to be evaluated. Even at the research library level, the conspectus has not lived up to the potential librarians ascribed to it when it was gaining acceptance as the method of collection evaluation in the mid-1980s. Ferguson, in discussing the barriers to cooperative collection development, cites the ownership paradigm, competitiveness, and autonomy as three reasons that cooperative collection development through the use of the conspectus has not been successful in research libraries.[11] The ownership paradigm says that the library must bring the patron and the material together, and ownership was seen as the most direct way to do this. This is the old concept that if you collect more, you will be more likely to have what patrons need and will not have to rely on anyone else. This concept had a trickle down effect as smaller and medium-sized libraries began to use the conspectus. They felt they had to have more resources to compete with the bigger research libraries. Competitiveness comes into play when libraries want to look better to one another, impress administrators that they have wonderful collections (or do not have them and need more money), or attract leading scholars to their institutions. Autonomy simply means that libraries want to control their own destinies and to be self-sufficient.

When the conspectus is used to reflect the ownership paradigm, not access, librarians feel that more resources are needed to obtain and acquire more material in order to raise the library's collection levels. Ferguson feels that the need for cooperative collection development was not adequately addressed by the conspectus for large research libraries, and unless it is modified to include access, its utility may be diminished in the future for other libraries as well. "The whole conspectus scenario imagined that once librarians understood each other's strengths and weaknesses, they would make reliance agreements and agree who would do what in areas of weakness."[12]

In order to communicate to each other specialized areas in which other large research libraries did not need to collect, RLG developed the Primary Collecting Responsibility (PCR) concept along with the conspectus methodology and guidelines.[13] In reality this concept did not really foster cooperative collection development—these were very obscure areas in which the other libraries were not interested. Faculty still objected if their favorite collected works were lent to another institution. The conspectus has not encouraged cooperative collection development, but it could be used to give libraries credit for the resources now accessible through the Internet, document delivery, or by fax transmission if the library provides adequate and reliable access to these resources.

THE GUIDELINE AND LEVEL PROBLEM

Guidelines and levels are not particularly clear even about ownership. They do not address access at all. Coffey discusses the inconsistencies of the RLG supplemental guidelines for education, women's studies, and philosophy. Education does not list any works for the minimal level, while women's studies gives resources for the minimal level and the percentage that the library should own from this resource.[14] He notes that other problems occur at level 3 since it is unclear if doctoral research is supported at this level or just the curriculum. The philosophy guidelines seem to suggest that material to support doctoral research should be available in a level 3 collection, while the women's studies and education guidelines refer to dissertation research at level 4. Blake and Tjoumas consider the RLG levels to be ambiguous since language in the definitions for levels 3 and 4 are so similar.[15] The wording in level 3 says that the collection is "adequate to support undergraduate and MOST graduate instruction"[16] (does this include some doctoral instruction?) with "a wide range of basic monographs, complete works of major important writers,"[17] while level 4 is to "include all the important reference works and a wide selection of specialized monographs as well as a very extensive collection of journals and major abstracting and indexing services."[18] The difference may be the difference in the journal collections and the extent to which the monograph collection deals with narrow research topics, while both levels 3 and 4 should include the important reference works.

The Pacific Northwest guidelines are guilty of extremes in overlap, a distinct problem if ownership is the only issue. For example, the 1988 guidelines list the percentage of periodical index coverage in the appropriate Wilson Indexes as 50 percent for level 3a and 75 percent at level 3b.[19] If the coverage falls somewhere "in between," the selector must use judgement to assign the level in one direction or another. The vagueness leads to wide variances in assignments among libraries, and all of the guidelines are quantitative. Even in such qualitative areas as list checking, the measure is still percentage of ownership. None makes any reference to electronic sources, much less to access to off-site sources. Another problem for medium-sized libraries is that the Pacific Northwest Conspectus guidelines do not deal with levels beyond three very effectively. The larger, but still not gargantuan libraries have difficulty coping with distinctions and with the fact that the guidelines use only such general indexes as the Wilson Indexes to measure subject level ownership.

The Pacific Northwest version of the conspectus addressed the problem of levels to a certain degree through the breakdown of the

RLG collecting levels 2 and 3 into 2a, 2b, 3a, 3b, and 3c, thus allowing smaller universities to describe smaller collections with more precision. There is no provision, however, in the current RLG or Pacific Northwest conspectus for the description of a library's access to new technologies or to materials held anywhere other than on site. Only owned holdings can be described.

The vagueness of the instructions in the RLG and Pacific Northwest manuals for conducting collection evaluations and the problems with determining the differences in levels are partly to blame for libraries' reliance on hard, quantitative numbers. Siverson, in his discussion of the conspectus implementation, says, "evaluators are in effect treating all items as *if the collecting level indicates nothing more than volume thresholds.*"[20] For example, what makes a collection a "research collection" versus an "undergraduate collection"? Methods such as list checking and shelf list measurement of owned library materials have been the traditional ways of evaluating a library's collection, thus reinforcing the concept that more ownership is better. Matheson believes that there are problems with the conspectus methodology since the differences between levels 2, 3, and 4 are so vague, and there is no indication of how many methods should be used to assess a collection.[21] Siverson says the conspectus has a "lack of empirical precision" and notes in the library literature "disquiet over the ambiguity of its definitions of levels and sublevels."[22] One solution to these problems is the proposal made by Stielow and Tibbo of using a two-dimensional model or grid when assessing a collection. They included monographs, serials, reference, government documents, primary (sources), and media in their grid, then assessed these collections at basic, survey, advanced, research, and comprehensive levels.[23] Access could easily be included in this grid, and the level of the resources could be indicated.

To summarize, the language of the RLG Conspectus guidelines are considered vague and ambiguous by many practitioners in the field of collection development. They are also out of date since many have not been revised since the late 1980s. There is no provision in the guidelines for access since electronic resources available to libraries today were not in wide use when the guidelines were written. Keeping the conspectus guidelines and manuals current does not seem to be a priority project for WLN, which is maintaining the RLG guidelines (the Pacific Northwest manual has also not be updated since 1988), but librarians have turned to them in the endless search for greater objectivity in the assessment process. Therefore, if the conspectus is to be used as an evaluation tool for library collections in the next century (unless everyone has access to a huge virtual library), access should be included as a factor in the RLG and other Conspectus guidelines.

HOW DO WE DEFINE ACCESS?

Some patterns of the use of access are already clear. The Internet will be an important vehicle for delivery of materials and for access to indexes and abstracting sources. For example, in Georgia, Emory University, the University of Georgia, Georgia Institute of Technology, and Georgia State University have cooperated to provide access to the science, social science, and arts and humanities modules of *Current Contents*. Access to the index is provided through the Peachnet connection to the Internet. The index is mounted on the mainframe at the University of Georgia, but holdings information from the cooperating libraries are included. The four participating institutions have agreed to check journal listings before a journal is canceled to be sure that the institution is not the sole owner of the source, in which case the library would check with its partners before discontinuing the journal. A system by which interlibrary loan requests can be sent electronically to the lending institution is being developed. Finally, the GALILEO project will broaden access to this source from all the libraries in the University System of Georgia. There ought to be a way that this access to the journal collections at the cooperating libraries could be reflected in the conspectus projects done in Georgia.

Other examples of access points include the Internet's role in document delivery. Over the Internet, access to services such as Carl UnCover, the Information Access full-text system, and other document delivery providers is easy and, in the case of the indexes to Carl UnCover, is free. Other document delivery systems use Internet transmission as a major vehicle for rapid delivery of articles. For example, the University Center in Georgia uses the Ariel System of scanning articles and then transmitting them to patrons within the system through fax and Internet transmission. The GALILEO Project is providing the full text of ABI Inform, Periodical Abstracts, and Business Dateline, among others, to the Georgia System libraries through the World Wide Web.

Finally, new technologies are blurring the distinction between ownership and access. Full-text and full-image products, such as Proquest and ADONIS, are providing alternative formats for delivery of journals to supplement, or in many cases, to replace traditional ownership. One library in the Georgia University System has simply canceled all of the print journals that are provided on its full-text system. Indeed, in some libraries the full-text system is not even mounted locally but shared among campuses through networking, as in the GALILEO Project in Georgia mentioned above.

Given all of these factors, is it time to design a conspectus methodology that includes access to materials in whatever format as a major component of evaluation? If the conspectus methodology is expanded to include access, there must be development of coherent and relevant standards for a library to claim access to materials in evaluation of its holdings. Some of those standards are emerging from the libraries' experience in using these new technologies.

Access standards must include the period of time necessary for delivery of information. The traditional two to three week interlibrary loan delivery time simply does not qualify as real access. Delivery must take place within 36 to 48 hours. Fax transmission, scanning, and online delivery by ftp are making these turnaround times possible, but libraries cannot avoid the necessity of the expansion of ILL staff and the increase in training which are required to accomplish this task.

Patrons must have easy access to sources that list, clearly and briefly, the methods by which they can access information. Such access should include an automated union catalog for easy identification of materials. The PALS system, used by Georgia State University, provides such a catalog. It includes the monographic holdings of 35 libraries of many types across the state. Periodical indexes can also be mounted and holdings displayed but only for the libraries that use the PALS system. Others cannot see specific holdings. An important element of providing this holdings information should be the provision of circulation information on monographs and serials. Providing this information to users is the hardest part of providing a union catalog, but it must be there to provide maximum access.

A union catalog is just the beginning. Adequate access to electronic resources has to be more than just "Why don't you try the Internet?" Horror stories abound about access to electronic resources. One library provided subscriptions to electronic journals, but access to the journals was provided on one workstation in reference and used so infrequently that none of the reference librarians knew how to access the e-mail account where the journals were stored. The journals were not listed in the catalog. Hypertext links to those journals from a cataloging record would have solved this problem neatly. Another case involved indexes that were loaded in an online catalog but not listed on the opening menu of the catalog. In still another case, indexes were loaded at another university, accessed through their catalog, and only available through complicated access to the Internet. The guidelines must weed out access which falls outside the readily available, user-friendly access. The minimum has to be a menu-driven system. A graphical user interface, such as access to the World Wide Web through a web browser like Netscape, is even better.

The conspectus model should also give some consideration to arrangements that include reciprocal borrowing privileges at institutions located close enough for easy access. The GALILEO universal borrowers database is in testing in Georgia, and other systems are already up and working, such as Ohio's OHIOLINK system. The conspectus methodology should allow for this type of access and perhaps give some weight to access as well as ownership. Many accreditation bodies already allow such access as a criterion for provision of information, and some count access as strongly as ownership. Recent visitation teams to Georgia State University have asked questions about access to other libraries and to the Internet. They have been satisfied with reciprocal borrowing and access to the Internet as criteria for provision of information resources, particularly journals.

The danger, of course, in relying on access is that enthusiastic administrators, finding a way to save some money, may cut budgets severely because, of course, users have access to other libraries. Part of access standards must be a clearer delineation of what constitutes the core that all libraries that offer, say, a Ph.D. program in history must have. We have begun the task with tools like *Books for College Libraries* that define a core collection for undergraduate libraries. We need to work to define a core through overlap studies and some statistical work that will provide a basis for establishing what every library must own to be considered adequate at each of the levels. This means that we have to work on those vague guidelines. Overlap and uniqueness studies, such as those based on OCLC cataloging records, can be very helpful in defining what the core is for a particular subject and finding out what strengths we have. Once we have established a core for levels 1 and 2 of the conspectus, then we could establish better and more substantive guidelines for what levels 3, 4, and 5 should be. The library community has enough experience in writing guidelines to avoid the pitfalls of guidelines that are on the one hand too particular to a local setting and on the other hand are so vague as to be meaningless. Once the core is established, access can be an important part of providing materials beyond the core. One of the barriers to cooperative collection development which Ferguson mentions is autonomy. Librarians "defend the need for autonomy because they are unsure of their own fiscal futures and distrust everyone else."[24] In addition, they exhibit "a general lack of information ... about the needs of their own users."[25] For both of these reasons, relying on access is frightening for librarians and for their institutions, but it is a reality in a world where not everyone can afford to own everything. Libraries cooperate or they become obsolete. There is no real choice. Librarians can begin to talk to their users using a variety of methods, both statistical and qualitative, that the profession has been developing over the years. They can also test through pilot projects and deal openly and honestly with the problems that will inevitably arise.

Document delivery is another method of access which must be accounted for in conspectus methodology. Expecting patrons to pay the full cost of delivery, which can run $18-$25 an article, is probably not realistic. To qualify for true access, the library may need to subsidize at least part of the cost to primary patrons of the library. When evaluating a collection, would more weight be given to the library that subsidizes more of the cost? Research libraries are already beginning to work toward standards for document delivery as evidenced by the ARL NAILDD Project, begun in 1993, which plans to "improve interlibrary loan and document delivery services for users, and to make them more cost-effective to research libraries."[26] Standards developed in this project could form the basis for conspectus evaluation criteria.

Delivery of material ordered by a variety of methods has in many libraries been improved so that the item is delivered directly to a patron's workstation. Most academic libraries are thinking about this kind of service, but it is fully available in only a few. The research libraries involved in the ARL NAILDD project, for example, are considering making this delivery method a part of standards for access. However, present conspectus methodology does not make internal delivery methods a part of evaluation of a library's collections, and it would require a major change to do so.

RECOMMENDATIONS

One of the problems with papers such as this one is that all too often no solutions are offered. In this case, the solutions are long term and require commitment and much effort to implement. However, the promise of conspectus methodology and cooperative collection development to save library collections for future generations rides on our willingness to commit to long-term, arduous solutions. Already, some paths that the library community must take are clear.

1. *Revise the conspectus worksheets.* Stielow and Tibbo have postulated a grid which, if used, might broaden and deepen the present conspectus worksheet methodology. The grid would establish levels based on different types of material—monographs, serials, reference works, government documents, primary sources, media. This recommendation would favor adding access as a seventh type of material. Levels would be assigned in these areas. [27] Revision would also have to include reconsidering using call numbers alone as subject indicators. Already the women's studies guidelines have recognized the problems with call number indicators. Dividing out the areas might make the rewriting of guidelines easier, since more specific criteria could be used.
2. *Revise the conspectus guidelines.* The conspectus guidelines have been a source of much controversy. If the multidimensional model proposed by Stielow and Tibbo were to be used, the guidelines would need to become more specific. In addition, most of the guidelines were written when access was not really an issue. Standards for access are emerging and can be used to evaluate quality.
3. *Establish a core.* At each level in the conspectus, there has to be a core. Overlap and uniqueness studies, verification studies, bibliography checking, and others can be used to establish the minimum basic standard for each level of the conspectus. The

problem with the first three of these recommendations is that they are very labor intensive. However, librarianship has both CMDS and CODES as organizations devoted to better collection development. If we cooperate (that word, again), the responsibility and the work could be shared.

4. *Define access standards.* The more experience libraries have with using access to augment collections, the more librarians will know about what constitutes acceptable access and what does not. The library community must be willing to say what works. As Schumann puts the issue, "The mission of librarians is not just to simply fill specific information needs. Our mission is to solve information problems."[28]

5. *Make the assignment of collection responsibility above the core possible and be flexible about the assignment.* One of the problems with assigning primary collecting responsibility has been the problem of autonomy that Ferguson mentions. Librarians do not have much faith in their fiscal future. Assignments need to be finite. None of us can promise for all time. And when responsibilities change, the responsibility can move to another institution. Duplicate PCR assignments would go a long way toward making the responsibility less onerous and transition easier. Including these considerations as a component of conspectus methodology and for satisfying accreditation requirements could be an important boost for cooperative collection development, which often snags on the need of individual libraries to prove ownership. It would be a step toward freeing academic libraries to work toward identifying and accepting responsibility for collection development in areas where they have strength and giving up responsibility for areas where their collections are not as strong. In the labor history example used earlier, the library would give up responsibility for comprehensive collecting in labor history and change its emphasis to working class history. Someone else would pick up the slack in labor history. The academic library would receive credit for access to the area of strength collected by another library and would be able to lower the collection goal for that area in its own library. Limited budgets could be spent more effectively if the responsibility for maintaining collection goals could be spread out.

The ultimate question is whether ownership, except of the most basic core collection, is outmoded in the brave new world of electronic access to information. It may be that inclusion of access points in conspectus methodology is an interim step. Eventually, access may be more heavily weighted than ownership in all but the largest and most heavily funded of academic libraries. Making access an integral part of the evaluation of collections is one way of integrating these choices into a thoughtful, carefully chosen mix of information sources, and the conspectus is one tool that libraries can use to foster better communication concerning these new resources.

NOTES AND REFERENCES

1. Frederick J. Stielow and Helen R. Tibbo, "Collection Analysis in Modern Librarianship: A Stratified, Multidimensional Model," *Collection Management* 11(3/4) (1989): 77.
2. Ibid.
3. Peggy Johnson, "When Pigs Fly, or When Access Equals Ownership," *Technicalities* 12 (February) (1992): 5.
4. Ibid.
5. Ibid., p. 6.
6. As quoted in Sheila S. Intner, "Differences Between Access vs. Ownership," *Technicalities* 9 (September) (1989): 5-6.
7. Stielow, p. 78.
8. Virgil L.P. Blake and Renee Tjoumas, "The Conspectus Approach to Collection Evaluation: Panacea or False Prophet?" *Collection Management* 18(3/4) (1994): 1-31.
9. Ibid., p. 11.
10. *Pacific Northwest Collection Assessment Manual* (Salem, Oregon: Oregon State Library Foundation, September, 1988), pp. 3-6.
11. A.W. Ferguson, "The Conspectus and Cooperative Collection Development: What It Can and Cannot Do," in *Collection Assessment: A Look at the RLG Conspectus* (New York: Haworth Press, 1992), p. 107.
12. Ibid., p. 108.
13. Ibid., p. 110.
14. Jim Coffey, "The RLG Conspectus: What's in the Numbers," in *Collection Assessment* edited by Richard J. Wood and Katina Strauch (New York: Haworth Press, 1992), p. 76.
15. Blake and Tjoumas, p. 22.
16. Ibid.
17. Ibid.
18. Ibid.
19. *Pacific Northwest Collection Assessment Manual*, pp. 41-42.

20. Scott E. Siverson, "Fine-Tuning the Dull Roar of Conspectors: Using Scaled Bibliographies to Assess Collection Level," in *Collection Assessment: A Look at the RLG Conspectus* (New York: Haworth Press, 1992), p. 55.
21. As quoted in Blake and Tjoumas, pp. 22-23.
22. Siverson, p. 46.
23. Stielow and Tibbo, p. 84.
24. Ferguson, p. 109.
25. Ibid.
26. Mary Jackson, "Research Libraries Redesign Access and Delivery Services," COLLEV-L, August 23, 1994, Subject: No. 584A-ARL ACCESS AND DELIVERY STATEMENT.
27. Frederick J. Stielow and Helen R. Tibbo, "Collection Analysis and the Humanities: A Practicum With the RLG Conspectus," *Journal of Education for Library and Information Science* 27 (Winter) (1987): 155.
28. As quoted in Wayne R. Perryman, "The Changing Landscape of Information Access: The Impact of Technological Advances Upon the Acquisition, Ownership, and Dissemination of Informational Resources Within the Research Library Community," in *Managing Technical Services in the Nineties* (New York: Haworth Press, 1991), p. 91.

USING THE WLN CONSPECTUS TO ASSESS A LAW LIBRARY COLLECTION

Elizabeth Thweatt

ABSTRACT

This paper describes a collection assessment performed in a medium-size law library using the WLN Conspectus software. It briefly defines the conspectus approach, outlines preliminary decisions made prior to performing the assessment, explains the process, and offers an evaluation of the work accomplished by the library.

BACKGROUND

A collection assessment "is an organized process for systematically analyzing and describing a library's collection, using both quantitative and qualitative measures ... based upon a descriptive approach to the subject information levels and formats available in the collection. It is not judgmental of the collection, but descriptive of its extent, age, scope, language, format, etc."[1] It attempts to measure the library's collection against the universe of materials.

Assessment data may be collected at the Division, Category, or Subject levels, or a combination of the three. There are 24 Divisions (broad areas) and approximately 4,000 subjects (specific areas) in the Conspectus. Assignment of collection code may be done by the five-point whole number or the more precise 10- point scale. It is important to decide which Divisions will be completed before the assessment process is begun, and also to determine the level for collection code assignment; determine the type and amount of data to be gathered; review existing documentation related to the collection; and determine appropriate techniques to use to get the needed data.

Collection management is most effective when the assessment is based on both *qualitative* and *quantitative* data used in combination with both *collection-centered* and *client-centered* techniques. Client-centered techniques measure how the collection is used by patrons. Collection-centered techniques examine the content and characteristics of the collection (size, scope, depth) compared with external standards.

PROCEDURE FOR GONZAGA UNIVERSITY SCHOOL OF LAW LIBRARY

Preliminary Decisions

Use the conspectus approach for collecting, analyzing, and recording data for the law library collection. Order and utilize the WLN Conspectus software and manual.

Measure the collection at the subject level (most detailed level) using the precise 10-point scale measurement for the Division LAW only, with emphasis on United States law. The other 23 Divisions in the Conspectus are not to be examined and analyzed, but related titles listed in the legal bibliographies will be recorded as appropriate as non-K/KF/JX supporting materials indicating whether or not the library holds the title.

Create worksheets to collect data from the library holdings and from subject bibliographies by subject and date of publication. Create a data analysis work sheet to record data on the book collection and record holdings of non-book materials.

Use—in part to determine collection assessment emphasis—a list of faculty teaching and research interests already compiled from faculty surveys conducted over the past three years as a guide for current collection development.

Also develop as a guide for further emphasis in the collection assessment process and for use in material selection emphasis, a list of subject offerings for 1982-1994 showing subject, times taught, and year last taught.

Order and analyze the WLN Gap Analysis and Statistical Summary Report. It is to include the holdings of 17 identified law libraries to be run against the Gonzaga Law Library's holdings.

The *quantitative* measures selected to analyze the collection, include counting the number of titles in the collection by subject and age using the electronic catalog and by examining the Interlibrary loan borrowing statistical analysis report. The Interlibrary loan lending statistical report will not be examined.

The *qualitative* measures selected to analyze the collection include checking our library holdings against titles listed in selected standard legal periodical indexes and standard legal bibliographies. The WLN Gap Analysis and Statistical Summary Report is to be used as a point of comparison with the data gathered from bibliographic searching.

The Process

Before any actual work could begin on the assessment, it was necessary to research methodology for collection assessment with particular emphasis on the conspectus approach. Once the research was completed and the preliminary decisions outlined below were made, following the standardized procedures was fairly straightforward.

The first two steps of the process were done almost simultaneously. The WLN Conspectus software was ordered; as soon as the libraries to be included in the WLN Gap Analysis and Statistical Summary Report were identified, that report was ordered:

Libraries in the WLN Gap Analysis & Statistical Summary Report

Alaska Court Libraries
Perkins Coie Library
Schroeter, Goldmark & Bender Law Offices

Short Cressman & Burgess Law Library
University of Idaho Law Library
University of Montana School of Law Library
Watcom County Law Library
Idaho State Law Library
Montana State Law Library
Washington State Law Library
Northwestern School of Law Library
Bogle & Gates Law Firm Library
Karr Tuttle Campbell Law Library
Lane Powell Spears Lubersky Law Library
Preston Thorgrimson Shidler, Gates & Ellis Law Library
University of Washington Gallagher Law Library
University of Puget Sound Law Library

The purpose for having this report run was to look to our own database where records for our collection reside and compare our library holdings against other law library collections recorded in the database. We reviewed the *WLN Membership Directory* to identify law libraries listed there. We could have asked WLN to request a purchase of other law library database records and load them into WLN to be run against our collection. We did not have a guarantee that this could be done, although there was a high probability that it could be, and we had no idea of what the cost might be, if it could be done. We decided to have the report run against the 17 law libraries we had identified. The holdings of the 17 libraries when deduplicated totaled 129,818 titles. Comparing our library holdings with this file produced the following results:

Matching records:	23,939	18.5%
Close matches (title only)	1,769	1.4%
Non-matches (the gap):	103,592	80.1%

For the LAW collection only, the report produced the following results:

Matching records:	19,346	24.0%
Close matches (titles only)	1,431	1.8%
Non-matches (the gap):	59,743	74.2%

The illustration shows a summary only. The detailed gap analysis report shows a line-by-line analysis of the collection by subject from the conspectus perspective.

Identifying the collections to be compared using the gap analysis report, having the report run, and ordering the WLN Conspectus software were the first steps taken after planning the project.

Examining the collection was a labor-intensive process. Some of the work forms are included in the Appendix to illustrate methods used to gather the information. The first step was to look at the collection by subject and date through individual title listing in EAGULL, the law library's electronic catalog. The online catalog is the most comprehensive file we have to identify our records in isolation from other library catalogs. The data gathered in this step give a picture of the collection by the subjects examined. A student assistant was assigned to record this information. This is a standard method used in collection assessment.

The second labor-intensive task in the analysis process was to perform bibliographic checking. Materials identified in the initial planning stage for this purpose included the *Index to Legal Periodicals, Current Law Index, Recommended Publications for Legal Research, Law Books Recommended for Libraries,* and, for comparative purposes, selected volumes of *Current Publications in Legal and Related Fields.* State legal materials listed in the bibliographies were checked against the titles in the collection but it appeared that Washington state was sparsely covered. To obtain a broader perspective, *Washington Legal Researcher's Deskbook 1994* was also used to examine Washington state materials in more detail. Well into the project, a request was made to do an analysis in an interdisciplinary area which had not been considered in the initial plan. Some staff members volunteered to do limited checking of the major bibliographies listed above but the work was completed primarily by the author and a student assistant. This portion of the project entailed checking item by item the titles listed in the periodical indexes and the titles divided by subjects in the bibliographies against the library's electronic catalog and recording each entry by date of publication on the tally form. The purpose of this step was to determine the strength of the collection in light of the universe of material. The goal in this step was to obtain a measurement not to make a judgement about the collection. This is another standard method traditionally used in collection assessment. The interdisciplinary subject—international business transactions—was examined after other work was completed.

Interlibrary loan reports that reflected the items borrowed by the library and loaned by the library over the past five years were analyzed and recorded for subjects and legal periodicals as a subject. A minor element of the interdisciplinary aspect was noted for selected legal subjects. Only items borrowed by the library were recorded in this instance.

A walk through the library to examine the physical collection was the next step. In this process, the audiovisual collection, the microforms collection, and the book collection were examined in light of the information collected in the bibliographic checking process. The tally had been consolidated onto a different form which totaled counts for each subject by date. Because of the nature of legal collections and the constant changing and updating of materials, the physical examination of the collection may have more importance for law than a variety of other disciplines. The collection needs to be examined to determine if it is properly updated, if the updates are on the shelves, and if they are not, whether the books are properly marked to indicate that. With the background information gathered in the bibliographic checking, it will be apparent if there are large gaps in any area of the collection. Preservation needs are also revealed at this point. It also becomes evident if the collection needs to be weeded.

Examining an interdisciplinary subject area and bringing the data into a comprehensive whole can be quite challenging. Lacking current comprehensive bibliographies, we approached the bibliographic searching in a variety of ways. We examined one older bibliography which centered on the subject being assessed. We examined an older general bibliography and a current general bibliography under a variety of related topics. We visited a college library with a strong teaching emphasis in the subject area. In the final analysis, the library visit had little value beyond identifying one bibliography. Finally, we performed selective bibliographic database searches of subjects identified in previous work, examined titles listed by the subjects, and checked library holdings for those records. The data was recorded in the same manner as it was for the other subjects but the work was much more intensive. The analysis was more tentative.

Evaluation of the Process

The assessment has enabled us to gain a knowledge of our collection strengths and weaknesses in precise subject areas. Gathering data, particularly the bibliographic checking, was much more time-consuming than anticipated. The information obtained is valuable and can enable us to develop our retrospective collection in particular areas. The assessment could have been carried out by taking samples rather than attempting to be comprehensive in each subject selected for examination. The time when a subject is selected for intense collection development is soon enough to do a comprehensive examination. Recognizing how much data to gather is critical to completing an assessment in a timely manner.

When using collection assessment software, a review of the subjects and the classification ranges before the data collection begins can be an important time-saving step. One valuable feature of the WLN Conspectus software is that it allows for local and interdisciplinary analysis. This allows for deviation from the standard examination of subjects and for combining a variety of subject aspects. For example, rather than collecting data on *Contracts KF801-1241,* I preferred to examine *Contracts* combining *KF801-870* (Contracts generally) and *KF898-905* (Construction Contracts) for a local analysis. Also, I received a request to evaluate *International Business Transactions*, which was not in the Conspectus. I had enough experience to know I could evaluate representative subjects within the discipline and obtain reliable assessment data. In this instance, I included *International Business Enterprises* (generally), *Foreign Corporations, Export and Import, Foreign Licensing Agreements, International Trade,* and *International Taxation.* Also, instead of searching comprehensively, I performed sample searches.

Standards for performing collection assessments have been in place for approximately 15 years. These standards transfer easily from one discipline to another. It is important to plan the process before the project begins and it is very helpful to know the unique characteristics of the discipline being examined. Using proper professional judgment is the key to resolving difficult issues.

APPENDIX: ILLUSTRATIONS AND FORMS

Standard Collection Codes:[2]

0   Out of Scope (library does not collect)
1   Minimal Level (library has few items)
    1a Minimal Level, Uneven Coverage
    1b Minimal Level, Even Coverage
2   Basic Information Level (a selective collection meant to introduce and define the subject)
    2a Basic Information Level, Introductory
    2b Basic Information Level, Advanced
3   Study or Instructional Support Level (a balanced collection of representative works current and retrospective adequate to support study but not to support research)
    3a Basic Study or Instructional Support Level
    3b Intermediate Study or Instructional Support Level
    3c Advanced Study or Instructional Support Level
4   Research Level (a collection that is adequate to support research at the dissertation or independent research level of a specialized discipline)
5   Comprehensive Level (a collection which attempts to include as far as possible all significant works in all formats and applicable languages for the subject)

Quantitative Guidelines for Assigning Collection Ratings

Percentage of Holdings in Major Subject Bibliographies:[3]

1b or less	5% or below
2a	less than 10%
2b	less than 15%
3a	15-20%
3b	30-40%
3c	50-70%
4	75-80%

Periodical Coverage[4]

    1b/2a   some general periodicals plus coverage in recognized special or major indexes

2b	2a plus broader selection and 30% of titles in recognized special or major indexes and access to the indexes
3a	50% of titles indexed and access to indexes
3b	75% of titles indexed and access to indexes plus access to nonbibliographic databases
3c	3b plus 90% of titles indexed plus access to major indexing and abstracting services

Table A.1. Assessment Data Gathering Work Sheet

Publication Year	Subject	Call Number		
		Have Collection	Have Bibliography	Do Not Own Bibliography
1900-1995				
1985-1989				
1980-1984				
1975-1979				
1970-1974				
1960s				
1950s				
1940s				
1930s				
1920s				
1910s				
1900s				
1800s				
1700s				

Note: This table is used to gather data from checking the library catalog and subject bibliographies.

Table A.2. Subject Collection Analysis by Age

Conspectus Line # _____
LC Call # _____
Subject _____

Publication Year	Collection Holdings	Bibliography Have	Bibliography Do Not Own
1990-1995			
1985-1989			
1980-1984			
1975-1979			
1970-1974			
1960s			
1950s			
1940s			
1930s			

(continued)

Table A.2. (Continued)

1920s	
1910s	
1900s	
1980s	
1700s	
Totals	

Note: This table is used to transfer data from the Assessment Data Gathering Sheet and to calculate percentage of holdings.

Table A.3. Physical Examination of Collection Work Sheet

Conspectus Line # _____	
LC Call # _____	
Subject _____	
Collection: # of Titles in Catalog	
Collection: # of Titles on Shelf	
Collection: # of Titles Checked Out	
Special Collections: AV, Micro, CD, Other	
Median Age	
Comments: Discrepancies in Data Gathered, Missing Titles, Currency, Preservation, Weeding, Others	

Note: This work sheet is used to view the collection in light of the information gathered from bibliographic sources, compare the physical collection with database or catalog holdings, and review the physical condition of the collection.

BIBLIOGRAPHY

Cerjan, M., P. Hazelton, P.R. Jarrett, M. McCluer, and M. Whisner. *Washington Legal Researcher's Deskbook 1994.* Seattle, WA: Washington Law School Foundation, 1994.

Current Law Index. Los Altos, CA: Information Access Corp., 1980-1992.

Current Publications in Legal and Related Fields. Littleton, CO: Fred B. Rothman, 1953, 1980, 1985, 1990, 1992, 1993.

Forcier, P., ed. *Pacific Northwest Collection Assessment Manual,* 2nd edition. Salem, OR: Pacific NW Conspectus Database, 1988. The first edition of this manual was used as a training tool and designed to teach librarians to perform collection assessments in a uniform manner, then contribute their data to the Pacific Northwest Conspectus Database. The second edition adds subject specific bibliographies and give more complete steps for the assessment process.

Index to Legal Periodicals. Edited by Joy London. New York: H.W. Wilson Co., 1994.

Jakubs, D. *Qualitative Collection Analysis: The Conspectus Methodology.* Washington, DC: Office of Management Service, Association of Research Libraries, 1989. This publication reports the results of a survey conducted in 1988. A wide variety of libraries and subject fields and assessment methods are represented.

James, E.R., et al., eds. *Index to Legal Periodicals.* New York: H.W. Wilson Co., 1928-1994.

Law Books Recommended for Libraries. South Hackensack, NJ: Fred B. Rothman, 1967-1976.

Miller, O.J., and M.D. Schwartz, eds. *Recommended Publications for Legal Research.* Littleton, CO: Fred B. Rothman, 1985-1992.

Olson, G.N., and B.M. Allen, eds. *Cooperative Collection Management: The Conspectus Approach.* New York: Neal-Schuman Publishers, 1994. The primary focus of this publication is the use of the conspectus methodology for management in cooperative library collection development efforts.

Powell, N., and M. Bushing. *WLN Collection Assessment Manual,* 2nd edition. Lacey, WA: WLN, 1992. Because I was using the WLN Conspectus software, I used this publication as my primary guide in performing the collection assessment for my library. The manuals represented here all refer to the same standards for collection measurements although the methods for performing assessments may vary.

WLN Conspectus Software User's Manual. Version 5.0. Lacey, WA: WLN, 1993. This manual accompanied the software used in the collection assessment at my library.

WLN Membership Directory. Lacey, WA: WLN, 1994. This publication was used to identify a wide range of law libraries to be included in the WLN Gap Analysis Report. The report provided information for verification purposes in the assessment process.

Wood, R.J., and K. Stauch, eds. *Collection Assessment: A Look at the RLG Conspectus.* New York, Hawthorn Press, 1992. This collection of papers looks at the development, history, and use of the conspectus approach to collection assessment.

NOTES AND REFERENCES

1. Nancy Powell and Mary Bushing, *WLN Collection Assessment Manual,* 4th edition (Lacey, WA.: WLN, 1992), p. 13.
2. Ibid., 32-33.
3. Ibid., 69.
4. Ibid., 69.

A COLLECTION ASSESSMENT MODEL:
A CASE STUDY AT THE GANSER LIBRARY

Sarojini Lotlikar

ABSTRACT

This paper describes a political science collection assessment project accomplished at Ganser Library of Millersville University, Pennsylvania. The assessment approach was holistic. Traditional list checking was combined with online checking of the circulation records of core titles, thus presenting a profile of student behavior and circulation statistics of core titles published during 1920-1988. Advantages of assessment using the online catalog and circulation module are emphasized, although the circulation picture was disappointing. Libraries cannot afford to be just warehouses. Librarians have to work aggressively with faculty to get the core titles used by students with current journal literature, thus advocating ALA's Information Literacy to prepare students for the twenty-first century.

Advances in Collection Development and Resource Management,
Volume 2, pages 93-104.
Copyright © 1996 by JAI Press Inc.
All rights of reproduction in any form reserved.
ISBN: 0-7623-0097-3

INTRODUCTION

A number of circumstances, including the author's sabbatical leave, led to this project. The new young faculty in the Political Science Department was in the process of revising the curriculum, and the newly established Center of Politics at Millersville University was bringing eminent speakers to the campus, thus attracting regional and national attention for election surveys. As a library liaison to the department, I was also involved in collection development for political science.

This was the first time that the Ganser Library had undertaken an indepth assessment project. The hope was that the study and the report would serve as a model for future discipline or program evaluations. The Ganser Library has established weeding guidelines and, over the last eight years, has weeded materials in some subject areas systematically with department faculty cooperation.

Periodic *assessment* studies are recommended by the collection development leaders including Blaine Hall, Mary Bushing, and Anthony Ferguson, but libraries are finding it increasingly difficult to undertake such studies with current responsibilities and pressure on librarians due to the Internet and other electronic services. "Assessing a library collection ... is a tool to enable libraries to be accountable for resources and to engage in decision making to enable them to move towards the accomplishment of unique missions."[1]

Blaine Hall and the Association of Library Collections and Technical Services Collection Management and Development Committee of American Library Association advocate "Regular systematic collection assessments are essential to a well managed collection development program. Assessments, when carefully planned and carried out, can tell you how well you are meeting your collection goals and the collection needs of your patrons."[2]

The objective of my sabbatical leave project was to assess the political science collection at the Ganser Library against the core titles recommended in the American Library Association's *Books For College Libraries* (*BCL*) and other authoritative lists. Because of time constraints, I decided to use *BCL* only. *BCL* includes a comprehensive list of core titles published by commercial presses, university presses, the U.S. government, state governments, and international agencies of the world. The titles are selected by subject experts from the major universities in the United States. Each selection may be viewed as a classic, that is, "a book or an article laying the foundation for a body of work which accumulates over a considerable time period."[3]

My second objective was to identify strengths and weakness in the collection, currency of materials, and to learn whether the library has adequate materials to support the Political Science Department current curriculum and satisfy student needs.

The 1993 Program Review document provided by the Political Science Department was helpful in identifying the current curriculum, new courses, discontinued courses and the direction of the department for the next century.

Ninety subcategories listed under political science in *BCL*, Volume 3, were matched with the courses offered in the Political Science Department.

The original plan was to check all the titles and their use in selected categories listed in the *BCL* irrespective of publication date. But within a day, it was noted that the library owned most of the titles published before 1970, although they were not much circulated. The focus was then directed to current materials published from 1970 to the present, a period showing higher circulation by students and faculty. With an emphasis on current core materials and using the online catalog, I was able to find current titles, related titles by the same author on the subject, and their usage. Sometimes, the library did not have the core title listed in the *BCL*, but it appeared that the related current title on the subject would satisfy user needs.

The collection evaluation approach I adopted was *holistic*, in that the assessment study included not only monographs, reference titles, and government documents, but also included periodical holdings, circulation statistics of monographs of 1920-1988, curriculum materials, video titles, and user behavior.

METHODOLOGIES USED

- Lockett, Barbara. 1989. *Guide to the Evaluations of Library Collections*. Chicago: American Library Association; and
- Hall, Blaine. 1985. *Collection Assessment Manual for College and University Libraries*. Phoenix, AZ: Oryx Press; were used to develop methodology and guidelines for my project. They are excellent.

- *Shelflist count* was used to study the quantitative analysis.
- *Books For College Libraries: A Core Collection of 50,000 Titles.* 1988. 3rd ed. Chicago: American Library Association.[4]
- "Outstanding Academic Books and Nonprint Materials." *Choice: Current Reviews of Academic Books.* Middletown, CT: Association of College and Research Libraries. 1991-1994 March announcements were reviewed.
- *SSCI Journal Citation Reports.* 1993. Philadelphia: Institute for Science Information.
- *Educational Ranking Annual.* 1993. Detroit: Gale Research Co.[5]
- *Circulation statistics for titles with imprint date 1920-1970.* A sample of circulation statistics survey for 100 titles chosen at random in Dewey Decimal Classification numbers of 320-329 (political science), 340-349 (law) and 350-359 (public administration) was generated on the Online Circulation module to study the profile of the usage of the old titles and user behavior.

ASSESSMENT RESULTS

1. *Shelflist Count*
- Total number of titles in Ganser Library: 18,150
2. *BCL Survey*
- Total number of *Core* titles listed: 1,795
    Pre-1970 = 701, 1970-1988 = 1,094
- Ganser has titles with imprint dates 1970-1988: 871 (77%)
- Number of titles circulated at least once from Ganser's holding of 871 titles: 326 (36%)

Titles from categories circulated more than once were identified in the following areas of political rights, political parties, elections, lobbying, civil rights, executive president, vice presidents, suffrage, women, Ku Klux Klan, Martin Luther King, slavery, the John F. Kennedy assassination, censorship of books, German politics, nationalism, Paine, Burke, Hobbes, democracy, liberty, John Mill, human rights, U.N. peace keeping, and constitutional history.

Most of the titles related to women in the field were used heavily. It proved very helpful to me as a liaison to the Women's Studies Program.

CIRCULATION STATISTICS OF TITLES PUBLISHED 1920-1970

Information on the *most circulated titles* and the *least circulated titles was highlighted to judge user behavior patterns and decide whether to withdraw or retain those titles. Those titles with the oldest imprints that circulated were also reviewed for inclusion as a classic or core title.*

a. *Political science* (320 to 329 Dewey Decimal Classification)
   Total number of titles surveyed: 1,400
   Titles circulated at least once: 326
   Titles circulated more than three times: 92

b. *Law section* (340 to 349 Dewey Decimal Classification)
   Total number of titles surveyed: 350
   Titles circulated at least once: 150
   Titles circulated more than three times: 34

The *most circulated two titles* in this section were Grant S. McClellan's *Capital Punishment* (New York: Wilson, 1961) and John C. Laurence's *A History of Capital Punishment* (New York: Citadel Press, 1960). These two titles circulated 25 times during the last three years. These older titles were still used heavily although there are current materials on the topic. Theodore Spies's *The Great Trial of Chicago Anarchists* (New York: Arno Press, 1969) circulated nine times. Books on the Peace Corps and abortion also circulated several times.

c. *Public administration* (350 to 359 Dewey Decimal Classification)
   Total number of titles surveyed: 350
   Titles circulated at least once: 52
   Titles circulated more than three times: 14

The *most circulated* title in this section is the *Lancaster County Planning Commission Annual Report.* (The 1982-1987 reports have a total circulation of 12 for the last three years.) A 1923 imprint, the oldest title circulated at least once during the last three years was Roy Nichols' *The Democratic Machine, 1850-1854* (New York: Columbia University Press, 1923). *Outstanding Academic Books: Political Science* (Choice) 1991-1994 lists were examined. The library has acquired 55 percent of the titles from the lists.

PERIODICALS HOLDINGS EVALUATION

The political science journal title holding list at the Ganser Library was checked against the political science basic title list in *Magazines for Libraries* (New York: Bowker, 7th ed., 1992). The library owns 60 of the 70 titles (85.7%). The library has a strong collection of political science journals supporting the undergraduate curriculum.

The list was also checked against the *1990 American Political Science Association Journal Information List* (Washington, DC: APSA, 1990). The Ganser Library has 35 of the 77 titles recommended for undergraduate programs (45.4%).

The following two categories from the 1993 *Educational Rankings Annual* were selected for checking: political science journals given top quality evaluations by American political scientists and political science journals with the strongest rating among American political scientists. The Ganser Library has all 10 titles listed in both categories.

1993 JOURNAL TITLE CITATION REPORT

The most cited journals under categories of political science, area studies, and international studies were reviewed from the 1993 report. The library has 28 of 73 journals (38%) in political science, 20 of 30 journals (66%) in area studies and 17 of 49 journals (34%) in international relations.

The result was encouraging for a periodicals collection of the size found in the Ganser Library and supporting an undergraduate program, considering that the report is a sophisticated, specialized assessment tool that reviews journals at the doctoral level.

INDEXES AND ABSTRACTS

The library is providing full access to journal and newspaper literature with subscriptions to all three major indexes in print format recommended in *Magazines for College Libraries* as well as CD-ROM titles including *Expanded Academic Index*, *UMI Newspapers*, *Marcive* (GPO), and some U.S. government document reference titles.

Circulation and ILL statistics for periodicals were not available by subject.

Currently, the library is evaluating its periodicals and urging academic departments to cut 20 percent of their subscriptions and maintain just core titles.

NONPRINT RESOURCES

The library has a collection of about 100 videocassettes supporting the political science curriculum.

The assessment study shows that the Ganser Library has maintained currency in its core collection by acquiring 77 percent of the *BCL* titles published between 1970-1988.

Currency is well maintained by selecting and acquiring a large number of government documents relevant to the university's political science and international studies curriculum through the depository program.

The library adds an average of 140 academic political science titles each year at an average price of $40.73.[6] This figure excludes reference titles, periodicals, and abstracts/indexes. The budget has been maintained without any growth, but a one-time supplemental budget was allocated to add titles in political theory and other areas.

Currency is also maintained in the reference collection and the curriculum collection through a separate allocation.

The library has developed a strong collection supporting courses in the U.S. Politics and Government, Constitutional Law (U.S.) and Germany.

During this project, the library withdrew 496 titles, duplicate copies, and older, out-of-date editions.

The Ganser Library has maintained currency in the collection to meet the needs of the program. The so-called classic or core titles are well represented, but they are little circulated. The Political Science Department faculty needs to consider this information. I did not recommend that the library acquire the core titles that the library lacks. Instead, focus should be on why the existing core titles do not circulate and how use can be generated. The faculty has to find creative ways in course assignments for students to see that the core titles are also used with current journal literature. Libraries cannot afford to be warehouses as they were in the past. W. David Penniman states, "Libraries must be viewed, first and foremost, as information delivery systems, not warehouses ... with an emphasis on output, not assets."[7] As Ferguson says, "Our bigger is better" paradigm is under fire.[8]

Recommendations were made to the library director that although currency is maintained by government documents and reference materials to provide information access as a starting point, a growing institution like Millersville University must maintain a balanced collection by acquiring adequate current materials for the main collection of the library in the following areas: public administration (federal, state, and local), international relations, United Nations, Africa and its major countries, Asia, Canada, Mexico, South America, Puerto Rico, the new Eurasian republics, Europe, Australia, and New Zealand. Textbooks in political science will be added to the curriculum center.

ADVANTAGES OF THE PROJECT

The project helped me to become knowledgeable about the curriculum, political science classics and scholars, and the strengths, weaknesses, needs, and gaps in the library collection. My relationship with the faculty involved in the project and my role as a library liaison were strengthened. The faculty became familiar with the library collections supporting the curriculum and the work involved in collection assessment. They also learned about a small part of the library operation. My sabbatical leave report with a color chart describing circulation statistics provided the faculty and administrators with a picture of the circulation record of core titles, student library use, and library needs.

The findings made me proud of how the Ganser Library Collection was built by librarians over the years in support of the curriculum. But circulation statistics raised serious questions. Why collect materials that are not used? Whose responsibility is it to promote use of these core titles? Can libraries afford to keep these titles if they are not going to be used? How can faculty and librarians promote research skills for students and prepare them for the twenty-first century?

CONCLUSION

I agree with Blaine Hall's suggestion that "Collection assessment should be a continuing process, not an occasional activity."[9] At Columbia University the following responsibility statement in selector job description is included: "Regularly review and assess parts of the collection and report the findings."[10]

Millersville University's Ganser Library is committed to an ongoing collection assessment program, although it is labor intensive. In the future, there may be ways to streamline the process. Thanks to a special grant secured by Sara Parker, former commissioner of libraries in Pennsylvania, 200 public and academic libraries in Pennsylvania will receive the WLN Online Collection Assessment Software. Using this software and our own computer-generated statistics on Dynix, we should be able to refine the assessment process and build even stronger collections in the future.

This collection assessment was a rewarding experience, but it would have been impossible without the administration support, classroom faculty cooperation, and involvement of various units in the library.

SELECTED BIBLIOGRAPHY

Books for College Libraries: A Core Collection of 50,000 Titles. 1988. 3rd ed. Chicago: American Library Association.
Bowker Annual: Library and Book Trade Almanac. 1995. New Providence, NJ: R.R.Bowker.
Hattendorf, Lynn C. Ed. 1993. *Educational Rankings Annual.* Detroit: Gale Research Co.
Ferguson, Anthony. 1992. "Collection Assessment and Acquisitions Budgets." *Journal of Library Administration* 17: 59-70.
Hall, Blaine. 1985. *Collection Assessment Manual for University Libraries.* Phoenix, AZ: Oryx.

Katz, Bill, and Linda Sternberg Katz. 1992. *Magazines For Libraries.* New Providence, NJ: R.R. Bowker.
Lockett, Barbara. 1989. *Guide to the Evaluation of Library Collections.* Chicago: American Library Association.
Martin, Fenton, and Robert Goehlert. 1990. *Political Science Journal Information.* 3rd ed. Washington, DC: American Political Science Association.
"Outstanding Academic Books and Nonprint Materials." 1991-1994. *Choice: Current Reviews of Academic Books.* Middletown, CT: Association of College and Research Libraries.
Penniman, W. David. 1993. "Shaping the Future for Libraries Through Leadership and Research." *Libraries and the Future: Essays on the Library in the Twenty-First Century.* New York: Haworth Press.
Powell, Nancy, and Mary Bushing. 1992. *WLN Collection Assessment Manual.* 4th ed. Lacy, WA: WLN.
Social Science Citation Institute (SSCI) Journal Citation Reports. 1993. Philadelphia: Institute for Science Information.

NOTES AND REFERENCES

1. Nancy Powell and Mary Bushing, *WLN Collection Assessment Manual*, 4th ed. (Lacy, WA: WLN, 1992), p. 13.
2. Blaine Hall, *Collection Assessment Manual for College and University Libraries*, (Phoenix, AZ: Oryx Press, 1985), p. vi.
3. Lynn C. Hattendorf, ed., *Educational Rankings Annual*, (Detroit: Gale Research Company, 1993), p. 395.
4. *Books for College Libraries: A Core Collection of 50,000 Titles*, Vol. 3, (Chicago: American Library Association, 1988), p. 358-458.
5. Lynn C. Hattendorf, ed., *Educational Rankings Annual*, (Detroit: Gale Research Company, 1993), p. 401.
6. *Bowker Annual: Library and Book Trade Almanac*, (New Providence, NJ: R.R. Bowker, 1995), p. 493.
7. David W. Penniman, "Shaping the Future for Libraries Through Leadership and Research," *Libraries and the Future: Essays on the Library in the Twenty-First Century*, (New York: Haworth Press, 1993), p. 14.
8. Anthony Ferguson, "Collection Assessment and Acquisitions Budgets," *Journal of Library Administration*, (1989) 17(2): 59.
9. Blaine Hall, *Collection Assessment Manual for College and University Libraries*, (Phoenix, AZ: Oryx Press, 1985), p. vi.
10. Anthony Ferguson, "Collection Assessment and Acquisition Budgets," *Journal of Library Administration*, (1992) 17(2): 65.

APPENDIX

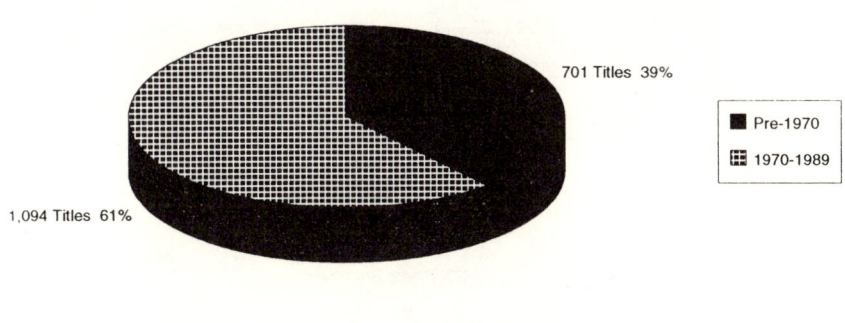

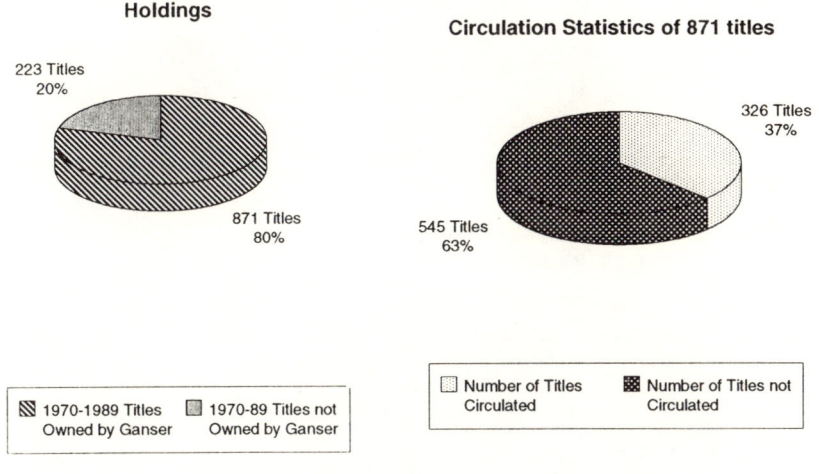

Note: Ganser Library owns a total of 18,150 titles in the Political Science collection.

Figure A.1. Ganser Library Political Science Collection Assessment

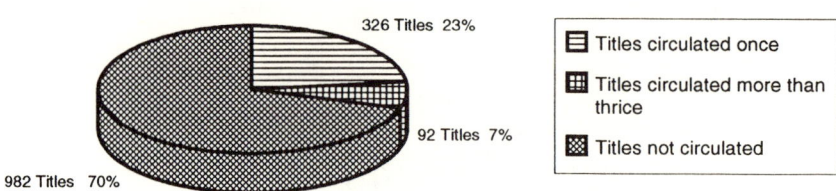
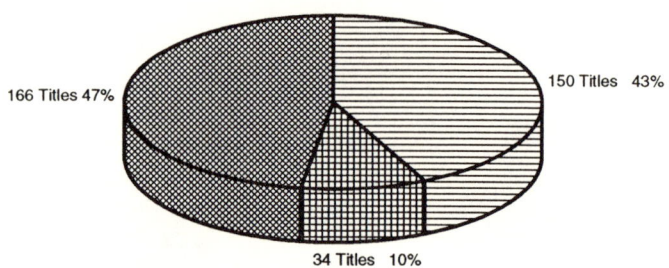
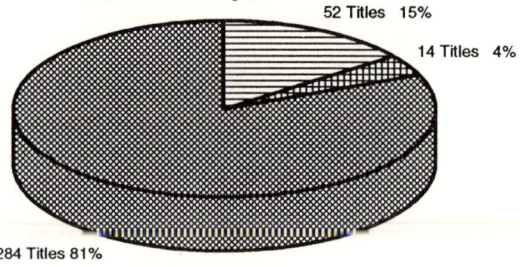

Figure A.2. Circulation Statistics of Titles Published from 1920 to 1970 (random sample)

USING THE WORLD WIDE WEB FOR ELECTRONIC SERIALS COLLECTION DEVELOPMENT

Brian Quinn

ABSTRACT

A search was conducted on the World Wide Web to identify electronic journals that Texas Tech University Library might offer its users as a menu item on the Library Information System, or on the library's Web page. Various Web resources were utilized, including Lynx, Mosaic, and Netscape. Several different search engines were enlisted in an effort to identify as many different electronic journals as possible in the areas of psychology and sociology. The search process as well as the results of the searches are described, and some possible selection criteria that might be used in collecting electronic journals are discussed.

INTRODUCTION

Recently, Texas Tech University Library decided to offer a broad range of electronic journals and scholarly databases to its users. The plan was to make the offerings available as a menu item on the Library Information System, as well as the library's home page on the World Wide Web.

The purpose of the project was to demonstrate to the library's users how much electronic information is available on the Internet in a variety of subject areas. It would also show them the role the library can play in organizing and disseminating electronic information. The library felt it was important to assume a leadership role in this area by positioning itself as the most important resource on campus for electronic information, as well as more traditional paper resources.

Given the preemptive nature of the project, the most rapid methods of assembling and organizing these electronic resources were needed. Consequently, the library decided to temporarily forego some of the usual procedures relating to serials selection and cataloging. There would not be enough time for members of the humanities, social sciences, or sciences teams to engage in lengthy review and debate the relative merits of various electronic serials or to argue about costs. Instead, the associate director of the library asked each of the subject librarians to recommend titles in their disciplines that would best illustrate the range of electronic serials available.

Rather than engage in the usual team debates associated with the serials acquisitions process, the administration decided to rely on the professional judgment of the subject librarians to determine the worth of each selection. It was also depending on the electronic research skills of the subject librarians to track down what would constitute the more important electronic serial titles in their particular subject area. In fact, subject librarians were not only asked to recommend journals but also to submit a brief justification statement for each title recommended. They were also told that they could recommend titles whether they were free or had a subscription cost.

As social sciences librarian, it was my responsibility to locate and recommend electronic journals for the areas of psychology, sociology, and social work. I was also asked to suggest titles for two other departments that I serve as liaison to—human development and family studies, and health, physical education, and recreation. In the interest of brevity, I will limit my discussion to psychology and sociology. Although I had done a considerable amount of "surfing" on the Internet, particularly in the area of psychology,[1] I was only aware of one or two of the better known electronic journals in the social sciences.

The first issue I had to grapple with was to determine what would be the best way to locate electronic journals in my subject areas. It was clear that I would have to conduct a thorough search of the Internet to see what electronic serials could be found. I decided to utilize a variety of search programs or engines, rather than rely on a single one. I wanted to conduct as comprehensive a search as possible, so I would have a range of titles to select from.

SEARCHING GOPHER USING VERONICA

I began my quest for e-journals on the Internet by searching Gopherspace. Gopher was developed in 1991 at the University of Minnesota, as a way to help users find information on campus. Gopher provides access to files on the Internet by organizing them into a hierarchy of menus or lists. You can select an item on a gopher menu by cursoring down to the item and pressing "enter," or by typing the number of the item.

You can also search Gopher using "Veronica," a program that provides keyword-based searches of Gopher directories. The name "Veronica" stands for "very easy rodent-oriented net-wide index to computerized archives." By simply typing in a key word, Veronica will initiate a search of the titles of menu items in Gopher.[2]

Veronica offers two basic choices for searching: only Gopher directories or all of Gopherspace. It is better to choose "all of gopherspace" for the most comprehensive search. Veronica allows you to search for more than one term and enables you to connect terms using "and," "or," or "not."

Using Veronica, I initiated a search of Gopherspace via PSI Net, by typing in the search terms "psychology and journal." This produced a list of approximately 50 journal titles. I went down the list of titles, examining the descriptions of each.

Included in the list were descriptions of one or two well-established journals, such as *Psycoloquy* and *PSYGRD-J*, which are currently published. The descriptions also included subscription information. Virtually all of the remaining listings, however, such as the *Journal of Applied Psychology* and the *Journal of Humanistic Psychology*, merely listed the tables of contents of one or two back issues, which were more than a year old, or contained no listing at all. In many more cases, after hitting the "enter" key, a message would appear reading "Server error: sorry access denied or file does not exist."

Thus Gopher, which had initially appeared to offer very fruitful search results, only produced one or two electronic serials titles. The same poor results occurred when I performed the same search using the search terms "sociology and journal." Overall, Gopher proved to be a very disappointing resource for electronic serials on the Internet.

SEARCHING WORLD WIDE WEB VIA LYNX

I next decided to search the World Wide Web in hope of better results. The World Wide Web is a hypertext-based system for finding and accessing Internet resources. "Hypertext" is a method of presenting information where certain words in the text serve as links to other documents that contain related information. This enables you to electronically jump from document to document in a kind of electronic free association.

The World Wide Web is an attempt to organize all the information on the Internet as a set of hypertext documents. The growth of the Web over the past several years has been phenomenal. Many Internet enthusiasts now consider the Web to be the richest source of information on the Internet. As a result, many new search programs have been developed specifically for searching the Web.

I decided to begin my search for electronic journals on the Web using a Web browser called "Lynx." It was created by programmers at the University of Kansas as part of an effort to build a campus-wide information system. Lynx is only capable of browsing text and cannot handle graphics or sound.

When Lynx displays World Wide Web documents, the "links" or connections to other resources are displayed as highlighted text. Up and down arrow keys move you back and forth sequentially through the links. The right arrow key jumps you to a highlighted link, while the left arrow key returns you to the previous topic. The space bar scrolls you to the next page and the minus key takes you back to the previous page. Typing the forward slash key ("/") will allow you to enter a string of characters which will be searched for in the current document.[3]

I initiated a search in Lynx by typing "lynx" at the Unix prompt. This immediately took me to the Yahoo directory, which is a list of resources available on the Internet. Yahoo (which stands for "yet another hierarchical officious oracle") is organized alphabetically by subject into broad categories such as "Arts," "Business and Economy," "Education," "Government," "Health," and also includes a category called "Social Science." Using the down arrow key, I highlighted this link, then used the right arrow key to select it. This led to a lengthy subdirectory of social sciences categories arranged alphabetically by discipline. There are separate categories labeled "Psychology" and "Sociology," so I highlighted the "Psychology" link and then selected it using the right arrow key.

In the Psychology link, one encounters a lengthy alphabetical directory of psychology resources. One of the links listed is titled "Journals," and I entered this link. Here I encountered a list of nine electronic journals in psychology.

The first of these, the *Journal of Behavior Analysis and Therapy*, was a new peer-reviewed journal that did not appear until 1996. Others, such as the *Journal of Cognitive Rehabilitation* and *Learning and Memory*, appeared to be paper rather than electronic journals that were merely advertising themselves on the Web. Several other titles, however, appeared to be bona fide electronic journals.

The legitimate electronic journals included *The Journal of Mind and Behavior*, which takes an interdisciplinary approach to psychology and related fields, *Psyche*, an interdisciplinary journal of research on consciousness, that is published in both electronic and paper versions, and *Psycoloquy*, a refereed electronic journal that is being sponsored on an experimental basis by the American Psychological Association.[4] In general, it is sometimes very difficult to distinguish between true electronic journals that publish their contents in full-text version on the Internet and paper journals that use the Web to advertise themselves. These "ads" will often include indexes of recent tables of contents of the journals and even abstracts of the articles, making it even more difficult to tell which journals are truly electronic and which are simply paper journals using the Web as an advertising medium.

I was able to locate one other psychology serial by returning to the Yahoo directory and selecting a link called "Social sciences server from Australian National University." There I found a publication called the *What's New in WWW Social Sciences Newsletter*. It is published bimonthly and includes annotated listings of interesting new Web sites in the social sciences, including their URLs (Universal Resource Locator, a kind of Internet address).

Besides the directory listings, Yahoo also offers a search feature, but when I typed in the search terms "psychology and journal," it produced the same list of psychology journals listed in the Yahoo directory. Still, Lynx and Yahoo proved to be more fruitful sources of psychology material than searching Gopher using Veronica. I returned to the Social Sciences subdirectory in Yahoo to see what might be found under the subheading "Sociology."

When I selected the "Sociology" link, it brought me to a list of topics similar to the one found under "Psychology." These include links titled "Criminal Justice," "Organizations," "Progressive Sociology Network," "Psychological and Sociological Technologies." and "Urban Studies." One of the links was titled "Journals," just as in the Psychology subdirectory.

I entered this link, and found two sociology journals listed. One was the *Electronic Journal of Sociology*, a refereed electronic journal based at the University of Alberta. The other is a journal called *Replika-online*. This is an electronic version of *Replika*, a Hungarian journal of anthropology and sociology that is based in Hungary and is published mainly in Hungarian. Fortunately, a full-text English version is also available through the same link as the Hungarian version.

When I returned to the list of topics in the Sociology link, the last topic listed was a link to the Sociology Index in the World Wide Web Virtual Library. This index categorizes information into very broad categories, with titles such as "Institutions," "Specialized Resources," and "General Resources." When I selected the "Specialized Resources" link, it led me to a list of sociology databases and archives that included *Ethnomethodology Newsletter*. This is published by the Department of Sociology at the University of Amsterdam and contains information about new developments in ethnomethodology research, including a bibliography of recent publications in this area. There is also a list of recently published papers in the field and news of upcoming conferences.

Again, I tried the Yahoo search option by typing in the search terms "sociology and journal." It produced a message that read "Sorry, no matches were found containing all the substrings (sociology and journals)." At the bottom of the Yahoo directory were links to several other World Wide Web and Internet search engines. These included Lycos, Webcrawler, Infoseek, and DejaNews. I decided to try some others.

SEARCHING WWW USING LYCOS

Lycos is another web search program that was developed at Carnegie Mellon University in July 1994. The name "Lycos" refers to the first five letters of the Latin name for Wolf Spider, Lycosa kochii. Lycos is a sophisticated search program that uses a probabalistic retrieval system.[5]

Lycos operates by taking a user's query and matching it to both the number of times the word appears in a document and how soon the word appears in the text. Lycos also has Boolean search capabilities, which means you can "and" two search terms together. It claims to index over 90 percent of the Web and can be very effective for broad searches.

I selected the Lycos link which took me to the Lycos Search Form. On the dotted line I typed in the search terms "psychology and journals." This produced a list of 21 matches, which I scrolled through using the space bar.

One of the matches that Lycos found was a link to a list of electronic journals compiled by the library at the University of Pennsylvania. These were arranged alphabetically by subject and contained links to both psychology and sociology journals. The psychology journals were ones I had encountered previously in the Yahoo directory in Lynx, but in the Sociology link I found two electronic journals that I had not come across previously.

The first one was the *Journal of World Systems Research*. This is an interdisciplinary electronic journal based at Johns Hopkins that focuses on scholarly research on the modern world-system. The other journal was titled *Social Science Japan*, which is the newsletter of the Institute of Social Science at the University of Tokyo.

At the bottom of the Penn Library electronic journals directory was a link titled "Directories of Electronic Journals." When I selected this, it produced links to several directories of electronic journals on the Web. One of these was a gopher site titled "Directory of Electronic Journals, Newsletters, and Academic Lists."

Before checking this, I decided to scroll through the rest of the findings. One of the links was titled "Psychology Sites Worldwide."

I clicked on this and was taken to a directory, which listed a link called "Journals." When I selected this link, it brought up a list that included a journal called *Psychiatry On-line*. This is an independent, free, peer-reviewed publication that is solely available on the Web and boasts a readership of 200,000.

I conducted a similar search for electronic sociology journals in Lycos using the search terms "sociology and journals," but this did not turn up any new journal titles. So I decided to see if I could locate any titles by visiting the gopher site I had come across earlier known as the "Directory of Electronic Journals, Newsletters, and Academic Lists." I typed the forward slash key, which allows you to enter a URL. The URL I typed in did not work, so I returned to Lycos, repeated the search, and reentered the Penn Library directory.

The electronic serials listed in the directory were all ones I had already encountered elsewhere, with one exception. *The Research Psychology Funding Bulletin*, which contains information about funding announcements and requests for proposals issued by both federal and private funding agencies, also turned up. When I tried a similar search for sociology, nothing new appeared.

SEARCHING THE WEB USING WEBCRAWLER

After checking the Penn Library directory in Lycos, I returned to the Yahoo Search page to try some of the other search engines. The next search engine featured on the page was Webcrawler. Webcrawler is a web search program developed at the University of Washington. It works by starting with a known set of documents, then identifies new places to search by examining the outbound links from that document, and then visits those links. The documents it finds are presented in order of increasing relevance and are given a score that appears on the screen to the left side of the query results.

When I tried searching in Webcrawler for both sociology and psychology titles, Webcrawler did not yield any new titles that had not already been found by Lycos. This raises the question of how many search engines it is really necessary to employ to search the Web. There appears to be much duplication of search results. Rather than waste time sampling the many engines available, it may make sense to limit one's search to a few of the more popular engines, so as to avoid duplication of effort.

SEARCHING THE WEB VIA MOSAIC

I was curious to compare how effective graphical Web browsers would be when compared to the text-based browsers I had just tried. So I typed "Q" for quit, and exited out of Lynx, hoping to find additional electronic journals using Mosaic. Mosaic is a graphical information browser developed in 1994 by graduate students in computer science at the University of Illinois. It is designed to search the Internet and display the files it finds in a graphical window.

Mosaic formats the information it finds in a colorful graphic fashion. Unlike text-based browsers like Lynx, it can transmit pictures, photos, film clips, and sound.[6] This can be particularly valuable when searching for electronic journals that rely heavily on visual images, as in the fields of art and architecture.

Since this is not generally the case for the social sciences, I could have ended the search with Lynx. But I wanted to try graphics-based browsers to ensure I had done a thorough search. It also seemed important to compare how effectively each of the browsers would search the Web.

I entered Mosaic by clicking on the Mosaic icon on my computer. This brought me to the Mosaic homepage, which listed a number of search options. I chose an option titled "An Index to Mosaic related documents." This brought me to a directory called the NCSA Mosaic Web Index. One of the options listed was "Starting Points for Internet Exploration."

I clicked on this link, and then scrolled through a directory until I reached a link called "Information By Subject." When I selected this link by clicking on it, it brought me to a directory called "The WWW Virtual Library." This directory contains a long list of links arranged alphabetically by subject. When I scrolled down the list, "Psychology" was listed as a subject but did not appear to be an active link, since it was not highlighted.

Under the "Psychology" heading were listed two active links: "*Psycoloquy*" and "Yale Psychology." *Psycoloquy* was an electronic journal I had already encountered in Lynx, but I decided to click on this link anyway, to see how the journal looked graphically. It turned out that recent issues of the journal were inaccessible, although archives were available for downloading to a file. When I next clicked on the "Yale Psychology" link, a Mosaic window popped up with a message that read "Error Accessing HTTP: File/directory does not exist."

I then scrolled down to the "Sociology" heading in the WWW Virtual Library to see if searching it might produce more fruitful search results than the Psychology link had. It appeared to be an active link, and when I clicked on it, I was transported to the "WWW Virtual Library: Sociology" page.

The page contained a short directory consisting of four headings: "WWW Virtual Library Related Fields," "Institutions," "Specialized Resources," and "General Resources." The "Related Fields" heading contains links such as "Anthropology," "Culture," "Demography and Population Studies," "Migration and Ethnic Studies," and "Human Rights." The "Institutions" link took me to a list of sociology departments and institutes organized into four geographic areas: Asia, Australia, Europe, and North America.

The link "Specialized Resources" contained a variety of links to archives, research centers, and institutes. Several electronic journals were also listed. One of these was called *C-Theory*, "an international electronic review of books on theory, technology, and culture." It is sponsored by the *Canadian Journal of Political and Social Theory* and contains reviews of "key books in contemporary discourse." When I clicked on this link, it brought me to a list of reviews that appeared to cover material that ranged from politics, literature, art and cinema, to media, gender roles, and cybernetics. It did not appear to be "sociology" in the sense of being primarily sociologists writing about sociology, although some of the topics could be termed "sociological," in the sense that they were related to society.

The question then arises as to whether this journal might properly be considered a sociology journal. My impression was that it could just have easily been classified as a literary journal, and that it therefore could not really be considered primarily sociology in terms of content. For this reason, I decided not to select it as one of my final choices. The journal is really interdisciplinary in nature, but there are so many of these, they would likely constitute a category in themselves.

Another new sociology journal that I had not come across previously was located in the link "ERCOMER," which leads to the Web Page of the European Centre on Migration and Ethnic Relations. They publish a journal called *New Community: The Journal of the European Research Centre on Migration and Ethnic Relations*. This is a spin-off of a paper journal called *New Community* that has been published in Britain since the early 1970s by the Commission for Racial Equality. The new journal has broadened coverage of migration and ethnic relations issues to include not just the United Kingdom but all of Europe. Only the journal's table of contents and abstracts are available electronically via the Web. The full text is available by subscription only. When I tried to click on a link that promised subscription information, a Mosaic window appeared with an "Error accessing—Connection timed out" message.

Two other electronic journals that appeared in the sociology directory were a publication called *Gray Areas*, which describes itself as an electronic journal of "Law, Music, Technology, Popular Culture, and Reviews." Its stated purpose is to explore the gray areas of life, which the editors define as subject matter that is illegal, immoral, or controversial. It also serves as an open forum for alternative lifestyles and deviant subcultures.

The question raised by this publication seemed similar to that of *C-Theory*. Can this really be considered a sociology journal? Again, if by "sociology" one means sociologists writing about sociology, then this journal would not fit the definition. It might better be termed "sociological" in that it covers social issues, but not from the standpoint of sociology as a discipline. Most sociologists would likely regard it as "journalism" rather than science. Some sociologists who specialize in the study of deviance might find it interesting, but for the rest it would likely prove to be of marginal interest. Again, I did not select this journal because it would not be considered "sociology" in the sense that most sociologists regard it.

Another electronic publication that turned up in the WWW Virtual Library for Sociology was called *Race Poverty and the Environment*. This publication is described by the editors as being a newsletter for social and environmental justice. When I clicked on the link, nothing appeared. But from the title and brief description, this would appear to be more a polemical publication than a scientific one. Simply because a journal covers social topics does not make it sociology per se. It must also treat these topics from a sociological viewpoint and use standard tools of sociological analysis and sociological concepts and vocabulary. It appears that there are a number of new "sociological" journals on the Web that might properly be considered "pop sociology" rather than bona fide social science.

When I returned to the WWW Virtual Library of Sociology directory, I tried clicking on the General Resources link. This took me to a directory listing various archives and associations. When I clicked on the European Sociological Association's link, it took me to the ESA's homepage, which has a link on it to *European Sociologist*. This is an electronic newsletter that focuses on issues of concern to European sociologists. It includes news of conferences, seminars, and events, as well as information about funding opportunities.

When I clicked on the "Newsletter" link, it brought me to a page giving author instructions for submitting material to the publication and announcing that the next edition of the newsletter was planned for November 1995. There was no sample issue to view or archive of previous issues, even though the announcement suggested that previous newsletters had appeared. Although the publication sounded promising, it was difficult to assess given that no version of it was available. I decided I would have to revisit this link at a later date but could not recommend it for possible acquisition by the library without having seen it first.

I again returned to the WWW Virtual Library for Sociology directory and continued browsing until I came upon a link titled *Social Research Update*. This is an electronic journal published quarterly by the Sociology Department at the University of Surrey in Britain. There is a hardcopy version that is available free to subscribers in the United Kingdom. Some of the topics covered in recent issues were social classification, analyzing qualitative data by computer, using diaries in social research, computer assisted personal interviewing, exploring the Internet, ethnographic writing, computer simulation of social processes, and telephone interviewing. Even though it was unclear whether this journal was peer reviewed, a quick survey of the contents suggested that it was a scholarly publication with high standards.

When I returned to the WWW Virtual Library for Sociology, I came across another link called "Socioweb: A Sociological Resource Center." When I clicked on it, it transported me to a directory listing various resources in sociology available on the Web, one of which was titled *SocioWeb 101*. I selected this link and was taken to a page that described the publication as "an electronic journal of undergraduate sociology." This journal describes itself as a WWW review of undergraduate sociology, the premise being that there are not enough forums for interesting work being done by undergraduates in the field of sociology. The editor intends *SocioWeb 101* to be a monthly publication which will be archived. Unfortunately, this is all speculative and no current issue exists, so this is another instance in which I could only plan to revisit the Web site at a later date to check for the journal's appearance.

Overall, it appears that Mosaic yielded mixed results when compared with search engines like Lycos and Webcrawler. These later text browsers proved to be better sources for finding electronic journals in psychology. Mosaic appears particularly weak in this area. The opposite was true for sociology. Mosaic was able to locate most of the journals found by Lycos and Webcrawler, as well as several not found by these text browsers.

Mosaic has two distinct disadvantages when compared with Lycos and Webcrawler. The first is that it is unreliable and often freezes during the course of a search. It failed several times during the course of my searches, and each time I was forced to exit Mosaic altogether and then restart it in order to continue the search. This sort of system failure never occurred using Lycos or Webcrawler.

The other drawback to Mosaic is its sluggish response time. Because it is a graphics browser, it will display images and graphics on the screen. This makes it a vastly more attractive medium visually than Lynx but also increases the time it takes to transfer these images. This slows down Mosaic considerably and makes it frustrating to use, especially when one is in a hurry.

Yet, it is also true that conducting a search for electronic serials in Lycos and Webcrawler is insufficient. In order to feel reasonably certain that one has conducted a thorough search, the text-based browsers alone are insufficient. This is likely to become increasingly true over time as more electronic journals begin to use graphics that will be more easily viewed using Mosaic. For the present, the most effective search strategy seems to be to utilize a combination of both text and graphics browsers.

USING NETSCAPE TO SEARCH THE WEB

My next strategy in searching for electronic serials on the Web was to try Netscape. It was developed in late 1994 by the same team at the University of Illinois that created Mosaic. In fact, it can be thought of as a second generation Mosaic with the same graphics browsing capability. However, Netscape provides greater access to a wider variety of Internet resources such as Usenet. It is also less complex and faster than Mosaic and tends to be less prone to glitches and breakdowns.[7]

To enter Netscape, I clicked on the Netscape icon on my computer screen, which took me to the Netscape homepage. I then clicked on the Net Search icon, which brought me to the Netscape Search page. This page lists a variety of Internet search engines, and one can go down the page and try each one, one at a time. This is what I did, searching each one by typing in the search phrases "psychology and journals," and "sociology and journals."

The first search engine I tried was Infoseek. When I conducted a search for psychology journals, it brought up a link titled "Cog & Psy Sci: Journals and Magazines." This took me to a long list of psychology journals, most of which did not appear to be electronic. There was one on the list, however, called *Psychological Science Agenda*, which is an electronic newsletter published by the American Psychological Association Science Directorate. It publishes news about the status of congressional legislation relevant to psychology and government funding of psychology research.

Another link that proved fruitful was called "Mental Health." It included a list of electronic journals in psychology compiled by John H. Krantz. The list included *The Canadian Journal of Behavioural Science* which publishes original full-text contributions in applied psychology. It publishes research on psychotherapy, child and developmental psychology, organizational behavior, personality, psychometrics, and social psychology, both in English and French.

Another full-text electronic journal that appeared on the list was called *Progress: Family Systems Research and Therapy*. This is a journal published by the Phillips Graduate Institute in California. Among the topics it covers are family stress, joint custody, adolescent sexuality, intimacy, childless couples, and other family-related subjects. Also appearing on the list was *TIP: The Official Newsletter of the Society for Industrial and Organizational Psychology*. This is a quarterly publication that contains articles on customer surveys, merit awards, and employee testing, as well as notices of conferences, workshops, and society news.

This exhausted all the electronic journals on Krantz's list, so I returned to the Netscape homepage and scrolled down to a link titled "W3 Search Engines." When I clicked on this, it brought up a whole list of search engines available for searching. I tried searching the CUI World Wide Web Catalog with no results. The Global Network Academy Meta-Library and Aliweb also proved fruitless, as did RBSE's URL database, NIKOS, JumpStation II, WWW Worm, Ph gateway, and UFN Search. Having tried all the W3 Search Engines, I returned to the Netscape homepage.

I initiated a new search for electronic sociology journals, beginning again with Infoseek. This did not yield any new titles not previously encountered before, so I again clicked on the W3 Search Engine link. A search using the terms "sociology and journals" yielded no findings in CUI World Wide Web Catalog, and the same poor result was true for Global Network Academy Meta-Library and Aliweb. RBSE's URL database turned up nothing, as did NIKOS, JumpStation II, WWW Worm, Ph gateway, and UFN Search.

Just as Mosaic had proved to be a good source for electronic sociology journals but not for psychology journals, the opposite appeared to be the case for Netscape. It yielded a couple of interesting electronic psychology serials but virtually nothing in the area of sociology. Once again, the lesson in this seems to be that any search of the Web for electronic serials cannot be considered thorough unless one tries several different search engines. No particular resource stands out on the Web as constituting anything approaching comprehensive.

Also, it appears that the number of electronic serials available may vary greatly from one discipline to another. Overall, my search yielded almost twice as many electronic psychology serials as sociology ones. This may be due to any number of reasons, such as the relative size of the disciplines, the ease with which "pure" journals may be readily identified (sociology is much more interdisciplinary in terms of content, making it more difficult to identify what might be considered "true" sociology journals), or the relative degree of computer literacy of psychologists compared to sociologists as a group.

SELECTION CRITERIA FOR ELECTRONIC SERIALS

Once I had identified some electronic journals that were being published in my subject areas, the next issue to grapple with was to decide what makes an electronic journal worth collecting.

Unfortunately, there are no good review sources to assess what is available on the Web. What then are the criteria by which one gauges the value of a particular electronic journal? There are a number of considerations that should be made before one succumbs to the temptation to acquire all the free offerings that are popping up all over the Web.

The most important criterion is relevance. One has to ask oneself how valuable will the publication be to a given department, faculty, or group of students. If the journal is unlikely to get much usage, it may not be worth the time and effort required to obtain and maintain it. Within my subject field, I tried to select electronic journals with the broadest appeal. More esoteric titles could conceivably be added later if the initial project proves successful. For example, at one point during my search I wondered if a publication such as *Ethnomethodology Newsletter* or *Social Science Japan* would be as useful to the overall campus population as more general publications like *Electronic Journal of Sociology*. In another instance, a journal called *Self Help and Psychology Magazine* appeared to be too "pop" in terms of content to be appropriate for an academic library.

Another important consideration is access. Electronic journals are sometimes easily accessible, sometimes not. On the Web, it is also possible to access a journal via various means. For example, a journal may be accessible by typing in a URL, or it may be available as a link in a directory. If the journal is not easy to access, if it has a long and complex URL, is it still worth collecting?

A closely related issue is how well an electronic journal is indexed on the Web. Do a number of major directories, such as Yahoo or WWW Virtual Library, include it as part of their listings? The more the journal is included in such gateway directories, the greater the likely awareness of it by patrons, and hence demand for it. Clearly, there will be more demand for a heavily indexed title like *Psycoloquy* than for more obscure publications like *Psychological Science Agenda*. Indexing will become an even more important criterion if indexing services decide to include e-journals in their coverage.[9]

Another important criterion is the degree of uniqueness of the electronic journal. Is the same information available in paper format? Or if the information is roughly equivalent, does the electronic journal convey the information faster, thus making it valuable for its immediacy? Speed of dissemination will likely become increasingly important, and at least in theory the electronic journal has the potential to deliver information much faster than paper journals. Tech Library already has one and in some cases several paper equivalents of many of the electronic journals I was able to find. Yet, they may be worth collecting simply for their preemptive ability. Eventually, most electronic journals may offer keyword access and searchable text.[10] This will give them another significant advantage over paper journals covering the same subject matter.

Language can also be an important criterion. Does the intended audience have enough language facility that they will make use of the journal? At one point during my search, I came across a sociology journal that was published entirely in German. Even though it appeared interesting, I did not ultimately select it because I was concerned that the faculty and students would not make much use of it. So in certain circumstances, language can be a critical factor.[11] It is rare that one comes across journals like *Replika-Online*, the Hungarian journal of sociology that also makes available an English translation, or the *Canadian Journal of Behavioural Science*, which publishes in English and French.

One very important criterion that has received more attention than perhaps any other is that of quality. Many librarians have raised the issue of whether electronic journals as an overall medium are better or worse than paper journals. From what I have seen, electronic journals as a group exhibit the same wide range in quality that paper journals do.

The real concern should be with trying to determine what is a quality electronic publication. One immediate distinction one can make is between peer reviewed journals and those that are unedited. High editorial standards are important if electronic journals are ever going to achieve the same level of respectability among academics that the best paper journals enjoy. Journals like *Psycoloquy* stand out from other electronic publications because of their rigorous review standards and also because of their regularity and consistency in maintaining those standards.

The value of being able to deliver a publication of high intellectual content on a regular basis cannot be underestimated in the world of electronic publishing. All too often a promising journal will appear at a site on the World Wide Web where it will sit for months without a second issue ever appearing. Or just as likely, a few initial issues will appear and then publication will suddenly cease without explanation. It is not enough to be intellectually rigorous, a journal must do it continually to be taken seriously.

Yet even with these considerations of quality in mind, I found myself selecting some electronic journals precisely because they appeared to be less rigorous than their paper counterparts. While a journal like *Psycoloquy* is admirable for its tight editorial control, a publication like *Psyche* may be valuable for its purely speculative qualities. The very fact that an electronic journal permits such material may make it valuable.

This is because many, if not most, paper journals in the social sciences have become so consumed in their quest for scientific legitimacy that they are open to charges of scientism. Social scientists like C. Wright Mills have argued that much of what filters through the system of peer review and appears in print is a kind of "dustheap empiricism."[12] Mills was referring to the trend toward studies that are methodologically rigorous from a scientific standpoint but that are so narrowly focused in their topic of investigation that their findings tend to be insignificant when placed in a broader perspective.

The content of many new electronic journals stands in marked contrast to this sort of arid empiricism. What makes them valuable from a collection development point of view is that they offer a valuable counterpoint to the kind of narrowly focused material that is appearing in many paper journals. If much of the cutting edge speculation in a given field is taking place in these new electronic journals, they would seem worth collecting just for that reason. Beyond tight editorial control, I looked for a certain intellectual richness and liveliness of dialogue. It would seem just as valuable to have a journal that encourages a certain boldness of thinking, so that our faculty and students can keep abreast of what is happening on the frontiers of a discipline.

Indeed, it may be a mistake to try to impose the same selection criteria commonly used for paper journals on electronic ones. To do so might be to overlook many of the most valuable attributes of the e-journal as a medium. If one of the more unique aspects of e-journals is their immediacy, then they could serve as an important source of precisely the kind of messy, speculative, adventurous thinking that most paper journals in the social sciences have virtually abandoned. This is not to say that refereed electronic journals are not valuable or needed. It is only to suggest that some of the more speculative electronic publications may be valuable to a collection because they permit such open thinking. A balanced electronic serials collection should include examples of both.

CONCLUSION

Several lessons can be learned from this project. First, the World Wide Web constitutes a rich source of electronic journal material that can be acquired easily and inexpensively relative to their paper counterparts. Many of these are fledgling publications, the quality of which is inconsistent, and which are issued on an irregular basis. There are a surprisingly large number of these electronic journals now published on the Web, and a handful appear to have established high editorial standards and a consistency of quality that rivals the best paper journals. It is likely that if electronic journals continue to proliferate on the Web at their current rate, the Web will be increasingly used as a collection development tool for electronic serials.

Tracking down electronic journals on the Web for collection development is sometimes a time consuming and frustrating process. Many links that initially appear promising often lead to dead ends, or the URLs do not work, or Mosaic or Lynx is not working properly. Sometimes one has difficulty finding one's way back to a site that one had just visited hours before. Because search engines on the Web are often crude, searches produce many false drops, and one has to wade through much irrelevant material before finding something worthwhile. In retrospect, it seems worth the effort, however, as patience and persistence in searching tend to yield more and better material.

No one particular Web search engine is thorough and effective enough to rely on for a comprehensive search. Using a variety of search engines will yield much better results. Netscape proved to be very effective, as did Lynx.

Indexing of electronic journals on the Web is poor. One frequently finds that journals that are not purely sociology or psychology in terms of content are nonetheless indexed under those subjects. Many new electronic journals are interdisciplinary, and it is not uncommon for a journal like *Postmodern Culture* to be indexed under both "sociology" and "literature," because it encompasses both of these subject areas. Yet, it is not properly a sociology journal nor is it solely a literary one. Subject headings are used very loosely throughout the Web. One learns not to trust headings and to check the actual contents of the journal before being sure of how to classify its subject matter.

There is a great deal of overlap of resources on the Web. Different search engines often produce the same group of electronic journals in their results. The same titles often reappear again and again, and one grows weary of seeing them repeated. One should not rely on a single search engine if one wishes to do a comprehensive search, but neither does it seem necessary to utilize the entire array that can be found on the Web. It is possible to conduct a reasonably effective search by utilizing a sampling of engines.

A final lesson to be learned is that one cannot fully apply the same selection criteria traditionally used for paper sources to electronic journals. Although some of the selection criteria may be similar such as relevance or overlap with other sources, other criteria, like access or traditional editorial rigor, may not be. To insist that all electronic journals maintain the same editorial standards as paper ones may be to sacrifice some of the immediacy and originality that make them a unique and valuable complement to paper journals.

NOTES AND REFERENCES

1. Brian Quinn, "A Guide to Psychology Resources on Electronic Networks," *Behavioral and Social Sciences Librarian* 13(2,1995): 35.
2. Betty Landesman, "Tunneling Through Cyberspace in Search of Adventure: An Introduction to Gopher," *The Serials Librarian* 25(3/4,1995): 19.
3. Greg R. Notess, "Lynx to the World Wide Web," *Online* 18 (July 1994): 81.
4. Stevan R. Harnad, "Psycoloquy: A Model Forum for Scholarly Skywriting," *Serials Review* 18(1/2,1992): 60.
5. Greg R. Notess, "Searching the World Wide Web: Lycos, Webcrawler and More," *Online* 19 (July/August 1995): 49.
6. Beverly K. Duval and Linda Main, "Exploring the Internet With Mosaic," *Library Software Review* 13 (Winter 1994): 269.
7. Warren Ernst, *Using Netscape*, (Indianapolis: Que Corporation 1995), p. 20.
8. Pat Ensor, "The Volatility of Electronic Collection Development, or the Care and Feeding of a Gopher," *Technicalities* 14 (July 1994): 12.
9. Paul Metz, "Electronic Journals From a Collection Manager's Point of View," *Serials Review* 17 (Winter 1991): 82.
10. Carol Harker, "Collection Development for Electronic Materials," *Against the Grain* 7 (April 1995): 21.

11. Anthony W. Ferguson, "Interesting Problems Encountered on my Way to Writing an Electronic Information Collection Development Statement," *Against the Grain* 7 (April 1995): 18.

12. C. Wright Mills, *The Sociological Imagination* (New York: Grove Press, 1961).

COLLECTION DEVELOPMENT AND MANAGEMENT IN THE DIGITAL LIBRARY

Sally Jo Cunningham

ABSTRACT

The increasing importance of electronic media, rather than the traditional paper press, in desseminating information is changing the nature of document collections and in particular affecting the way that documents are indexed, stored, and distributed to the user community. The current subject-specific digital libraries have primarily concentrated on building a initial collections and solving technical problems in providing access to research literature. As these collections and their user bases grow, maintenance and development issues will become critical. These issues are both technical (in ensuring that hardware and software supports users needs, that user searches are processed efficiently, and that the integrity of the index is preserved in the face of the fluctuations of the Internet) and institutional (in preserving a focus in the collection that meets the needs of the library's user community).

INTRODUCTION

Large amounts of research literature have become available over the Internet as university departments and research institutes have made their technical reports, pre-prints, and publications available electronically. Access to these documents has been limited, however, by the difficulties involved in locating items of interest. The original method for obtaining these documents was through anonymous FTP, a file transfer protocol that allows a user to copy files from an appropriately setup system but does not allow that user to modify existing files or add new ones. If the name and location of an interesting document were known, any user could access that file over the Internet. Of course, the problem was learning about the existence of a particular document of interest. Searching for documents involved first discovering the name of a machine containing an anonymous FTP collection of documents; logging in to that machine and searching for the "README" file, present in most collections by convention, that briefly describes the documents contained in the file system; noting the names of potentially interesting files (which could itself be difficult, given the terse nature of the "README" descriptions); then downloading the chosen files. This cumbersome process would then have to be repeated with each FTP site.

General purpose tools such as Archie, WAIS, and Webcrawler have since been developed to search Internet and WWW resources (generally including anonymous FTP sites). These programs are useful for locating known documents but less helpful in performing more general searches over a topic. Moreover, these tools are indiscriminate browsers of the Internet—where quantity is not a problem, but quality may be questionable. There is a growing recognition that many users are better served by subsets of the "raw" Internet, and that these subsets should be augmented by improved means of access and discrimination in selection of documents for the collection.

Recently a variety of "digital library" schemes have been implemented to explore issues in collecting, cataloging, storing, searching, and delivering electronically held information over the Internet. Some efforts focus on what Levy and Marshall term the "broadly-construed" library, a dynamic collection composed of a wide variety of resources intended for a wide variety of users.[1] Maintenance and development in these collections is considered in detail by

Ackerman and Fielding.[2] The majority of formally administered digital libraries are "narrowly construed," providing a focused range of materials to a well-defined set of users. These libraries generally provide search interfaces for one or two types of documents (technical reports, journal articles, pre-prints, or conference proceedings), for a single discipline. The full text of documents are often available, as well as indexing or bibliographic records. They are maintained by professional societies, universities, research laboratories, and even private individuals; their intended user base is a group of active researchers in the collection's defining discipline. Access is generally free, both to search and to download documents.

The emergence of these subject-specific digital libraries is particularly important given the pattern of access to materials presently employed by research scientists. Information exchanges of pre-prints, reprints, and photocopies of papers passed on by colleagues currently are major venues for the transmission of scientific information between researchers. In a study of how scientists locate and retrieve documents, the dependence on these sources ranged from 12 percent (for chemistry) to 39 percent (for mathematics) of all papers cited.[3] For specialized subjects this dependence on informal or extra-library dissemination can be much higher. Ginsparg reports that high energy physics has traditionally relied heavily on formal paper pre-print exchanges between research institutions.[4] The high price of these exchanges limited the number of sites that could participate, while the time delay in the academic publishing process made participating in the research front difficult without access to the pre-prints. The high energy physics digital library (HEP-TH) has democratized research in the field by providing ready, inexpensive access to information sources that were already preferentially utilized by scientists in the field. Researchers in less developed countries report access to current work through HEP-TH that their local libraries could not afford to acquire through conventional journals.[5] The problem of timely scientific information distribution in Third World nations, and its deleterious effects on both research production and effective utilization of existing results, has been widely documented in recent years.[6] The subject-specific digital libraries promise alleviate these problems by increasing the availability of these important types of scientific documents through provision of cheap and convenient access to them.

This paper concentrates on problems in developing and managing a "narrowly construed," subject-specific electronic collection and explores the extensions that are required for traditional collection development and maintenance methods. First, we describe exemplar systems that are currently in use. The technical problems involved in creating and providing a uniform access to a widely dispersed electronic collection are discussed, and the implications of different architectures to supporting user searches are discussed. Finally, the problems of maintaining a growing collection are discussed: selectively adding new materials, dealing with documents that are relocated or that disappear, and enforcing collection size limits (as dictated primarily by hardware resources).

DOCUMENT SOURCES

A number of systems currently exist to provide searching and indexing for subject specific electronic document collections. Currently, most of these systems specialize in computer science, physics, and other hard sciences—representing the interests of the earliest inhabitants of the Internet.[7] The document collection techniques developed for these disciplines are appropriate for other subjects and indeed are seeing use as the population of the Internet broadens (see, e.g., the management, philosophy, and economics digital libraries[8]).

The collections are generally constructed in one of three ways:

- *By harvesting existing documents.* Documents relevant to the subject are located and indexed, with the index alone stored at a central site while the documents themselves remain at their original locations. Examples of this type of organization include UCSTRI,[9] the HARVEST tools,[10] and the New Zealand computer science technical report libraries.[11]
- *By providing a uniform interface for a limited set of sites.* Participating sites agree to standard formats for document storage, and a central index provides uniform search access for all sites. The WATERS system, for example, indexes technical reports from 14 universities,[12] and the DIENST system provides an interface to the computer science technical report repositories for an additional 14 leading universities (formally known as the CSTR library).[13]

- *By building a collection of (primarily) donated materials.* The digital library is a central location for a discipline, to which authors send descriptions of their papers (i.e., title, authors, institutional affiliations, etc.) and either a URL location or (less commonly) an electronic form of the paper itself. The physics e-print archive is a primary example of this type, and its architecture has been successfully transferred to a number of other disciplines.[14]

DOCUMENT FORMATS

For most of these systems, it is assumed that the digital library user will be able to retrieve full documents, rather than bibliographic surrogates. For this to be possible, the documents are required to be in some common format that users can be expected to possess software to interpret or print such as PostScript, HTML, or perhaps a common text processor output (TeX, Word, LaTeX, etc.).

A major advantage of traditional libraries is that they offer a standard, long-lasting access format for documents: paper texts. Digital libraries have no existing standard format, and most accept only a subset of existing documents types, only PostScript, for example, in the New Zealand digital library.[15] The disadvantage lies not only in the documents arbitrarily excluded from the digital library by format but also in the uncertainty of the continued usability of the required formats. Access to documents preserved "forever" in 1981 on 5 1/2 inch floppies in long-forgotten word processors for the CP/M operating system is, to all practical purposes, not possible; similarly, it is unclear that the standards of today will be accessible for the users of tomorrow.

COLLECTION FOCUS

Systems that archive only for a given number of participating sites generally define their collection by document location: for example, a collection concentrating on the field of computer science will index documents held by a handful of university computer science departments, which are assumed to be appropriate for the collection. The participating departments are expected to make quality and relevancy determinations rather than the central indexing site.

Harvesting libraries operate similarly in that they index documents from likely locations; for example, a computer science digital library would include documents found in the anonymous FTP repositories of computer science departments. These latter systems make a further assumption that all documents held in a selected archive are indeed research reports—which may not hold true, as lists of abstracts and other summary material may be included in these locations. The integrity of these collections depend to a large degree on the intelligence of the harvesting system in culling these irrelevant files from the collection.

Digital libraries that depend on author donations have varying degrees of control over document acquisitions. In general, these digital libraries accept submissions that the author feels is appropriate to the focus of the collection. While it is possible that the collection administrator may exercise control by rejecting inappropriate articles, no such instances have been reported in the literature. The research communities that use these digital libraries appear to enforce a topic coherence and quality control through consensus, effectively ignoring documents outside the collection focus (i.e., by not citing these documents or not using them as a basis for further scholarly discussion). It is notable that the original libraries of this type were equipment-intensive subdisciplines of physics. It could be expected that these relatively cohesive communities of authors/users would be successful in self-policing the quality of documents in the collection and that the high cost of conducting research in these areas would minimize quack submissions. It will be interesting to observe whether this type of collection control will be as successful when applied to other disciplines, as is currently initiated in the HEP-TH inspired philosophy pre-print archives.

SEARCHING AND INDEXING FACILITIES

The method for creating the collection dictates the type of indexing and searching that the digital library can support. Since libraries built on author submissions generally require the authors to catalog their own works, these digital libraries generally offer the same types of search that are available in other online bibliographic systems: by author, title, date of publication, and others. Author-provided cataloging obviously lessens the effort required on the part of the system maintainer—generally a practicing researcher who oversees the digital library in spare time. Unfortunately, the records produced are often of mixed quality. For example, consider the following entries selected from the HEP-TH (high energy physics) archives:

1. Authors: A. Yu. Alekseev, V. Schomerus
2. Authors: Adel Bilal and Ian I. Kogan
3. Authors: Paul S. Aspinwall and David R. Morrison (with an appendix by Mark Gross)
4. Authors: A.H. Chamseddine and Herbi Dreiner (ETH-Zurich)

In this case, typical for this type of digital library, there is no standardized format for authors' names (here, appearing with full names, initials plus last name, and a mixture of the two); no standard convention for separating author names (either a comma or "and" are used), and parenthetical information can include a variety of information such as the name of an associate author or the institutional affiliations of an author.

Many of these problems are avoided in systems like DIENST, which index documents only for specially designated sites. These participating sites can exercise much more control over the cataloging of their documents than is possible—and indeed may even designate a site librarian to administer their portion of the collection. The cost, of course, is that enforcing cataloging consistency at the local level necessarily limits the number of sites that can participate in the digital library.

Digital libraries that harvest existing documents do not have user-supplied document descriptions available and must index on other types of document surrogates. UCSTRI, for example, provides a searchable text index based on text obtained by parsing the index ("README") file that is present by convention in most FTP directories of technical reports. As discussed previously, this document description is generally terse (often including only the title and author names) and provides a very small number of terms for indexing. Moreover, the parsing procedure is sensitive to the format of the index file; since these files do not have a standard format, the parsing cannot be guaranteed to succeed. And, of course, the "README" file may not even exist at a given site. Another system, HARVEST, has an essence subsystem that extracts "content summaries" for indexing. Unfortunately, the quality of these summaries varies widely. ESSENCE is based on filetype-specific procedures to extract relevant information from the document itself; for example, markup information in LaTeX documents can be parsed for author and title information. Different document formats yield different levels of cataloging information, and the degree to which a given author adheres to a given format will also affect the summary contents—given that the document format is recognized by essence. In general, the types of search (and reliability of those searches) is highly variable in harvesting digital libraries. The base level search is generally a simple keyword search over the extracted document surrogate, which provides very uneven access for author and date queries in particular.

The New Zealand computer science digital library addresses this problem by permitting the user to limit a search to the initial page of a document, which typically contains the author, title, and the institutions with which the author is affiliated. The publication date field is approximated by searching on document timestamps (the date at which they were entered into their original repositories). Given that many sites are currently digitizing their older paper reports, this type of search is likely to produce erratic results (since the timestamp can only record the date that the report was inserted into the database, not the date that it was originally produced). However, this type of search will become more accurate as the repositories catch up on their retrospective conversions. An intelligent document parser, such as HARVEST's ESSENCE summarization system, potentially provides more precise bibliographic information, and by extension more precise searching, but at the expense of requiring a significantly more complex and filetype-dependent indexing system.

COLLECTION MAINTENANCE

The major focus for the current digital libraries has been building the initial collection. As these libraries emerge from the prototype stage and develop established user bases, they must consider issues in enforcing the integrity of the collection's focus and supporting search software.

Stability is not, unfortunately, one of the characteristics of the Internet. A major problem in maintaining an existing collection is simply ensuring that documents in the collection continue to exist. UCSTRI, for example, reports "frequent maintenance problems" caused by changes in the technical report repositories that it indexes, such as files being renamed or removed from the collection.[16] Maintenance agents (autonomous or semi-autonomous software) ensure the integrity of the document collection by periodically examining the source sites of the digital libraries and updating the collection index accordingly. For those libraries that index exhaustively from individual sites, the same agent can add new documents to the collection by locating new files in the known repositories.

How are new *sites* added? Currently, new sites containing documents relevant to a collection focus are detected manually by monitoring existing lists of relevant sites for new additions, scanning Usenet newsgroups that cover relevant subjects, and encouraging users to e-mail suggested new sites to a central coordinator.

The implicit assumption for digital libraries that index on participating repositories is that those repositories will enforce both quality and focus on the documents they provide. This trust seems well-placed, as the existing libraries of this type report no problems as yet with significant numbers of inappropriate or low quality documents entering the collection. And, of course, a simple sanction exists for any contributing site that violates the library's document standards: exclusion of the site from the collection.

As noted above, enforcing collection focus and quality standards is potentially more difficult for digital libraries that receive document donations from individual authors. These libraries tend to have a much narrower focus—a subdiscipline of physics, for example, as opposed to the entire discipline of computer science. It appears that the relatively small size of these research communities supports a user-based consensus for collection growth. For example, the HEP-TH high-energy physics archive is the original physics library. As the usefulness of this digital library was recognized by other subfields of physics, they established their own specialized libraries (rather than expanding into the HEP-TH collection).

On a more technical level, the size of a digital library's collection is limited by the hardware needed to support it. Computer science research has contributed efficient architectures, data structures, and text compression algorithms to minimize hardware requirements. The common architecture described previously, in which only the index is stored in a central site and the document files themselves remain distributed with their providers, significantly reduces the memory requirements for digital library providers (as compared with storing both the index and source documents in a central location). For example, the New Zealand computer science technical report library currently (August 1996) indexes 22,000 documents that occupy 17 gigabytes in their repositories. An index to the full text of that collection, stored in the central site, occupies only 300 megabytes—a mere 2 percent of the size of the original PostScript document files.

However, an all-inclusive information collection policy is basically unscalable and will become infeasible as the number and size of Internet-accessible and machine-readable documents grows. While as yet none of the newly-established digital libraries have reported reaching the limits of their memory resources, several techniques for culling collections have been proposed. One possibility is to monitor every participating user's access to the collection and note the sites or documents that see the least use. These sites/documents are prime candidates for removal when the size of the collection becomes unmanageable. This technique is attractive in that the rate of growth of the collection, and hence the resources that it consumes, is governed by the size, diversity, and level of activity of the user population rather than by the rate of growth of the bibliographic universe.[17] Further, this pattern of use is easier to track and can be measured more accurately than in a conventional library. "Use" of a document comes when it is selected for downloading from its host site—certainly easier to detect than physical documents being read in a traditional library's stacks.

In some collections it may be possible to use the characteristics of the documents themselves to determine what to delete. Technical reports, for example, are typically most useful shortly after their publication. In computer science in particular, they tend to receive half of their citations within two years, and the rate of citation falls off rapidly as time passes.[18] Given this usage pattern, technical report collections might consider eliminating the more elderly documents, as they are more likely to be obsolete.

CONCLUSION

The current crop of subject-specific, research-oriented digital libraries has concentrated on technical issues in collection development, that is, building an initial collection and providing efficient search software. As these libraries mature, issues in maintaining an appropriate collection focus and size are emerging. Libraries such as the CSTR archives, which simply provide an additional, electronic form of access to a small set of technical reports that have previously been available only in paper, can continue to rely on traditional collection development and maintenance methods. Digital libraries incorporating new materials and collection organizations require new solutions to the development/maintenance problems.

Because of the diversity of documents available in electronic format and the dynamic nature of the Internet, these issues promise to be even more significant than in traditional libraries. Novel, imaginative technical methods are emerging, for example, agent software that autonomously adds new documents to the collection. Other solutions rely on the unprecedented ability of the user community to directly influence the nature of the collection both by facilities through which users can add to the collection directly (or suggest additions to the collection administrator) and by the techniques suggested previously for culling documents based on usage. This increased user influence on collection development emerges from the fact that fine-grained information is available in the digital library about user preferences in individual documents and their sources.

A more formidable difficulty lies in the general architecture adopted by most of the digital libraries discussed in this paper, the central indexing site, with distributed document storage. In effect, this architecture requires document providers to handle long-term collection maintenance. They must ensure that their contributions continue to be available, accessible, and in an understandable format. The sustainability of this system architecture over the long term remains to be seen.

NOTES AND REFERENCES

1. D.M. Levy and C.C. Marshall, "What Color Was George Washington's White Horse? A Look at the Assumptions Underlying Digital Libraries," *Proceedings of Digital Libraries '94*, 1994, pp. 163-169.

2. M.S. Ackerman and R.T. Fielding, "Collection Maintenance in the Digital Library," *Proceedings of Digital Libraries '95*, 1995, pp. 39-47.

3. J. Hallmark, "Scientists' Access and Retrieval of References Cited in Their Recent Journal Articles." *College and Research Libraries* 55(3,1994): 199-210.

4. P. Ginsparg, "After Dinner Remarks: 14 Oct '94 APS Meeting at LANL," 1994, <URL:http/xxx.lanl.gov/blurb>; and "First Steps Towards Electronic Research Communication," *Computers in Physics* 8(4,1994): 390-401.

5. Ibid.

6. W.W. Gibbs, "Lost Science in the Third World." *Scientific American* (August 1995): 76-83; M. Odedra, M. Lawrie, and M. Bennett, "International Perspectives: Sub-Saharan Africa: A Technological Desert," *Communications of the ACM* 36(2,1993): 25-29.

7. A list of many currently available science digital libraries is available at <URL:http://www.larc.nasa.gov/org/library/abstr.html>.

8. Locations:

    management: <URL:http://www.gnn.com/gnn/wic/bus.05.html>
    philosophy: <URL:http://phil-preprints.l.chiba-u.ac.jp/IPPE.hyml>
    economics: <URL:http://www.epas.utoronto.ca:5680/wpa/>

9. M. van Heyningen, "The Unified Computer Science Technical Report Index: Lessons in Indexing Diverse Resources," *Proceedings of the Second International WWW Conference*, Chicago 1994, pp. 535-543, <URL:http:///www.cs.indiana.edu/ucstri/paper/paper.html>

10. C.M. Bowman, P.B. Danzig, U. Manber, and M.F. Schwartz, "Scalable Internet Resource Discovery: Research Problems and Approaches," *Communications of the ACM* 37(8,1994): 98-107.

11. I.H. Witten, S.J. Cunningham, M. Vallabh, and T.C. Bell, " A New Zealand Digital Library for Computer Science Research," *Proceedings of Digital Libraries '95*, 1995, pp. 25-30.

12. K. Maly, E.A. Fox, J.C. French, and A.L. Selman, "Wide Area Technical Report Server," Technical report, Department of Computer Science, Old Dominion University, 1994, <URL:http://www.cs.odu.edu/WATERS/WATERS-paper.ps>; and J. French, E. Fox, K. Maly, and A. Selman, "Wide Area Technical Report Service: Technical Reports Online," *Communications of the ACM* 38 (April 1995): 45.

13. J. Davis and C. Lagoze, "'Drop-In' Publishing With the World Wide Web," *Proceedings of the Second International WWW Conference*, Chicago 1994, <URL:http://wwww.ncsa.uiuc.edu/SDG/IT94/Proceedings/Pub/davis/davis-lagoze.html>.

14. Ginsparg, "After Dinner Remarks: 14 Oct '94 APS Meeting at LANL," and "First Steps Towards Electronic Research Communication."

15. Witten, Cunningham, Vallabh, and Bell, "A New Zealand Digital Library for Computer Science Research."

16. M. van Heyningen, "The Unified Computer Science Technical Report Index: Lessons in Indexing Diverse Resources."

17. Witten, Cunningham, Vallabh, and Bell, "A New Zealand Digital Library for Computer Science Research."

18. S.J. Cunningham, N. Empson, and R. Kamau, "Bibliomania: What Can We Learn From the Research Literature?" *Proceedings of the New Zealand Computer Society Conference*, 1995.

THE TEAM APPROACH TO THE MANAGEMENT OF A GOVERNMENT DOCUMENTS COLLECTION

Eileen Theodore-Shusta and Ray Wang

ABSTRACT

A federal depository collection generally consists of three components—public/reference service, access/circulation service and processing/technical service. While most libraries choose to set up a department that has all three components, others have mainstreamed government publications into their general collections. Binghamton University Libary has yet another approach—it has assigned the different service components to corresponding units in the existing library organization, for effective resource sharing.

INTRODUCTION

Organizational boundaries were often not felt in the old environment where each unit within a library had well defined tasks. However, as automation affects the technical core of the organization, boundaries between traditional divisions within the library become evident and need to be spanned or bridged. "The traditional organizational separation of public, technical and collection services does not accurately reflect how the work of the research library is accomplished and contributes to unnecessary and debilitating bureaucracy and conflict.... Work is increasingly accomplished through project teams."[1]

Nowhere else is this so clearly illuminated as in the government documents area of the library. Existing as a library within the library, all services were traditionally offered from that point. The documents librarian was expected to have expertise in receiving, processing, shelflisting, perhaps cataloging, reference, circulation, and collection management. As these services become increasingly automated, increased levels of expertise are needed. The following are among reasons which account for such challenges.

- Manual shelflisting has given way to online cataloging through national cooperative cataloging efforts and commercial vendoring of those records.[2]
- Electronic access has replaced traditional print resources, moving quickly from floppy disks to CD-ROM products to full-text access via the Internet.
- Most institutions report increases in stacks maintenance, circulation, and reference services after the cataloging on their OPACs of government documents. Circulation statistics grow by as much as 200 percent to 300 percent.[3]
- Proliferation of materials produced in computer file formats, principally CD-ROM, and in full-text via the Internet.

An alternative to expecting the documents librarian to maintain the levels of proficiencies needed is the use of cross-divisional teams, where each member provides his or her subject expertise. The following case study is an example of such a model.

THE PROBLEM

The organizational structure of Binghamton University Libraries is a traditional hierarchy, with services arranged into four divisions: Information and Research Services (I&RS), Technical Services, Access Services, and Systems. Each of these divisions is administered by an assistant director. The libraries select 55 percent of federal depository documents with a heavy concentration in microfiche, 100 percent of New York State documents in microfiche, some local documents, United Nations documents in fiche, and a highly selective collection of documents from other states.

In 1993, the Government Documents Unit fell within I&RS. Staffing consisted of one documents librarian (MLS), a half-time paraprofessional, and one clerk. The librarian, who reported to the head of Reference, was responsible for oversight of collection development, reference, receiving, processing, and stacks maintenance within the Documents Collection. Following the resignation of the documents librarian in 1993, the paraprofessional was reassigned full-time to General Reference.

When inspected in 1994 by GPO, the Documents Collection was cited as being noncompliant in the area of staffing, with staffing at .5 FTE Librarian and one FTE Clerk. It should be noted that an informal survey conducted in 1993 of other comparable depository libraries showed a significant difference in staffing, with most collections supported at or above GPO standards of one professional librarian and support staff at one hour per percentage of collecting (e.g., 55 hours for a 55 percent depository).

Along with the staffing problems, the 1994 GPO inspection failed the collection in the area of bibliographic control, because inadequate staffing did not allow for the maintenance of a shelflist for receipts. The Documents Collection did not have a record of holdings and had not for the past three inspections. Organization of a rapidly burgeoning CD-ROM collection was desperately needed, particularly with regard to access and maintenance of titles mounted onto the public workstations.

In 1993 the library was faced with the following challenges:

- Noncompliance with federal regulations in the areas of bibliographic control and staffing;
- An vacant documents librarian position;

- Training issues in all areas; and
- Lack of formal procedures for administering the collection.

THE SOLUTION

The librarian position remained vacant for close to a year. During the year's vacancy, other staff assumed the collection oversight and development responsibility. A librarian from I&RS was assigned liaison responsibility to Technical Services regarding the Documents Collection during the year. A working group was formed which consisted of the I&RS librarian, the head of Cataloging and the documents processing clerk. The group met on a weekly basis, resolving operational concerns. Arbitrary decisions were made for materials which needed immediate processing. Other items were categorized and placed aside for the documents librarian to handle when the position was filled.

The working group proved to be a good working model for the best use of the libraries' personnel resources. Concerns ranging from staffing to training of student assistants were discussed and resolutions were suggested within the group. Each team member was responsible for communicating information back to her division.

After the new documents librarian was hired, it was decided that this model would continue. A formal work group was formed, temporarily coordinated by the head of Cataloging Services (later coordinated by the documents librarian) and included the head of Circulation, the processing clerk, and other staff as the need arose. The group met weekly, addressing such topics as training, work flow, and coordination of effort.

ORGANIZATION

Receiving, processing, and claiming was placed within Cataloging Services, as the Book Preparation operation was already located in that unit. A mandate for the libraries was to integrate cataloging records into the NOTIS database, Elixir, an integrated OPAC. The documents clerk received an introduction to MARC format and copy cataloging to assist in problem resolution.

Responsibility for stacks maintenance was given to Access Services, supervised by the head of Circulation. These responsibilities included shelving, shelfreading, and removal of superseded materials, tasks performed by 15 hours of undergraduate assistants, supervised by the floor manager. Training of staff was performed by the paraprofessional formerly assigned to the area.

The documents librarian's position was redesigned, resulting in a 50 percent assignment performing documents collection development and oversight, and 50 percent general reference responsibility. It should be noted that the Documents Collection and the Reference Collection are located on different floors, as is Documents Receiving and Processing.

All CD-ROM titles are cataloged, stored in a cabinet in Reference, and are arranged in SuDoc number order. Titles of signifant interest have been loaded onto two public workstations. A program of updating superseded materials is in place.

THE PROCESS

As materials are received in the libraries, they are delivered to the processing clerk. Brief shipping list records are loaded into the libraries' online catalog via FTP from the vendor, Marcive. The clerk physically processes each item and notates the brief cataloging record with receiving information. The brief record now serves as a shelflist, putting the libraries into compliance in the area of bibliographic control. Full-MARC records are sent monthly to overlay the brief records, providing complete description, subject access, and shelflisting in the library's OPAC. A resource file of our retrospective database was created, allowing for conversion of these records, beginning with Congressional Hearings (Y4s). The clerk reviews all shipping lists and technical reports for information regarding new item numbers and superseded information.

New documents are then staged for review by the documents librarian. This ensures the level of knowledge about the collection needed by the documents librarian for reference and collection management. Items of some note are set aside for display by Access Services on a New Book Shelf.

The remaining documents are then sent to Access Services for shelving and superseding. Flags with instructions are placed in items needing superseding by the processing clerk. These instructions are processed by Access Services staff if possible or routed to the documents librarian for his attention if complex. Looseleaf materials and pamphlets are sent directly to the documents librarian for filing. Additional graduate and undergraduate students have been assigned at each stage of the process to help offset staffing concerns.

PROBLEM RESOLUTION WITHIN THE TEAM

As an example of the benefits of the work group, a proposal was made at the administrative level to shift the various collections within the libraries to maximize the remaining space in the building. The shifts were coordinated by the head of Circulation, a member of the group. A principal part of the move included the Government Documents Collections. In anticipation of the move, the group recommended the Federal Depository Collection be reviewed for superseding and weeding as appropriate. No systematic review of the collection had been performed in the immediate past. Using the Superseded List, each item when received was flagged with retention information by the processing clerk. Shelved by Access Services staff, the title in question was reviewed, and materials were identified for withdrawal. Complex retention decisions were routed by Access Services to the documents librarian for interpretation and resolution.

To facilitate the process, the group recommended the hiring of additional student assistants, namely a graduate assistant and approximately 20 undergraduate hours. The undergraduates were assigned to Access Services to aid in shelving and simple superseding. The graduate assistant was assigned to the documents librarian for a general review of the collection. Over 12,000 items were superseded or weeded within the next several months, freeing 375 valuable shelves.

CONCLUSION

The coordination of effort and the level of communication within the group work together to make the process of handling government documents and resulting projects highly successful.

Utilization of the skills, talents, and knowledge of staff in the various divisions of the libraries has aided the libraries in the organization of this collection. Staff have been trained to the levels needed to perform assigned tasks. Procedures are in place for effective control of the collection. The noncompliant areas from GPO inspection (staffing and bibliographic control) have been corrected. The documents librarian is now able to spend much more time than before in providing reference electronically to patrons. In a little over a year's time, many of the problems concerning the documents collection have been resolved. All this was accomplished with no more staff or resources. It was achieved through the implementation of a concept—the concept of team work.

NOTES AND REFERENCES

1. James G. Neal and Patricia A. Steele, "Empowerment, Organization and Structure: The Experience of the Indiana University Libraries," *Journal of Library Administration* 19 (1993): 82-83.
2. Darlene M. Pierce and Eileen Theodore-Shusta, "Automation: The Bridge Between Technical Services and Government Documents," *Cataloging & Classification Quarterly* 18 (1994): 75-84.
3. Thomas Kinney and Gary Cornwell, "GPO Cataloging Records in the Online Catalog," *Reference Librarian* 32 (1991): 259-275.

TOTAL QUALITY MANAGEMENT, CULTURE, SYSTEMS, AND CUSTOMER SERVICE:
APPLICATIONS FOR COLLECTION DEVELOPMENT

Theresa C. Trawick and Rhae M. Swisher, Jr.

ABSTRACT

Every organization—whether business, government, or academe—has its own definition of total quality management (TQM) and its own ideas of how to implement it in the ever changing organization. This paper discusses the elements of TQM applicable to any organization but specifically addresses it as an integral part of managing an academic library and its collections. The focus is on the two major components of an organization: its culture and its systems. The success of the library in the 21st century will depend on management's profound knowledge of work cultures, its ability to choose library personnel who have leadership abilities, and acceptance of the concept that library service quality will be defined by and emanate from a strong collection development nucleus.

INTRODUCTION

One of the most succinct definitions of TQM comes from a study group of the Total Quality Forum, a consortium of business and academic leaders; the Forum defines TQM as:

> a people-focused management system that aims at continual increase in customer satisfaction at continually lower real cost. TQ is a total system approach (not a separate area or program), and an integral part of high-level strategy. It works horizontally across functions and departments, involving all employees, top to bottom, and extends backwards and forwards to include the supply chain and the customer chain.[1]

The pioneer of TQM was Dr. W. Edwards Deming, who early in his career worked with Dr. Walter Shewhart of AT&T Bell Laboratories as Shewhart developed the cycle known as Plan, Do, Check and Act; Deming later modified the cycle as Plan, Do, Study and Act (PDSA). Planning charts were not linear but circular, representing the systems flow in an organization. Not by design but by experimentation, this circular system became a part of the collection management endeavor at the main campus library of Troy State University (to have been educated in PDSA would have been less painful).

Deming's own country, the United States, was slow to explore the TQM concepts; in contrast, Deming's management principles were adopted by the Japanese after World War II, making Japan a major player in the global business community. In a humorous tone that very well expresses the spirit of business in the West and East, Masaaki Imai, author of *Kaizen: The Key to Japan's Competitive Success,* said that the Western world has an expression "If it ain't broke, don't fix it" while the Eastern world has an expression "If it

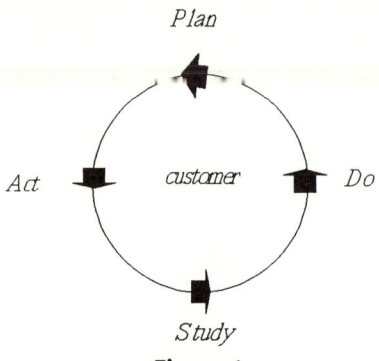

Figure 1

isn't perfect, make it better."[2] It was not until the late 1970s that U.S. corporations began looking at Deming's management approach to "making it better." By 1990, a survey found that about 50 percent of *Business Week's* 1,000 top companies had initiated a quality improvement program of some type.[3] TQM is now being taught in academic programs and being practiced in federal agencies, the armed forces, and non-profit organizations, such as libraries. Pressure from the business community and public administrators brings TQM to academe even while some schools are untangling what it is and how to initiate it.

HIERARCHICAL ORGANIZATIONS AND THE WORK CULTURE

In a hierarchy, management is government or authority by an elite group or by person(s) ranked higher. In management of organizations, a simple interpretation is that the employer tells his workers what to do. In contrast, total quality management (TQM) focuses on systems and processes, not on linear decisions; therefore, typical administrators, who are not grounded in systems and/or who have not experienced daily operations from the ground up, disregard or underestimate the TQM movement. These administrators remain happy with their title and decision-making status. How does the hierarchical management so familiar to most organizations affect the culture of the organization? Why do some attempts at total quality management fail? The answers are in the cultural environment of the work place, where the administrators' and the workers' attitudes build or tear down the quality of service. Even though TQM is associated with change in the work place, it must be emphasized that TQM does not mean unpredictable change and instability for employees—TQM brings stability because the employees are an active part of the decision-making process and have participated in planning how and when change is to be implemented.

As early as the 19th century, Vilfredo Pareto, economist and sociologist, held the belief that emotion and instinct, not reason, drives an organization. Such beliefs have held through the 20th century: James R. Fisher, consultant to American and international business for more than 30 years, delineated in his book *Work Without Managers* (nothing or no one is in control in American business) the cultural types or "six silent killers" in a chapter dealing with "The

Mad Monarchs of the Madhouse." The six characteristics of the "madmen" are as follows:

- *Passive Aggression Behavior.* Coming to work late; leaving early; doing as little as possible to get by, not as much as one is capable of doing.
- *Passive Responsive Behavior.* Never doing anything until one is told; never doing anything that one is not specifically told to do; leaving one's mind at home while bringing one's body to work.
- *Passive Defensive Behavior.* Always having an answer for why something isn't done; always having a memo for every contingency; or being an expert finger pointer.
- *Approach Avoidance Behavior.* Accepting assignments that are never completed; volunteering to support initiatives but never coming through or even showing up; indicating a desire to be challenged but avoiding sacrifices and inconveniences.
- *Obsessive Compulsive Behavior.* Being obsessed with what one does not have and is not, at the expense of what one does have and is; always seeing the grass as greener on the other side of the fence.
- *Malicious Obedience.* Withholding information critical to the successful conduct of business; doing what you're told even though you know it is wrong; circulating disinformation or misinformation, inventing rumors.[4]

Knowledge of the cultural environment and the characteristics of workers must exist before leaders can institute a total quality program. Whereas total quality management nurtures strong leadership, cooperation, and learning to build an emotional environment conducive to continuous quality improvement, a hierarchical management creates rigidity and distance among employees. "A man dare not take a risk. Don't change a procedure. Change might not work well. What would happen to him that changed it? He must guard his own security. It is safer to stay in line."[5] The staff who are to do as they are told do not feel that their ideas are appreciated. Even if formal internal reporting occurs among different departments, it is usually shallow and fragmented. Managers work in an environment of competition as they vie for the attention of senior management. The customer is forgotten.

The impact of the work environment on the quality of service cannot be underestimated. Sweeney's opinion is that the most important aspect of the redesign of systems is people relationships. "These relationships can be either supported or diminished by the organizational structure."[6] Fisher warns that an organization should consider the following edicts before restructuring:

- Individual behavior always follows that of the organizational structure.
- Organizational structure generates unique cultural biases, which translate into collective behaviors.
- To change individual behavior requires giving attention first to cultural biases and then to the organizational structure. You cannot change the structure (*system*) before you change the predominant way in which workers think and feel (*cultural bias*) about work, management, the organization, and themselves.
- Attempts to change behavior by ignoring either the cultural biases or organizational structure contribute to, at best, a temporary remedy.[7]

HIERARCHICAL ORGANIZATIONS AND SYSTEMS

A major downfall of managers in the "ranked" organization involves goal processing. Managers may lay out goals but do not plan or convey the "detailed" means (resources) for achieving the goals. Even more debilitating is when management does not listen to those workers carrying through on goals, nor gives workers the authority to act on a decision. In a hierarchy, the manager and his subordinates attempt problem solving, but the solution is usually a quick fix or putting out the brushfire. Rarely do managers seek solutions to problems beyond their defined parameters, even though most problems cross departmental lines and changes or modifications by one department may adversely affect the next department. Managers from the different "departments" do not meet together to consider work flow from the beginning of the process to the end or to consider thought processes needed to analyze the problems. In fact, most managers are held to their job descriptions that outline responsibility in their segment or slice of the organization.

Knowledgeable managers have found that a small portion of causes of poor products, once discovered, can solve 80 percent of the problems. Vilfredo Pareto, previously mentioned, is known for the 80/20 principle applied to income distribution, and Joseph Juran, another guru of total quality management, adapted the Pareto principle as "80% of problems can be traced to 20% of causes." Hierarchical organizations, because of the segmentation, have difficulty in pinpointing causes. Greg Bounds and cohorts, authors of *Beyond Total Quality Management: Toward the Emerging Paradigm* define failures in a hierarchy as "excessive control, narrow accountability, social isolation, constrained and suppressed communication, incidental customer value, power brokering, overgrown/misused systems, imposed results with no delegated means, and lack of cross-functional responsibility.... Like Humpty Dumpty, an organization with hierarchical management is reduced, divided and broken into pieces, but no one ever puts it back together again to optimally serve customers."[8]

TOTAL QUALITY MANAGEMENT

How does the cultural and systems environment of TQM compare with hierarchical management? Richard T. Sweeney, who wrote "Leadership in the Post-Hierarchical Library," espouses that the "post-hierarchical" library is an "antibureaucratic" one.

> It is an organization which is much more focused on patron or user service and much less bound by inflexible rules and the paperwork tradition.... The post-hierarchical library is not just a change in the traditional library but rather a radically changed concept of a library—i.e., a reengineered library.... It effectively uses many new information technologies, but its most unique characteristics are the new patterns and structures in which people work.[9]

Miriam Drake offers a similar view:

> Survival for many academic libraries will depend on successfully managing the transition from the storage of paper and film containers to a center of learning and information service. Transforming the traditional library into a customer-oriented learning and service center—where people, problem solving, and intellectual content are more important than books and physical objects—is one of the greatest challenges facing academic librarians today.[10]

Drake indicates that the TQM shift for library staff at the Georgia Institute of Technology, where she is dean, began after librarians, administrators, and faculty campus-wide attended a seminar given by Milliken & Company (a Baldridge Award Winner). Drake states that Milliken believed that "TQM practices, so successfully adopted by business, could be applied to institutions of higher learning given time, hard work, and total commitment."[11] In Drake's interpretation of TQM for academic libraries, she indicates that traditional service where librarians find citations to articles or hand books to patrons will not suffice; content and accessibility issues will be addressed by librarians who have a strong customer focus and are willing to create an environment for continuous improvement.[12] Susan Jurow, director of the Association of Research Libraries, Office of Management Services, offers the following: "In a TQM environment, the service focus is not simply an isolated or separate activity or event, rather, *it is an integral part of the entire organization process for accomplishing work and achieving objectives.*"[13]

This integral management style is outlined in Deming's "14 Points"; condensations of each of the points by Rosanna M. O'Neil are given below:

1. Create constancy of purpose for improvement of product and service. Deming explains that problems of the future command "first and foremost constancy of purpose and dedication ... and that to solve these problems management must undergo a transformation" (Deming, pp. 24-27).
2. Adopt the new philosophy.
3. Cease dependence on mass inspection.
4. End the practice of regarding business on price tag alone.
5. Improve constantly and forever the system of production and service.
6. Institute training.
7. Teach and institute leadership.
8. Drive out fear. Create trust. Create a climate for innovation.
9. Break down barriers between staff areas.
10. Eliminate slogans and targets for the work force.
11. Eliminate numerical quotas for production.
12. Remove barriers that rob people of pride of workmanship.
13. Encourage education and self-improvement for everyone.
14. Take action to accomplish the transformation.[14]

TQM AND COLLECTION MANAGEMENT

Deming's principles formed the foundation for collection management at Troy State University (TSU). The following narrative on a TQM approach to collection development at Troy State University main campus library will discuss Deming's principles from a (1) social-cultural and (2) systems-operations viewpoint.

In the mid-1980s at TSU library, the term total quality management was unknown and the term customer not used. Before this time, the library was a hierarchical structure. Supervisors ran a department, respected the boss' wishes and executed his wishes as best as possible in this traditional setting. The TSU director proved to be a visionary who saw the library as part of learning resources and embraced television, radio, and media as information delivery sources. He worked in a fairly stable environment. He and an associate director were the senior administrators. As a result of the Southern Association of Colleges and Schools (SACS) visit in the early 1980s, Troy State University began to hire additional librarians. The associate director had dreams of collection development within the reference department but needed a force to make it happen. The environment was no longer reasonably stable; technological advances were defining the library beyond the four walls; inflation was consuming the materials budget; programs were growing and changing; and the information world was being redefined (librarians or information specialists?).

After several decades, during which the library was managed on a hierarchical basis, the director retired, and TSU hired a new director (mid-1980s), who had a strong background in management, a strong commitment to the development of his staff, and a strong commitment to public service and technology. At the same time, a new head of reference and collection management was hired. Both were in an advantageous position to redefine the management style as new staff were added. Whereas monographic selection had formerly been the responsibility of acquisitions, it became a part of the broader aspect of "collection management" that the collection development committee favored. The leaders played a crucial role "in ensuring the success of quality management," because it was the "leaders' responsibilities to create and communicate a vision to move the firm toward continuous improvement and to provide formal and informal support to enable the creation and sustenance of an organizational system ... receptive to process management practice."[15] Admittedly, in the early phases of establishing quality management, much of the support was informal and rudimentary. An obvious first step was to study work flows. For example, the committee gathered information on the means to inform collection development committee members about serial cost changes and title changes and developed a system that would allow exchange of such information across departments. During a period of years, surveys were created and revised with the goal of having a feedback mechanism. Reference transaction forms filled out on survey days indicated course work and sources used. This information was used to support collection development goals. University-wide, annual, and five-year planning statements were written and applied to budget plans. Year after year, quality evaluation and continuous improvement cycles became more formal and became a routine part of collection management work.

What began as a collection development committee within the reference department became a collection "management" committee of six to eight members, including the dean. Even though called a committee, the library leadership gave the committee the authority, as well as the responsibility, to act on decisions. Staff from other departments met with the committee as needed. The committee had the advantage of "wearing many hats"; consequently, they could see the "whole elephant" (or most of it). The committee responsible for reference services and selection crossed departmental lines to find out more about the process that occurred after materials were selected through the process that the customer experienced in retrieving them. The term "process management" was unknown. The committee also gave library instruction, coordinated interlibrary loan (later to include document delivery), planned budgets, designed measurements, and served as subject specialists and systems staff. Of course, this multi-tasking was driven by the size of the organization, but a system in which the same staff plan, do, study, and act is one exhibiting total quality management. The entire staff in reference, on every level, became a major player on the problem-solving committee.

The committee developed because of the library leadership; in turn, the library unit was directly affected by the leadership of the university. In the 1990s, TSU revised mission statements, promoted strategic planning, and established an Office for Institutional

Effectiveness. TSU staff from all levels met to problem solve the new TSU administrative system. The new provost encouraged communication and input from all levels. Even though the university was not officially endorsing TQM, the management style included some important aspects of TQM.

This change evolved slowly and painfully. Often change was interpreted as "criticism" of how things were done in the past and staff had difficulty getting beyond this basic emotion. One specific example of reluctance to change revolved around the request made in the 1980s for an OCLC workstation. Neither the justifications nor the actual purchase of one was the issue; problems centered on the emotion that OCLC workstations had traditionally belonged to cataloging. It became a challenge to make some of the staff comfortable with public service "owning" one, too.

Because of its leadership and the culture of public service, the collection management committee seemed to be a "natural" team. However, establishing horizontal links to the circulation and technical services departments proved to be a difficult task, since some department heads feared extra work load and/or feared loss of power in sharing knowledge of "their" processes and/or were threatened that their subordinates would not be loyal. "In cooperative environments, persons A and B work together to achieve mutually beneficial goals; by cooperating, both individuals can achieve more than each could through independent or competitive actions."

Constance F. Towler promotes the team approach where a "multiplicity of people in an organization perform three separate functions: (1) The team members bring in all of the aspects of a given problem or, at least, more than any individual could encompass. (2) While the team is coming up with the problem solution, each 'fix' to the problem is made in relation to all other aspects of the problem, so that the solution the team comes up with is one they have agreed can work. (3) The team then takes its solution and implements it on a day-to-day basis, fine-tuning it and making modifications as necessary."[16]

Cooperation

Cooperative efforts among the members of the collection management committee (team) during the past 10 years have been too numerous to count. Some specific examples of cooperation are related to fund allocation and budget management. The TSU Troy collection management committee was actively involved in the formulation of the annual budget in April and any projected budgets in relationship to annual planning/strategic planning statements. Annual goals established in March dictated a program-type budget that evolved into a line-item budget. Major changes were presented to top management in written format. An example of changes in line items resulted from a proposal made by collection management which asked for a new line for document delivery; the new line was funded. Departments were alerted to possible budget cuts and assisted the dean in defending cuts or deciding where cuts were least detrimental. A rule-of-thumb was that each budget would cover inflation for serials at 10 to 15 percent and inflation for books at 5 to 7 percent. Another rule-of-thumb was that the budget would include replacement and maintenance cost for equipment at one-third the original capital cost. A third rule was that new programs would require new funding at a level commensurate with the needs identified in new program cost analyses conducted prior to implementation of the program. The committee distributed 50 to 60 percent of the entire book line to the major subject areas (humanities, social sciences, sciences, business, and education) to support faculty requests and to purchase other materials for academic programs as found in standard bibliographies and review tools. The unallocated portions of the book budget provided discretionary funds that were spent for reference materials, special collections, browsing books, accreditation needs, or other needs as dictated by collection management. Discretionary funds were always set aside so the collection management group could defend the need for support of a new program or the need to heavily develop one area, such as in agreements for shared collections within the state of Alabama. The chairperson was charged with overseeing the expenditure of funds in a manner designed to maintain a strong and consistently developed collection within the parameters of the university and library mission/planning statements and collection management policies.

In supporting programs, collection management adopted a holistic approach: all aspects that affected collections (format, document delivery) were considered when solving the problem of support. If a team member recommended more videos in a subject area, he justified the reasons to the team and, on agreement, could transfer monies from books to videos. Because many of the schools on campus offered education courses, team members would collaborate to see that educational materials in a particular subject area were strengthened to support both education and the subject area. For 10 years, there were numerous "robust" discussions among the team members, but shows of hostility or self-promotion did not occur as is often the case in a traditional setting. Internal strife was a "taboo" because of the committee and leadership's attitudes toward the work environment.

This team kinship was evident in the subject specialists efforts. Because staff turnover was a constant, it was critical that members be able to mentor one another, sharing developments in their respective areas; each had to carry additional or different areas of subject responsibilities. Five years ago, the social sciences subject specialist accepted another library's offer; the periodicals supervisor agreed to relinquish duties to replace the departing librarian. Similarly, a retired dean of the TSU School of Business agreed to work part-time as the subject specialist in business. With a background in finance, management, and law, he became a great asset to collection management and exhibited great team spirit (even though he was much older than his colleagues).

In addition to *internal* cooperation, TQM promoted *external* cooperation. Like most collection management staff who collaborate with networks, the TSU staff worked closely with the Network of Alabama Academic Libraries (NAAL) in its efforts toward shared collection development. NAAL provided a guideline for written policy that rendered benchmarks for collection levels. These, along with American Library Association Guidelines, formed the backbone for the written policy for TSU that was published in 1991, *Collection Management: Assessment and Policy.*

Another external partner important to the library's collection management program was Information Access Corporation (IAC). Because of the lasting relationship with this major supplier of databases, TSU was one of the first libraries in the United States offering ASCII full text: Health Reference Center, Expanded Academic Index, and BusinessFile ASAP via a local area network. IAC's willingness to collaborate with the main campus to furnish full text to the "outlands" of University College in support of military education was a major part of continuous improvement in services.

The genesis of University College was in 1981 under the name College of Special Programs inclusive of all off-campus locations outside of campuses at Montgomery, Dothan, and Phenix City, Alabama. The college was renamed University College in 1990. The educational programs were designed to meet the needs of the clientele of the region. Most programs, in support of the needs of military personnel, were developed under the guidance of the educational services officers. Library services were the responsibility of the dean of Libraries at the Troy campus.

In regard to University College, the geographical spread of programs presented difficulties in managing collections. Variations that existed in teaching on military bases were great. In 1993-1994, site inventories were made to confirm the premise that inconsistency prevailed (an antithesis to quality development). The collection management team on main campus served when called upon but could not forge the horizontal links necessary to expand TQM to sister campuses. A firm link was established in 1994 between the main campus library and University College through the addition of a University College librarian. However, variations such as staff turnover and changing contractual agreements negatively affected total quality. Limited staff could not plan, do, study, and act quickly enough to respond to customer needs; yet the main campus efforts to "plan, do, study and act" in regard to University College needs have resulted in the Troy State University Administration adopting a five-year incremental plan to improve the quality of services offered by University College. The plan was a collaborative effort among representatives from University College, the Office of Institutional Effectiveness, the Provost, dean of Libraries, and the collection management team. The plan included a five-year incremental budget that would increase University College library support by $2 million. Guidelines addressing the categories of libraries, management, finances, personnel, facilities, resources, and services were drafted. A statistical format for reporting expenditures was given. Model agreements were included. A vital part was the inclusion of the library's Six Points of Institutional Effectiveness, setting goals, measurements, and actions.

Pride

No matter the setting, the institution cannot be effective (even with increased budgets) unless employees are satisfied and fulfilled. Job commitment, according to Anderson, represents "the extent of agreement between the employee and the fundamental values and purpose of the organization. To the extent that agreement exists, an employee is more motivated to expend energy on reorganizational tasks and to provide high process, product, and service quality to satisfy the organization's customers." Employees who are encouraged to have pride in their job will work hard even when tasks are not liked. Anderson suggests that pride of workmanship originates from three highly interactive sources:

1. The pride of accomplishment or achievement of product and service quality, obtained from being able to deliver a quality product or service to the customer. The TSU Library has received heartfelt oral and written recognition from the University Administration for quality library services. The library has known the pride felt when managers share results of users surveys that consistently rate assistance from staff as excellent.
2. The pride of knowing that one has improved the process that is producing the quality product or service, derived from the satisfaction of having improved the quality of how the work task will be accomplished by oneself and others. The TSU Library committed to full-text delivery because users did not only want bibliographic tools for locating articles but wanted the articles. TSU was on the cutting edge in giving users full text. The pride in setting up delivery of electronic full text just in time to the customers even before an integrated library system was in place at TSU was a "risk" that proved to be right for the organization.
3. The pride of having personally and successfully engaged in learning, brought about by the realization that one has used and applied existing knowledge and experience to generate new knowledge and advance what one already knows. Deming stresses that waste, such as waste of materials is a misfortune but "waste of knowledge, in the sense of failure of a company to use knowledge that is there and available for development, is even more deplorable." (Deming, p. 466) The expertise of the collection management team in the development of book, media, and periodical collections was extended into the arena of electronic delivery of collections. The policy for delivery basically stated that criteria for selection of materials are basic,

no matter the format. The introduction of actual text-via-computer, especially in business, law, and health, added more specialized and more current materials than the library had been able to collect inhouse. The skills of the collection team in developing policy and procedure so that, even with limited staff, Internet resource use could be taught, also contributed to a great sense of pride.

Learning

If education is crucial to pride in workmanship, how can one learn? One can learn from recognizing, then optimizing opportunities. Whether generating or adding to knowledge, learning does not merely take place in the classroom. One seeking knowledge finds myriad ways to learn. A significant fact is that learning and finding solutions to problems go hand in hand.

Collection management used meetings to share and explore ideas and discover solutions. The committee met once a week to discuss aspects of reference service. Collection management issues were discussed every other week for two or three hours in a fairly formal meeting. Informally, the group brainstormed as well—over a cup of coffee or during a walk. Minutes of collection meetings were disseminated to other staff, other campuses, and the university administrators. Collection management had no time to waste on negativism; it was too busy brainstorming about mission, customer satisfaction, and measures. The group actively participated in Academic Council meetings, the All-University Committee on Teacher Education, and other knowledge-sharing activities on campus. The time spent on planning, doing, studying, and acting was well spent; time could have been wasted on quick fixes, on repetitive/cumbersome procedures, or in apologies to customers.

In fact, quality assurance processes put into place can have only overwhelming results, according to Ann Lawes. She emphasizes that TQM provides:

> a vital link in the unit's relations with administrative and managerial decision makers. The effect is that we become proactive rather than reactive, and we no longer simply react to an administrative mandate asking us to produce results, justify our worth, and relate, what we do to our host organizations and their strategies and goals. Indeed, we do much more. With quality assurance, we initiate the mandate.[17]

An important part of quality assurance is learning from others. In addition to informative meetings, collection management used visits to other libraries as a learning tool. A trip to the regional U.S. government documents depository library answered many questions about the selection and use of U.S. government documents within the collection development scheme. Since travel funds were limited, inexpensive internal workshops became important. Team members agreeing to cover a particular database or resource met on selected Saturday mornings to have breakfast and a learning session.

While meetings and workshops contributed to increased knowledge, the PDSA cycle definitely reinforced learning. Participants in PDSA built a "sensitivity to the evolutionary nature of problems."[18] Thought processes, such as self-studies for SACS and the university's strategic planning initiative, which included Annual Planning Statements and Long-Range Plans were beneficial because the planning was not done linearly but within PDSA. Such planning contributed to better service.

Application of the knowledge established through the years by collection management was reflected in the planning of the revised copy of *Collection Management: Assessment and Policy*. Since teaching how to find information was a big part of the library's mission, the team supported the idea that instruction and collections were strongly tied together. Using Lori Arp's article, "Connecting Bibliographic Instruction and Collection Development: A Management Plan," as inspiration, the team set requirements for information to be included in the new policy, which included accreditation groups, program levels, subject areas to be emphasized, and campuses to be supported. This information was gleaned during sessions with departmental faculty. Library instruction given during the past two years was to be described: what guides were prepared, what teaching techniques were used, and what was implemented because of evaluation results. The subject specialist held sessions with faculty to plan general and advanced instruction for a department. The results were similar to that stated in the conclusion to Arp's article: A "streamlined collection and a flexible and dynamic instructional curriculum, each of which is responsive to the changing needs of the faculty and students."[19]

A document such as *Collection Management: Assessment and Policy* is only as effective as its authors want it to be. The recurring theme of Plan, Do, Study, Act builds the expertise and knowledge

Applications for Collection Development

necessary to see results. A holistic view of the organization is a prerequisite for actions taken as in the writing of this policy. As part of seeing the whole elephant, the library's strengths and weaknesses have been defined and studied. As previously mentioned, collection management actively practiced PDSA, which developed an awareness of opportunities to build on strengths and develop problem-solving skills to correct deficiencies. As defined by the team, strengths of the TSU library were as follows:

1. Bibliographic records of library materials are created in accordance with national standards for form and accuracy. Bibliographic records are in machine readable format and are entered in a national bibliographic database.
2. The library has excellent statewide agreements for interlibrary loan services and regional networks.
3. Reference services, including bibliographic indexes and other sources, identify most existing knowledge.
4. The staff is well qualified and trained to provide access to information sources for the administration, faculty, and students.
5. Computerized information sources have been carefully selected to support the curricula needs of the university.
6. Through the information theory and application program, the librarians introduce most beginning freshmen to basic resources that are available in the library's collection and target special programs for upper-division students who need more indepth instruction.
7. The library supports and shares with the administration national library guidelines, policies, and standards, for example, *ACRL Guidelines for the Preparation of Policies on Library Access.*

Weaknesses were outlined as follows:

1. Faculty do not fully accept the library's role in curricula planning and development.
2. The university is limited in equipment and staff to implement system-wide accessibility to information.
3. According to the American Library Association collection development guidelines, many areas of the library's collection are at a basic information level.

In addition to cyclical planning, the team advanced in its knowledge of library budget (the greatest of learning mastery). A specific illustration of mastering the budget was the team's early move to include all costs of electronic resources (including hardware and software) as part of the serials budget, not equipment budget. Hardware/software access provision had to be a continuing cost, rather than one-time or "enhancement" cost. In addition, the team (including the director), combed each line item to assure that services were as cost effective as humanly possible.

Whether engaged in the budget process or other processes, knowledge improved processes. There are two types of knowledge, according to Anderson, that team members must acquire: profound knowledge and process task knowledge. A profound knowledge base builds on bits of knowledge from other organizations, from experts in areas of librarianship, and other areas of expertise that are applicable to collection management, for example, total quality management. Jurow specifically mentions (1) meeting management and (2) problem solving as examples of the kinds of skills expected to be known by staff but "for which training is seldom provided."[20]

Within the TSU library, another example of expected skills has been that of office management. Within the serials department, recent problems occurred not simply from unfamiliarity with serials but the lack of office management skills to make processes work. Sweeney contends that "every staff member on a team must possess operating knowledge and skills of core processes and also specialized knowledge in one or two domains of importance to the team."[21]

Another aspect of profound knowledge involves the understanding of the importance of the social/psychological make-up of the organization. The Myers-Briggs Type Indicator was given to all levels of management at TSU, results of which were communicated to the library staff. The fun of guessing the personality types created a relaxed atmosphere; long-term effects have included having more patience with one another's personalities.

Documentation

Profound knowledge and process task knowledge must be closely acquired. As these two knowledge bases are built, sharing through documentation must result. The importance of documentation cannot be overstated. In fact, the TSU Library's *Collection*

Management: Assessment and Policy manual proved that documentation can pay dividends. This manual formed the groundwork for small but incremental increases in the materials budget on main campus over the last decade, during a time when comparable schools were dropping periodicals and losing book budgets to automation. Taking risks, the library added 179 journal titles in 1990-1991 with one-time enhancement funds; the following year, the university committed to the enhancement money becoming part of the regular periodical line. Increased material budgets meant an additional 100 titles added in 1994-1995. Titles were evaluated by indexing coverage, interdisciplinary aspects, coverage in bibliographies, faculty/student recommendations, and citation analysis.

Another type of documentation of major importance has been the library's *Policy and Procedures Manual* available on the local network. It has aided the learning process for new staff. In every phase of each PDSA cycle, the team has written summaries, recommendations, reports, news releases, and minutes and distributed them consistently to the university administration, students, and faculty. The communication has been consistent and planned; when documentation is hastily done or is too informal or is written on demand to "put out a fire," it quickly becomes ineffective or weakened.

Customer Focus

Besides the employees, the most important person is the customer. There are two broad categories of customers: external and internal (Table 1). The services and their quality are varied as indicated in Table 2. These services are not different from those expected by the customers of any other customer-oriented organization. Collection management, with its complexity of systems, will be ineffective if customer satisfaction does not remain the focus. Who is the customer? Karou Ishikawa, the well-known Japanese quality guru, profoundly asserts that *"the customer is whoever gets your work next."* How can the customer best be served especially in the *changing* environment?

- Take action.
- Follow-up on customer needs and complaints.
- Be accessible to the customer.

Table 1. Collection Management Customers

External to Main Library	Internal to Main Library
TSU—all Campuses	Acquisitions
Students	Cataloging
Faculty	Serials
Staff	Interlibrary loan/Document delivery
Affiliated	Circulation
Community	Reserves
Administration	Systems
Libraries	Administration
Network of Alabama Academic Libraries	Instructional design
Southeastern Library Network	

- Really listen.
- Schedule periodical meetings with customers.
- Conduct scheduled meetings with colleagues to share ideas.
- Sustain the communication loop consisting of the user, the library, and the parent institution.
- Be aware of other organizations' successes. Richard M. Hodgetts, author of *Blueprints for Continuous Improvement: Lessons From the Baldridge Winners*, which was published by the American Management Association in 1993, shares the strategies and programs that have been productive for the winners of the Baldridge awards in providing quality services.

People and Processes

The overall conclusion that can be drawn from the previous paragraphs is that people make the organization. Even though many

Table 2. Quality

Service	Material
Reasonable cost	Reasonable cost
Quick response	Ease of use
Easy return	Well stocked
Quick delivery	Variety
Knowledgeable staff	
Personal interest in customer	
Pleasant atmosphere	
Consistent service	

fields of study, from psychology to operations research, are involved in developing organization theory, each field promotes the necessity of leadership, communication, learning, and participation. "Viewing an organization as one large open system means that managers must address how to integrate horizontal and vertical flows of work and information. The customer value strategy developed by strategic leaders must be deployed throughout all levels of the organization down to operations. The flow should be two-directional" (Anderson). What is an operation? An operation is the daily work, for example, checking in periodicals, done on materials, or information. A process is the flow of information or of products regardless of departmental lines. For instance, the *collection development process* involves many steps:

- Environmental analysis: What are the characteristics of the world in which customer needs for collections are to be met?
- Financial analysis: What does the present budget look like? Should zero-based budgeting (creating a budget as though one did not previously exist) be applied to verify that dollars and needs coincide?
- Customer analysis: Who is the customer? What does the customer need or want? What will his needs be in the future? What quality level does the customer want—for which he is willing to pay?

In its purest form, process management leads to work units being formed around related tasks, for example, collection management processing equals selection, bibliographic control, access, and document delivery. To treat these tasks separately in isolation is detrimental to the health of the program. "[O]rganizations often attempt to solve a problem in the middle of a process without rethinking the entire process.... Each 'fix' has the potential for unforeseen consequences that can lead to new problems."[22] Fowler, program director for quality process at Harvard says, "*As a culture we have been trained to solve problems quickly, to get the solution behind us and get on to the next task in a hurry; therefore, we have often rushed to the fastest solution. As a consequence, some of us spend too much of our time fighting fires which are often caused by hasty **partial** solutions. We are so accustomed to this practice that we believe it is part of our job.*"[23]

There is no quick fix nor beginning and end to total quality management. TQM centers on people and continuous quality improvement. Cross-functional teams that are familiar with operations, organizations that are built on leadership, cooperation, and learning—all reinforce the concept of continuous improvement. Since getting a team started may be a difficult hurdle, Deming contributes questions to help a team to start as proposed by Edward M. Baker of the Ford Motor Company.

Your organization:
a. Where in the total organizational structure does your department fit?
b. What products and services does it provide?
c. How does it provide these products and services; what processes are used?
d. What would be the effect if your organization (unit, section, department) stopped producing its products and services?

You:
a. Where do you fit in your department? What is your job?
b. What do you create or produce; that is, what are the results of your work?
c. How do you do this (e.g., give a general description of what you do.)
d. How do you know if you produce good results or poor results; that is, are there standards or criteria of good performance?
e. How were these standards established?

Concerning your customers:
a. Immediate customers
   i. Who receives directly the products or services that you produce? (He is your customer.)
   ii. How does your customer use what you produce?
   iii. What would happen if you did not do your job right?
   iv. How do your errors affect them?
   v. How do you find out if you are not meeting the needs or requirements of your customers (e.g., from customer, boss, reports)?
b. Intermediate and ultimate customer
   i. How far beyond your immediate customer can you trace the effect of what you do?

Applications for Collection Development

Concerning your suppliers:
a. How is your work initiated (e.g., assignment from boss, request of customer, self-initiated)?
b. Who supplies you with material, information, services, and other information that you need to do your job (e.g., boss, customer, co-worker—same group, people in other areas)?
c. What would happen to you if your suppliers did not do their jobs?
d. Do they have performance standards?
e. How do their errors affect you?
f. How do they find out if they are not meeting your needs or requirements? Are you working with them? Are you fulfilling your obligation to them?[24]

The vocabulary used to describe these groups can be project team, task force, or quality circle. Choice of words is not important; the people and the quality of work to be achieved are the important factors. Gary Fellers, consultant, articulates his predictions of successful management "teams" and articulates his predictions even stronger than Capezio: "Smaller, effectively managed interdepartmental teams are the modus operandi of the future. In fact, they are a necessity for survival beyond five to ten years."[25] It is teams that will have the capability to improve processes. Process improvement is:

> Continuous endeavor to learn about all aspects of a process and to use this knowledge to change the process to reduce variation and complexity and to improve customer judgments of quality. Process improvement begins by understanding how customers judge quality, how processes work and how understanding the variation in those processes can lead to wise management action.[26]

The process improvement that Capezio is requiring from team effort can be accomplished in many ways. To practice continuous improvement as a collection management team, informal and formal means have been used. Brainstorming is a must. Through team interaction, a problem is studied and alternate ideas are considered. A more formal approach is studying all possible causes and all possible solutions using a fishbone diagram (Figure 2). The fishbone is a graphical presentation introduced by Karou Ishikawa, a well-known Japanese quality guru.

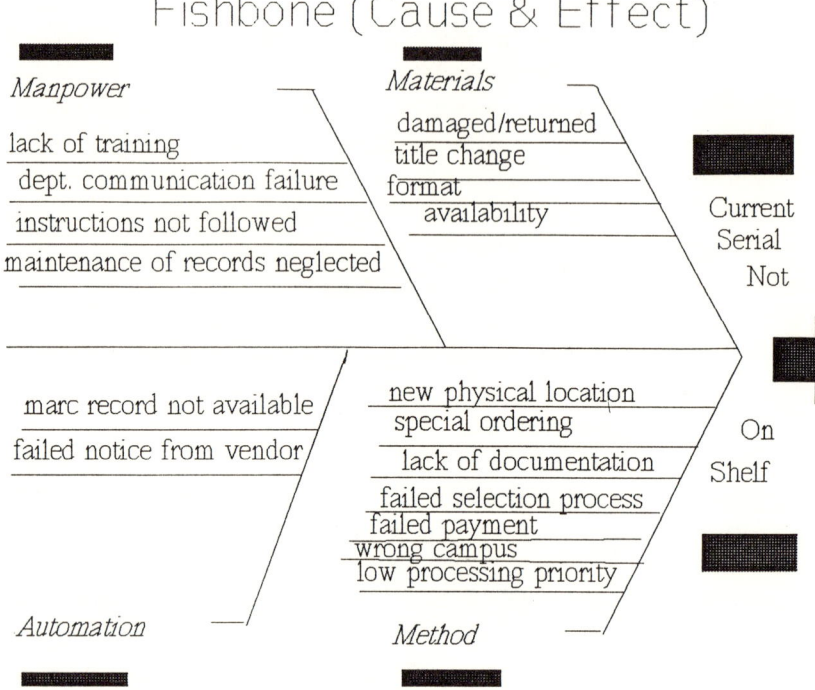

Figure 2. Possible Causes of Serial Not Available on Shelf

An important factor of the PDSA cycle within an organization committed to quality improvement is measurement of the quality. One type of measurement supported by followers of TQM is benchmarking (continuous comparison). It is a means whereby an organization chooses the best "models" to study to find out why an organization or a standard is considered the best. Benchmarking can be a complex methodology involving statistical analysis or can be a simple process. A simple process might include (1) choosing one process or service to improve, (2) visiting other organizations to gather information, and (3) using the Deming cycle for planning quality improvement. According to Capezio, there are four general types of benchmarking: (1) internal, (2) competitive, (3) world-class operations, and (4) activity type.[27] The first type, internal benchmarking, is when other departments or divisions within the organization are studied for their outputs, thus alerting participants to resources available internally. A case in point is the output from the university's Office of Institutional Effectiveness, statistics essential in the PDSA cycle. Usage reports from the local area network also provides internal benchmarking. The second type, competitive benchmarking, involves the study of competitor's products, services, or processes. For the collection management team, the Network of Alabama Academic Libraries (NAAL) has provided standards for libraries in similar organizations. NAAL meetings have provided opportunities to share and to find out what other libraries are planning/doing. The third type, world-class operations benchmarking extends beyond the library and its sisters to the world. Publications, such as *Blueprints for Continuous Improvement: Lessons From the Baldridge Winners* by Richard M. Hodgetts, can provide libraries with ideas worth adopting or adapting. The collection team at TSU looked to the publishing world for an external standard. As written collection policy, the book publishing output in a given year was communicated to the administration. In the document, each subject specialist then indicated a percentage of this annual output that was judged necessary to support a particular subject area. Standards from accreditation groups have also played a critical part in benchmarking. The fourth type, activity type benchmarking, is aimed at the key factors involved in processes or activities. At TSU, an example of activity type involved the reference survey. Instead of using tally marks to simply count the number of customers helped, the collection team studied other libraries' measurement tools, attended workshops, and designed a form that would answer some of the questions that the collection management team wanted answered, such as which collections were being used and for which discipline. "Because the benchmarking process is generally undertaken by those engaged in the work, it also builds a profound commitment to make the proposed changes work."[28]

"A fundamental truth of the TQM movement is that you cannot manage what you cannot measure."[29] No matter the measurement techniques used, an organization must remember that the ultimate benchmark is customer satisfaction. Measurements of customer satisfaction during the past decade at TSU have varied. Surveys have been filled out by users at the door; evaluations have been filled out by undergraduates and graduates within the classroom; essays have been written by students as a writing-across-the-curriculum assignment to evaluate library resources and services for a particular class; reference transaction surveys have been filled out that indicate the major of the student and the resource(s) used to help him or her;

and informal interviews have been conducted. Student workers have been sent out of the library onto the campus as "roving reporters" with a list of questions to be asked so that people who do not use the library could be polled.

Each measure has had one result in common: the collections are of high quality; however, the volume of holdings are too small. This measurement result has driven collection management efforts to increase materials budgets, offer electronic full text, and provide document delivery (free to those users meeting established criteria). In a recent article on benchmarking, Fleisher indicated that "The key to measuring ... is to establish clearly visible action targets." One action target established by collection management as a result of measurement efforts was that patrons have a chance to find at least 50 percent of the materials that they needed "just in time," with the library willing to deliver the other half as quickly as possible. The library drew these conclusions after many forms of evaluation/measurement had been used. Deming stresses that misuse of statistical measurement and the lack of understanding of what statistics are indicating is common in the work place. Studies to define common causes and special causes are needed before a stable system of control can be put into place. Deming recommends that statistical experts be used to design the measurement program in the work place.

In the chapter titled "Diseases and Obstacles" in *Out of the Crisis*, Deming relates his ideas of how management misuses employee evaluations and how measurement is reduced to counting. "One of the main effects of evaluation of performance is nourishment of short-term thinking and short-time performance. A man must have something to show. His superior is forced into numerics. It is easy to count. Counts relieve management of the necessity to contrive a measure with meaning."[30]

Measurement is only one vital component of the planning and studying that occurs in collection management. Changes that have occurred during the past decade at Troy State Library are still being cycled through plan, do, study, act. Any activity or process that affected collection management was within the domain of the team to analyze and to improve. Some of the collection management actions are described in the following paragraphs.

Physical Locations

A special music collection named after the renowned bandmaster Paul Yoder was cataloged and removed from a locked room to improve access. The U.S. government documents collection and the reference collection have physically been rearranged. Wrap-a-round shelving was dismantled so that straight rows of shelving with classifications posted rendered easier access. Art books shelved behind the circulation desk for restricted use were moved to their appropriate place in the circulation collection. Over-sized volumes were labeled and placed on low shelves. *Congressional Quarterly Weekly Report*, historically shelved in the reference collection, was moved to periodicals, a more logical place for the users to find the issues. The team worked closely with the School of Education and library users in establishing a test collection. The test collection became a part of the new instructional design department. The department housed a browsing audio-visual collection (the audio-visual collection had previously been in closed stacks and retrieved by accession number), a children's/juvenile book collection, and a textbook collection. Also in this area, multimedia was loaded on Macintosh computers; team teaching of its use was the responsibility of the education librarian and education faculty.

Book Ordering

Since the collection management team usually had current bibliographical information for ordering purposes, much of this searching no longer took place in acquisitions. *Books in Print Plus Reviews* on CD-ROM was purchased to assist in the selection effort. Book order forms were continuing to improve. Problems with documenting titles received through memberships or as gifts were being resolved. Staff from acquisitions and collection management have worked on fund coding. Guidelines for what orders have highest priority and how long to wait before canceling items have been written as a cross-functional effort. Reference books were to be acquired even if orders were carried into another fiscal year. Reference and science books were not priority items for the bindery.

Finding Tools

The TSU Periodicals Directory in paper has been improved in various ways over a period of time. Discussions across departments and streamlining of periodical processing have made the task of keeping information in the directory accurate and current much easier. Clerical staff interviewed students to get first-hand input about the difficulty of use. One of the obstacles was the alphabetical ordering wherein acronyms were at the beginning of each alphabetical section. Cross-referencing greatly improved chances of finding titles beginning with acronyms. The OCLC identifying number that had been included for the convenience of ILL personnel was being confused with LC classification. Taking out the number reduced confusion, and a directory with the numbers was printed separately for ILL. Terminology was standardized. Entries for titles of book serials covered in major indexes were revised. Older editions of the directory were routed to faculty offices. Periodical control will ultimately be impacted by the library's installation of the SIRSI Unicorn Management System. This tool will also offer excellent searching capabilities to customers, whether the database is internal or external to the library building.

Bibliographic Control

The TSU Library historically housed a few titles near offices to assist in bibliographic searches. From this small beginning, a bibliographic collection grew up and was assigned a four-letter symbol in OCLC; BIBL appeared over the call number and all "bibliographies" were shelved together. The collection team led the effort to have the books changed to reference (REF). Another collection, uncataloged TSU theses and dissertations, were kept wherever a spot was vacant on the shelf. In this case, collection management and cataloging decided to include theses and dissertations as part of the circulating collection and wrote guidelines to indicate which fields in the bibliographic records were to be used and what information needed to be included for easy access. A similar process took place to provide cataloging records for pamphlet collections, such as American Enterprise Institute and National League for Nursing. Collection development and cataloging agreed that the 508 field for media would be used for feature length films, documentaries, classic films, art films, animated films, or other cases where the technical contributors to the production were judged to be important access points. The willingness of the cataloging department to listen, along with rationalizations from the collection team on the need to browse shelves, resulted in the Z classification being dropped in favor of materials assigned a subject LC classification. In the mid-1980s, U.S. government documents were not cataloged. A TSU systems analysis class followed guidelines for bibliographic control composed by collection management to design a database in DBASE III so that items to be considered for disposal could be listed, new titles could be generated, and subject bibliographies produced. This "electronic shelflist" proved to be a worthwhile interim; the shelflist was discontinued several years later when the team worked with cataloging to begin the OCLC Document Service. Near this time, the team, after much study, recommended that the U.S. government documents, except for indexed periodicals, be classified SuDoc and housed together. Since government documents had previously been divided with some in reference and some in circulation, dummies were placed on shelves to help direct patrons. Unfortunately, some sets, such as *Public Papers of the Presidents*, are split until retrospective conversion can take place. Even though the change was difficult, the team agreed that for long-term access the agency designated SuDoc numbers would aid browsing by users. With the commitment by the government to electronic formats, the PDSA cycle in regard to U.S. government documents will continue.

In regard to machine-readable data files (MRDF), the cross-functional approach taken by the staff has led to guidelines for cataloging of electronic resources. Ongoing are rough drafts of guidelines to handle materials that are only MRDF, periodicals accompanied by MRDF, books accompanied by MRDF, and MRDF accompanying books. The staff in several departments are studying the cataloging efforts where Internet resources are concerned.

Electronic Resources

Electronic delivery over the past five years has impacted library services so greatly that process management is more necessary than ever. At TSU 10 years ago, titles such as *Biological Abstracts* and *America: History and Life* were dropped in paper because customers could better be served through electronic searching. Services, such as FirstSearch, have given the customer more searching capability in more databases than ever before (not to mention document delivery). Cost-effective educational programs, such as that offered by Mead Data Central as the Lexis/Nexis/Medis database service, are contributing greatly to the training of future citizens. The 1992 Lexis educational program that provided a legal library, a full-text library of newspapers and journals, and a medical library cost TSU $1,983 for its initial on-line period, whereas standard commercial rates for the same searching would have cost $37,680.

Other remote delivery of indexing/full-text searching by major providers like Information Access and UMI is being considered. These tools delivered remotely mean less maintenance on the part of TSU and wider distribution. The delivery of Internet resources is another ever changing challenge. Keeping in mind Miriam Drake's belief that librarians must do more than hand out books and citations, the TSU library staff must utilize as many TQM processes as possible in order to deal with content quality, vendor database services, and the massive Internet. Close relationships among data processing staff, library staff, and customers must be maintained in order to cost effectively deliver needed information.

In terms of cost effectiveness, when campus networking was in its infancy, the collection management group explored commercial delivery of Internet resources and opted to use CLASS. Because of limited number of staff, the use of the Internet was limited to team teaching with classroom faculty. At present, the library is planning a homepage, from suggestions of subject specialists, on which Internet resources should easily be accessible for faculty and students. Subject specialists will choose resources in accordance with present selection policy for subject areas and in accordance with policy for electronic delivery of collections. Collection teams "shooting at moving targets" need all the management skills they can assemble as the move to the digital information world takes place. Meanwhile, the collection team has opted to continue paper subscriptions to the major Wilson indexes as a security net during the digital transition.

Serials

As most library staff are aware, serials control is one of the greatest challenges in the library, mainly because of the variations involved.

Historically, serials processing spanned departments; therefore, locating causes of breakdowns or problems was difficult or impossible. As more collection management staff learn process management, the chore should become easier. Electronic serials control has improved tracking, but turnover in serials staff has had a negatively effect on this function. The knowledge of those staff involved in daily operations involving serials is so critical. Staff who are grounded in serials work, along with much systems analysis from a team approach and electronic tracking provide powerful serial control. Familiar serials problems are related to which and how many pieces come with a subscription, how payments to an on-line service should be dealt with to be most cost effective, how do local data fields affect union lists, and what statistics are needed to assist in TQM.

During the academic year 1993-1994, the collection team added serials to its holdings. Several objectives to be met included improved library holdings to ensure support of the curriculum, more efficient use of materials budget, and increased current awareness of key resources. Baker & Taylor's *Continuation List of Core Titles*, standard bibliographies, faculty consultation, similar source comparison, and other means were used to justify standing order status.

CONCLUSION

> We as individuals all have the potential for never-ending quality improvement, both incremental and breakthrough, in the way we do our work and lead our lives. The principles of quality are as applicable to services as to manufacturing. They are as applicable to individuals as to organizations, and individuals can put them into effect more rapidly than can organizations. Moreover, although we often complain of poor quality in our organizations, our personal quality may be equally in need of improvement.... We are all responsible for our work and can dramatically impact the quality of that work.[31]

Once we take personal responsibility for quality, then the frequently asked question of how to implement TQM becomes answered: it begins with the individual and permeates the work place over time. Workers become willing to accept the responsibility and authority necessary to improve quality. Managers become willing to share the responsibility and authority. *Management's role ...* is to *lead* and *to serve* its first customer, the organization's workers:

- *Lead* the organization, and it will realize its opportunities and adjust to its challenges.
- *Serve* the workers, and they will serve the organization ... and, in turn, serve everyone.[33]

"The ABCs of Total Quality Management" by Susan Pike captures the main points to remember about TQM and will serve as a summary.

A. Adopting the New Philosophy.
B. Benchmarking.
C. Continuous Quality Improvement.
D. W. Edwards Deming—Quality guru who promoted quality management theory and practice. Led Japan in TQM efforts to rebuild their economy. Wrote the 14 points of TQM.
E. Employee Empowerment.
F. Flow Charts/Fishbone Charts.
G. *Goal* (North River Press, 1986). Written by Eli Goldratt and recommended as the "quality bible."
H. Honest Communication.
I. Kaoru Ishikawa, a leader in the Japanese quality movement.
J. Joseph Juran—Deming's rival and the elder statesman of TQ Control.
K. Keep At It.
L. Leadership.
M. Mission Statement.
N. Numerical Quotas eliminated.
O. *Out of the Crisis* (MIT, 1986). Deming's 14 points.
P. Pareto.
Q. Quick Fix is not an answer.
R. Remove Barriers that Rob People of Pride in Their Work.
S. Statistical Quality Control Techniques.
T. Training. Teaching.
U. Users.
V. Value = Quality, Price, and Service.
W. Mary Walton, author of *The Deming Management Method* (Putnam, 1985).
X. Xerox, winner of the 1989 Baldridge Award. Known for benchmarking and customer focus.
Y. You. Quality begins with you.

Z. Zero Defects. Quality experts disagree on achieving but encourage improvement of processes toward no defects.[34]

NOTES AND REFERENCES

1. J. Rampey and H. Roberts. "Perspectives on Total Quality," *Proceedings of Total Quality Forum IV*, (Cincinnati, OH, November 1992), quoted in Greg Bounds et al., *Beyond Total Quality Management: Toward the Emerging Paradigm*, (New York: McGraw-Hill Inc., 1994), p. 4.
2. Stanley Brown, "Measures of Perfection," *Sales & Marketing Management* 147 (May 1995). Electronic full-text from BusinessFile ASAP, Information Access Corporation.
3. Susan Jurow and Susan B. Barnard, "Introduction: TQM Fundamentals and Overview of Contents," in *Integrating Total Quality Management in a Library Setting*, edited by Susan Jurow and Susan B. Barnard, (New York: Haworth Press, 1993), p. 2.
4. James R. Fisher, Jr., *Work Without Managers: A View From the Trenches*, (Tampa, FL: The Delta Group, 1991), pp. 94-156.
5. W. Edwards Deming, *Out of the Crisis*, (Cambridge: Massachusetts Institute of Technology, Center for Advanced Engineering Study, 1986), p. 109.
6. Richard T. Sweeney, "Leadership in the Post-Hierarchical Library," *Library Trends* 43(1, Summer 1994): 68.
7. Fisher, p. 208.
8. Bounds, pp. 308-309.
9. Sweeney, p. 64.
10. James M. Matarazzo and Miriam A. Drake, eds., *Information for Management: A Handbook*, (Washington, DC: Special Libraries Association, 1994), p. 11.
11. Crit Stuart and Miriam A. Drake, "TQM in Research Libraries," *Special Libraries* 84(3, Summer 1993): 131-136. Special issue titled "Benchmarking, Total Quality Management and the Learning Organization: New Management Paradigms for the Information Environment." Electronic full-text from BusinessFile ASAP, Information Access Corporation.
12. Stuart, "TQM in Research Libraries."
13. Tim Loney and Arnie Bellefontaine, "TQM Taining: The Library Service Challenge," in *Integrating Total Quality Management in a Library Setting*, edited by Susan Jurow and Susan B. Barnard, (New York: Haworth Press, 1993), p. 86.
14. Rosanna M. O'Neil, Richard L. Harwood, and Bonnie A. Osif, "A Total Look at Total Quality Management: A TQM Perspective From the Literature of Business, Industry, Higher Education, and Librarianship," *Library Administration & Management* 7(4, Fall 1993): 245.
15. John C. Anderson, Manus Rungtusanatham, and Roger G. Schroeder, "A Theory of Quality Management Underlying the Deming Management Method," *Academy of Management Review* 19 (3, July 1994): 472-509. Electronic full text from BusinessFile ASAP, Information Access Corporation.

16. Constance F. Towler, "Problem Solving Teams in a Total Quality Management Environment" in *Integrating Total Quality Management in a Library Setting*, edited by Susan Jurow and Susan B. Barnard, (New York: Haworth Press, 1993), p. 98.

17. Ann Lawes, "The Benefits of Quality Management to the Library and Information Services Profession," *Special Libraries* 84(3, Summer 1993): 142-146. Available full-text from BusinessFile ASAP, Information Access Corporation.

18. Towler, p. 111.

19. Lori Arp and Gerald (Jay) Schafer, "Connecting Bibliographic Instruction and Collection Development: A Management Plan," *RQ* 31(3 Spring, 1992): 402.

20. Jurow and Barnard, "Introduction," p. 8.

21. Sweeney, p. 73.

22. Susan Jurow, "Tools for Measuring and Improving Performance," in *Integrating Total Quality Management in a Library Setting*, edited by Susan Jurow and Susan B. Barnard, (New York: Haworth Press, 1993), p. 116.

23. Towler, p. 97

24. Deming, pp. 90-92.

25. Gary Fellers, *The Deming Vision: SPC/TQM for Administrators*, (Milwaukee: ASQC Quality Press, 1992), p. 27.

26. Peter Capezio and Debra Morehouse, *Taking the Mystery Out of TQM* (Hawthorne, NJ: Career Press, 1993). p. 276.

27. Capezio, pp. 187-188.

28. Jurow, "Tools," pp. 124-125.

29. Craig S. Fleisher and Sara Burton, "Taking Stock of Corporate Benchmarking Practices: Panacea or Pandora's Box," *Public Relations Review* 21(1, Spring 1995): 1-20. Electronic full text from BusinessFile ASAP, Information Access Corporation.

30. Deming, p. 105.

31. Harry V. Roberts and Bernard F. Sergesketter, *Quality is Personal: A Foundation for Total Quality Management* (New York: Free Press, 1993), p. 131.

32. Fisher, p. 308

33. Fisher, p. 163.

34. Susan Pike, "The ABCs of Total Quality Management," *New Jersey Libraries* 26 (Fall 1993): 24-25.

COLLECTION DEVELOPMENT:
A COLLABORATIVE EFFORT

Cynthia H. Shabb and Judith L. Rieke

ABSTRACT

Traditionally when one thinks of developing collections at colleges and universities, faculty and their role in selection come to mind. However, building better collections should also involve other players on the information delivery team. As libraries have static budgets, and as more materials are available to purchase, the selection process and providing access to information becomes more difficult. The emphasis on collection building is different today due to rapid changes in technology, the economy, and our culture. Bibliographers, as part of the information delivery team, need to work in a collaborative network of many individuals in order to fulfill their collection development responsibilities and to respond to the information needs of their constituents. With this team approach, bibliographers can develop a support network to assist in making sound collection development decisions. This article gives bibliographers some concrete methods for developing effective mechanisms of communication with the full information delivery team.

INTRODUCTION

Traditionally, when one thinks of developing collections at colleges and universities, the teaching faculty and its role in selection comes to mind. However, building better collections and providing access to information should also involve other players on the information delivery team. When libraries have static budgets and as more materials are available for purchase, the selection process becomes more difficult. The emphasis on collection building is changing due to "technological, economic, and sociocultural forces."[1] Bibliographers, as part of the information delivery team, need to work in a collaborative network of many individuals in order to fulfill their collection development responsibilities and to respond to the information needs of their constituents.

To be most effective, the network should include faculty, colleagues from within and without the library, library staff at all levels, administrators and other campus support, vendors, and publishers. Extending the network beyond the library setting broadens the perspective. Campus connections in administrative positions give the library credibility and can have a positive effect on budgeting and funding. Maintaining positive alliances with vendors and publishers can also contribute to the enhancement of collections and provide better information for everyone. John R. Secor states that "publishers, vendors, and librarians make up a community" and that the interactions among the three should lead to long-term, mutually beneficial goals.[2]

Bibliographers are often called "renaissance people ... who can walk on water."[3] With this team approach, bibliographers can develop a support network to assist in making sound collection development decisions. This paper gives bibliographers some concrete methods for developing effective mechanisms of communication with the full information delivery team.

FACULTY AS KEY PLAYERS

"Librarians and faculty have at least two things in common: a desire to acquire a major share of the information in their fields of interest and lack of funds to satisfy that desire."[4] Collections that are solely selected by faculty are not always of interest and assistance to all levels of users in an academic library. How can bibliographers work with faculty to tailor collection building and provide information to meet the needs of undergraduates, graduate students, faculty, and staff?

In an article by Drummond, Mosby, and Munroe, "traditional public relations" was encouraged to foster collaboration between librarians and faculty.[5] Several articles describe various techniques or tips for new bibliographers working with faculty.[6] Effective communication methods and public relations are emphasized. Bibliographers must be willing to learn departmental interests, allow faculty several modes of communication (e-mail, voice mail, librarian and faculty initiated communication) and to offer enhanced bibliographic services. It has been said that "to build and strengthen faculty relations, two things are needed—one is enthusiasm and the other is the willingness to take the initiative."[7]

FACULTY CONTACTS

For new bibliographers, setting up the initial meeting with the faculty liaison is important. This meeting can be arranged by the head of collection development or by the bibliographer. In some disciplines, gathering a group of faculty liaisons might be successful. More questions tend to arise in an individual setting; however, bibliographers may learn more about the department when a group convenes. Ideally, it is best to experience both situations.

During the first meeting, budget information and a review of the ordering time line can be shared. Current approval plans can be described. Many times, additional subjects of interest are uncovered.

The goal of the bibliographer is to learn as much about departmental research interests as possible. Review the current catalog. Look at the course titles to see what is being taught and note the degree programs being offered. Auditing courses to enhance knowledge about a subject can be rewarding for the bibliographer as well as the faculty member. Faculty members genuinely appreciate a bibliographer's awareness of their teaching and research interests.

Attending faculty meetings can be helpful to bibliographers. Another time to talk to faculty is during their scheduled office hours. If bibliographers are given an opportunity to describe some of the specialized services that they offer, they might be called upon by faculty to assist at a later date.

D'Andraia states that the "business of libraries is staying in business." He advocates aggressively reaching out to library users.[8] Bibliographers can facilitate this process by providing "value-added" services that go beyond the traditional level of assistance.

VALUE-ADDED SERVICES

What are some of the important value-added services that bibliographers can provide to faculty? Bibliographers might suggest particular books or electronic resources of interest to the department. Periodically providing faculty with a list of pertinent new reference materials can be helpful. Volunteering to offer an instructional session or specialized reference service for a class would be appropriate for those with research components. Extending access to databases at no charge for a trial period can be productive for both the liaison and the library. For example, free FirstSearch cards can be given to new liaisons where the databases are relevant to their field of teaching and research. Offering faculty an opportunity for hands-on experience in a particular database might generate interest in an electronic source that the library is emphasizing. Assistance with electronic sources that might be accessible from faculty offices can be valuable. This specialized assistance might lead a faculty member to ask the librarian for instructional sessions for classes. They might also realize the convenience of electronic access. This awareness can help create positive relationships between faculty and the library.

Noontime seminars emphasizing some aspect of the library—a database, methodology of a paper, a targeted print or electronic source—can help bibliographers gain credibility. Faculty observing librarians in their element might lead to a class assignment.

When faculty do not contact the library about class assignments, librarians should initiate the contact. When libraries recognized that chemistry students were struggling with written assignments, the bibliographer for chemistry offered the professor a handout to assist the students. The handout opened the door the next semester for a 15-minute presentation, a brief library tour, and a handout. The following semester, the bibliographer was invited to deliver a

35-minute presentation, and the students were given an opportunity during their lab time to learn how to use the library. This faculty became an ally who told others about this service. Consequently, the librarian was invited to assist with other classes. Building relationships with faculty requires an investment of time.

Providing faculty with information about the library can be a real help, too. Librarians think about libraries day in and day out, but faculty with different responsibilities cannot be expected to be aware of all of the library services and issues. As one example, Sapp discovered that during a serials review, information about the journal situation had not filtered down from departmental administrators to individual faculty members.[9]

In the electronic environment, libraries can develop homepages and set up links to sites of special interest to faculty. A list of bibliographers' e-mail addresses on the homepage could be helpful to faculty—especially in areas other than their own. They may know their own bibliographer but have a need to contact someone in another area.

Finally, bibliographers need to be empowered with budget information so that they can respond to faculty questions. When faculty ask a question, it is most helpful if bibliographers understand the financial limits. Information should be given out expeditiously. This helps all librarians appear credible and knowledgeable about library operations.

EXPANDING THE TEAM

In the electronic environment, our colleagues might be in our own library, in another library within the state, or even libraries in other states and countries. Within the library, regular meetings with specific agendas involving bibliographers, access services, technical services, computer services, and special collections staff are important. This allows a forum for discussion and provides the staff with an opportunity to appreciate the full nature of collection development and the effect that collection decisions have on all levels of activity.

Staff throughout the library influence collection development decisions. Schad notes that, "collection development integrates work and staff, cuts across departmental lines."[10] Access services, including interlibrary loan staff, can notify selectors of heavily used materials. It may cost the library more to acquire an item through a document delivery service than it would to have the source in the library. That may be a good indication that the item should be purchased if possible. According to Malcolm Getz, "there's a tipping point between when you ought to buy and when you ought to borrow." This number is fluid and each case needs to be considered individually.[11]

Involving technical services staff, especially individuals in acquisitions, is essential. Someone placing an order for a book often catches details that the bibliographer does not. For example, acquisitions staff can alert the bibliographer that the cost of a paperback is substantially lower than the hardbound price. This information may be relayed to the bibliographer so that the format decision can be reevaluated.

Technical services staff also often realize that an earlier edition is in a special location and can ask the bibliographer where they want the most recent edition to be shelved. It is beneficial for bibliographers to acquaint themselves with technical services processes, so that all parties speak the same language. Users want information expeditiously. Anything bibliographers can do to speed the ordering and cataloguing process means faster service.

Serials staff may have knowledge regarding usage of the periodical collection that can be helpful during serials reviews. Staff can also provide statistics, if available, and may be aware through their service on public desks of which titles are most popular. In addition, they know the publication problems of various titles because of their daily contact with them. They could provide evidence regarding irregularities and make recommendations as to whether or not they meet expected production standards. They are also often the first to be alerted when a serial increases in price.

In the world of downsizing and outsourcing, technical services staffs are performing more complex tasks. As libraries outsource cataloging, the straightforward, easy to catalog material is gone, leaving the specialized for the local library. These materials often help define the unique strength of a collection. Today, support staff do many of the tasks that once were performed by professional librarians. It is helpful for bibliographers to recognize that the duties of technical services staff are ever-changing.

The rationale for making decisions can be better documented by tracking the use statistics of electronic services. Computer services librarians and bibliographers should examine use statistics in tandem. Use statistics tell bibliographers which products need to be promoted, discontinued, or replaced. Computer services librarians are instrumental in establishing connections to various electronic services. Given the wide variety of computer equipment in a campus setting, computer services librarians often need to work individually with faculty to provide access to information resources. For electronic products to achieve maximum results, the computer services librarian and the bibliographer need to collaborate.

Special collections staff are often model players in the field of collection development. Their collection development goals are outlined within a specific policy, and they seek primary and secondary resources to match these goals. Their mission focuses on preserving historical records that document the political, economic, social, and cultural heritage of a designated geographical area or subject field. Special collections staff also collect appropriate published resources and have an in depth knowledge of the publishing world for that particular area or topic. As significant collections are acquired, special collections librarians should share information about them and the associated trends in historical research. Highlighting the receipt of significant collections provides the library with public relations opportunities.

Collaborative efforts can exist within a campus environment and among libraries within the state. For example, on the University of North Dakota (UND) campus, the Library of the Health Sciences combined its efforts with North Dakota State University (NDSU) in order to share an electronic database. Another project between UND, NDSU, and other institutions in North Dakota is in the beginning stages. A primary serials vendor for these institutions is preparing a uniform list of holdings as a possible way of streamlining collaborative collection development decisions.

MINITEX, a multi-type library resource sharing network in Minnesota, North Dakota, and South Dakota, has developed a list of bibliographers and their collection development responsibilities so that bibliographers with similar collection responsibilities could share ideas. MINITEX has also sponsored several conferences on cooperative collection management to encourage networking among bibliographers in the region.

The capability to communicate with others has been enhanced with today's technology. Correspondence with colleagues about products and services all over the world is facilitated with e-mail and listservs on the Internet. Although these informal exchanges may affect collection development decisions, many will never officially be recorded. Professional meetings offer other opportunities to meet people with similar interests and also lead to unrecorded influences.

THE COACH'S ROLE

Collection Development Officers and Library Administrators

Empowering bibliographers with knowledge about library budgets, policies, and the mission of the library helps their work with faculty. When library administrators include bibliographers in day to day operations decisions, they are better able to pass on information to faculty. "Empowerment of librarians is a prerequisite to their partnership with faculty."[12] For example, if a faculty member wants a particular journal they would much prefer to have their bibliographer be able to describe the process rather than have to speak to the head of collection development or the director of the library. If a library wishes to be user-friendly, employees need full authority to perform their responsibilities.[13] Administrators can facilitate this by providing bibliographers with the information they need to perform their jobs.

Administrators can alert bibliographers to future goals of the university and keep them apprised of new academic programs and accreditation requirements. Sharing information gained from curriculum meetings and discussions with faculty is beneficial to bibliographers.

Administrators should encourage bibliographers to visit faculty in their offices. After these meetings, bibliographers can write reports and note any follow-up action required along with comments or observations. These reports may simply be informative or they may alert administrators of challenges that lie ahead. If follow-up action requires a response by either the head of collection development or an administrator, the report can serve as a reminder.

Academic Administrators

Academic administrators outside of the library are potential advocates. Informing administrators of services that the library offers will help administrators recognize the role the library plays. Requests for information from administrators should be conducted expeditiously since nothing succeeds like success. Satisfaction with the library's service is important in formulating opinions about their competence. Administrators have an interesting vantage point that enables them to understand the total programs of the institution and their relationship to one another.[14] It is wise to gain support from administrators prior to embarking on a major change in policy, or a serials review, so that they can act as positive reinforcement.

Promoting the Team

The development office can help create a large pool of library advocates.[15] Involving members of the development office at the outset in a fund-raising activity can be advantageous. Their expertise in identifying donors among alumni can save unnecessary money on mailings that might not reap any benefits. As brochures, publicity, and information are put together for potential donors, it is a good idea to consult them or have them design the material. It is important for brochures to speak to a wide audience, so their experience with alumni can be an asset to the library.

Bring in Special Teams: Vendors and Publishers

Recently, librarians' relationships with vendors and publishers have been stormy and fraught with discontent. The primary reasons for this are the ever escalating costs of journals and the continual expansion of published material. Librarians blame publishers and publishers deny any wrong doing, citing the mounting tide of publishable manuscripts as the culprit. Vendors feel squeezed in the middle as subscription cancellations roll across their desks and book orders decline. Resolution of the problem is not around the corner. While all parties explore ways out of the quagmire, there are still opportunities to learn from each other. Collection builders need to understand more about vendors and publishers and to look objectively at how they can help us. Vendors and publishers can function in the same manner as special teams, bringing reinforcements at critical times during the game.

Vendors

In the library setting, the acquisitions staff is most likely to fully understand the role that vendors play in developing library collections. They work closely together in a symbiotic relationship. Vendors aid in acquisitions staff work flow by physically ordering, invoicing, and claiming library materials directly from publishers for libraries. Their collaboration in collection development happens in other more indirect ways as well. Vendors produce a wealth of information and services for libraries. These can take many forms, and librarians should look carefully at how to utilize them. As Lee states, "A library's collection development efforts can often be enriched by well-planned cooperation with materials vendors."[16]

One particularly helpful service that vendors provide is notifying bibliographers of new publications. The question might arise as to why one would need notification of new publications from vendors when advertisements from publishers flood mail boxes on a daily basis. Relying on vendors has several advantages. Their notifications arrive consistently and can be accommodated into an organized work flow. The information is neutral and unbiased. A designated audience is indicated along with subject analysis and classification. If the publication is part of a series or a reprint of an earlier edition, this information is clearly stated. The format of publication notifications varies from newsletters to pre-order approval slips.

Book approval plans can be viewed as another way that vendors inform librarians of current publications. This method has the advantage of actually allowing librarians and faculty members to examine the books before committing to purchase them. Seeing and browsing through materials makes for easier and more informed decisions. The negative side to these plans is the process of returning books that were not appropriate or are too expensive. However, the selection profiles for both slip and book approval plans can be adjusted as needed. For example, approval profiles can be limited by subject, price range, and specific publishers.

Vendors can provide a multitude of special management reports. Many serial vendors have historical price analysis data for titles that a library owns. Bibliographers can use this to trace the subscription fluctuations for journals in their subject areas. When making the decision to add a subscription, vendors can provide helpful indexing and abstracting reports. These list the names of the secondary sources that index the serials, thus assuring bibliographers that the new title will have maximum usage. It is possible to obtain lists of a library's journal subscriptions arranged by Library of Congress Classification Number and by Internationl Standard Serials Number. Some vendors will also provide templates for librarians to use in assessing and evaluating their collection of serial titles.

Book vendors can provide many of the same types of reports, including price increases, dollars spent by subject areas, and the number of titles available.

Librarians should look for ways to share these reports with faculty members. Serials vendor reports on price histories can show the dramatic changes in subscription rates. Lists of subscriptions by subject can be produced and used by faculty when they are confronted with the need for departmental cancellations.

Serial and book vendor discounts and service charges can be discussed with interested faculty. It might help them understand why the library chooses a particular vendor and presents evidence that the library strives to get the best value. Faculty often give librarians suggestions about how to acquire a book or journal. If faculty are knowledgeable about the vendor process, they will accept why the library cannot always use their advice.

If asked, vendors will visit libraries to explain service charges and discounts. Their perspectives on events and trends can help clarify choices and facilitate decision making. Vendors offer librarians the opportunity to benefit from their work with other librarians and publishers. According to Larry Price, "In a sense, the supplier acts as a consultant who has a keen interest in the success of the library."[17]

Vendors are often technologically sophisticated. Online ordering and claiming are commonplace. Some provide check-in services and systems. Adherence to communications standards and EDI protocols enables vendor systems to interface with local integrated library systems. Most have established homepages on the World Wide Web that describe their services and present ordering options. Some allow their databases to be searched. The databases can provide a valuable bibliographic resource even if not used for purchasing.

Lee described how vendors can match a library's holdings (if supplied in machine-readable format) to their databases.[18] Thus, titles available but not held in the library are identified. This service can be used to build retrospective collections in a subject area when new programs are added to the curriculum.

Publishers

Librarians are reluctant to use publishers as a resource in their collection building activities. Several contentious issues beyond journal pricing keep librarians wary, copyright being one of the most obvious.[19] Schuman, in "Librarians and Publishers: An Uneasy Dance," describes several others. The privatization of government information and disagreements over discounts have also made librarians anxious. Despite these disagreements, Schuman contends that "There are some obvious commonalities of missions and self-interest that should mandate mutually supportive collaborations between librarians and publishers; clear and frequent communication should be a top priority."[20] This becomes even more crucial in the electronic environment where author and user are directly connected.

The role of publishers in the production of information is often misunderstood even though library educators advocate learning about publishing characteristics.[21] Publishers tend to respond to the needs of their authors and end users. They react first to their editors' demands and focus on the content of the research reported. Bibliographers can become exposed to these points of view by attending conferences and meetings where publishers are present. It is especially helpful to attend smaller meetings that promote communications among all participants, such as the Charleston Conference, the North American Serials Interest Group (NASIG), and the Society for Scholarly Publishing.

Pricing of products, particularly journals, is as indicated earlier a sensitive and complex issue. While librarians repeatedly question publisher practices and generally remain skeptical of their explanations, publishers have recently started releasing subscription prices earlier. This practice allows librarians to begin working with faculty when cancellations are inevitable. Price projections facilitate planning. Vendors are often the vehicle for distribution of this information.

Publishers appreciate opinions on their products, and librarians can contribute to that process. Bibliographers should offer to assess them if given the opportunity. Bibliographers would be able to contact faculty members and others who might provide additional perspectives. This is especially beneficial with new electronic endeavors. Some publishers are partnering with libraries in the advancement of the desktop delivery of information. These opportunities all give librarians a way to influence the development of these products.

Bibliographers should realize that publishers are in the business to sell their products. They use several different types of promotional materials: complete catalogs, subject clusters (catalogs and brochures), general brochures, and ads in other publications. Although at times they duplicate each other, they can serve useful purposes that may provide information overlooked in other selection strategies. It is possible to review and discard the brochures quickly, while gaining an overview of trends and areas of emphasis. Look to this information for the first announcements of the latest products. Complete catalogs can be retained for reference, and subject-oriented material can be passed onto faculty members.

Publishers are developing a very strong presence on the Internet, and accessing their information electronically can help relieve the volume of discarded paper. Many have their catalogs available on the World Wide Web and offer direct online ordering. Especially helpful are the journal publishers that provide tables of contents and instructions to authors. This new mode of communication promises continued growth and access to information for bibliographers.

If problems arise and librarians have questions that are not answered directly by publishers and vendors, there are mechanisms to assist them. Several professional library organizations have committees that will mediate and try to resolve differences. ALA, under the Association for Library Collections and Technical Services (ALCTS), has the Publisher/Vendor-Library Relations Committee, and the Medical Library Association has the Publishers and Information Industries Relations Committee (PIIRC). These committees serve as conduits for communication between parties and can alert the library community of exemplary, as well as disreputable, practices.

CONCLUDING THOUGHTS

Collection development involves a team of people. All must work together to meet the needs of library users. Effective communication between team members greatly facilitates building collections that will be used. It is overwhelming for libraries to deal with static budgets, increased serial costs, proliferation of information, and the ever-changing technological environment. Partnering with the full collection development team will facilitate the selection and access to information process. All of the members have a genuine interest and a desire to create a winning environment for sound collection development decisions.

If bibliographers are given ample opportunities to interact with the full team, they will be in a better position to coordinate collection development efforts. Selection of materials and providing access to information is essential. In order for libraries to thrive, demands of users must be met. Providing specialized services to library users will help ensure that libraries will be winners.

NOTES AND REFERENCES

1. Harry S. Martin III and Curtis L. Kendrick, "A User-Centered View of Document Delivery and Interlibrary Loan," *Library Administration and Management* 8(4,1994): 226.
2. John Secor, "Ignorance Is Bliss," *Library Acquisitions: Practice and Theory* 15(1991): 379-383.
3. Scott R. Bullard, "Educating Rita—Part II: Training for Collection Development," *Library Acquisitions: Practice and Theory* 8(1984): 243.
4. Eveline L. Yang, "Psychology Collection Review: A Cooperative Project Between Librarians and Departmental Faculty Members," *Collection Management* 13(3,1990): 44.
5. Rebecca C. Drummond, Anne Page Mosby, and Mary H. Munroe, "A Joint Venture: Collaboration in Collection Building," *Collection Management* 14(1-2, 1991): 65.
6. *Liaison Services in ARL Libraries,* Issued as SPEC Kit 189, (Washington, DC: Systems and Procedures Exchange Center, Office of Management Services, Association of Research Libraries, 1992); Julie Ann McDaniel, "Leading the Way: In-House Collection Development Training for New Selectors." *Library Acquisitions: Practice and Theory* 13(1989): 293-295; C.E. Pasterczyk, "Checklist for the New Selector," *College & Research Libraries News* 49(7,1988): 434-435; "RASD: Guidelines for Liaison Work," *RQ* 32(2,1992): 198-204; Connie Wu, "Effective Liaison Relationships in an Academic Library," *C&RL News* 55(5,1994): 254,303.
7. Anne B. Commerton, "Building Faculty/Library Relationships: Forging the Bond," *The Bookmark* 45(1986): 17-20.
8. Frank A. D'Andraia, "The Business of Libraries Is Staying in Business," in *The Dynamic Library Organizations in a Changing Environment*, edited by Joan Giesecke, (New York: Haworth Press Inc., 1994), pp. 81-91.

9. Gregg Sapp and Peter G. Watson, "Librarian-Faculty Relations During a Period of Journals Cancellations," *The Journal of Academic Librarianship* 15(5,1989): 287.

10. Jasper G. Schad, "Managing Collection Development in University Libraries That Utilize Librarians With Dual-Responsibility Assignments," *Library Acquisitions: Practice and Theory* 14(1990): 166-167.

11. Julie L. Nicklin, "Colleges Rethink the Effectiveness of Interlibrary Loans in Cutting Expenses," *The Chronicle of Higher Education* (July 7, 1993), p. A37.

12. Helen L. Gater, "The Price of Partnership," in *Creative Planning for Library Administration: Leadership for the Future*, edited by Kent Hendrickson, (New York: The Haworth Press Inc., 1991), p. 91.

13. Julie Brewer, "Service Management: How to Plan for It Rather Than Hope for It," *Library Administration and Management* 9 (1995): 208-209.

14. Mark Sandler, "Organizing Effective Faculty Participation in Collection Development," *Collection Management* 6(3/4,1984): 65.

15. "RASD: Guidelines for Liaison Work," *RQ* 32(2,1992): 202.

16. Lauren K. Lee, "Library/Vendor Cooperation in Collection Development," in *Vendors and Library Acquisitions,* edited by Bill Katz, (New York: The Haworth Press Inc., 1991), pp. 181-190.

17. Larry Price, "Book Wholesaling: Looking Toward the 21st Century," in *Vendors and Library Acquisitions*, edited by Bill Katz, (New York: The Haworth Press, 1991), pp. 21-28.

18. "RASD: Guidelines for Liaison Work."

19. Carol A. Risher, "Publishers, Librarians, and Copyright," *Library Acquisitions: Practice and Theory* 13(1989): 213-216.

20. Patricia Glass Schuman, "Librarians and Publishers: An Uneasy Dance," *Wilson Library Bulletin* (1994): 40-43.

21. Edward G. Evans, *Developing Library and Information Center Collections*, (Littleton, CO: Libraries Unlimited, 1987).

DUPLICATES EXCHANGE UNION:
FROM WORLD WAR II TO THE WORLD WIDE WEB

Rebecca House Stankowski

ABSTRACT

Almost since their inception, libraries have joined in cooperative ventures to enhance their collections by sharing duplicate items with each other. Traditionally, these have been labor-intensive manual processes, that is, preparing lists of available titles, distributing the lists, then searching through each incoming list for needed items. The request must then be returned to the list originator, who in turn finally mails the needed item to the requester. It is therefore welcome news to find that this valuable resource has seen several technological advances in recent years and through the use of the Internet, E-mail, and the World Wide Web, there is now an on-line duplicates and exchange program that is effective and easy to use.

THOSE VALUABLE DUPLICATES

Nearly every morning at libraries all over the nation, assistants appear and ask their supervisors for daily duty assignments. On the occasions when they hear the dreaded words, "duplicate exchange," their faces often fall into mock grimaces at the prospect of several hours of tedious work. They may even protest, "Oh, are there very many? They take so long to do!" But now it is possible to tell then that even though there may be several, it will not take that much time to process them all. Why? Because, finally, the tedious process of manually searching through list after list has been replaced by a centralized on-line system that is indexed, allows Boolean searching, and is easy to use. But even after all of this is explained, the long-suffering assistants will still be doubtful.

Libraries have always had to be adept at finding methods to stretch their perpetually limited resources, and one successful strategy has been the cooperative exchange of duplicate materials. Many of these exchange programs concentrate on single issues of journals that libraries use to replace lost, stolen, or mutilated items which have created gaps in their holdings, but books, government documents, and out-of-print materials are also often available. Many different types of exchange programs have evolved over the years—the first may have been the American Association of Law Libraries Duplicate Exchange Committee, which was formed in 1906.[1] In the intervening years many cooperative programs developed by various library associations, academic institutions, and international cooperatives scattered from New York to New Delhi have enjoyed varying degrees of success. The enduring popularity of such programs is not hard to understand; studies analyzing the expenses associated with duplicates and exchange programs (which often include only staff time and postage) have concluded that the cooperative exchange of materials is very cost effective for participating institutions.[2] And it is also often the only method of obtaining that one journal issue that is no longer in print or otherwise available at any price.

COOPERATIVE PROGRAMS

Usually duplicates and exchange programs are developed by a group of like-minded institutions who agree to participate in this cooperative venture. Many are organized through a common interest (groups of medical and law libraries come to mind), and some like the Christian Colleges Periodical Exchange[3] serve a very narrow clientele. Participation in these programs is easy. A member library simply prepares a list of items that are available for exchange and then reproduces this list and mails it to all other member libraries. The recipients can read through these incoming lists, mark items they need, and then return them to the originating institutions. The requests are filled in order of receipt, and postage over a predetermined threshold (usually $1-$3) is reimbursed. Transaction completed.

While this manner of operation is simple, it is also labor-intensive and not very efficient. Preparing and duplicating the lists take time and money, so each participant may only issue two or three lists per year—some even fewer. But since lists usually carry an expiration date of four or six weeks from production and many items are "taken" shortly after new lists appear, they have a relatively short shelf life. Members of large programs will receive many lists, necessitating many hours of student or clerical (or even professional) labor to process. But even considering these drawbacks, many libraries find that the benefits of duplicate exchange programs still far outweigh the disadvantages.

DUPLICATES EXCHANGE UNION

Some of the most durable exchange programs are those sponsored or developed by professional organizations, such as the American Library Association's Duplicates Exchange Union, operated under the auspices of the Association for Library Collections & Technical Services (ALCTS). This program enjoys a long history, having been organized as the Periodicals Exchange Union in 1940 by Neil Van Deusen, librarian of Fisk University in Nashville, Tenn.[4] At that time the union was sponsored by the Association of College and Reference Libraries (later becoming the Association of College and Research Libraries). The American Library Association's Resources and Technical Services Division took over sponsorship in 1961.[5]

Van Deusen decided that the informal exchange of material that had been going on for years needed to be officially organized. He approached a number of libraries to determine interest, and in June

1940 he officially established the Periodicals Exchange Union with 64 members. He had developed a plan that allowed participants to exchange material at no cost and with no attempt to match "gives and gets" on a one-to-one basis. His plan, however, did involve a rather elaborate set of procedural instructions. Each participating library would be listed on a routing sheet in order of their periodicals budget, largest on top. This list was distributed to all members, who then attached a copy of their duplicates list to the routing sheet and sent it to the first library on the roster. When the first library had requested whatever it wanted, the list went to the second library, and so on down the line. The program worked—routing sheets were generated, duplicates lists went out, and exchanges were made. Van Deusen supervised the project for a year, then in May 1942 the ACRL appointed a three-person committee to manage the exchange.

In retrospect, there were some obvious problems with the Van Deusen plan. Of course the top library (the one with the largest budget) always got first pick, often leaving libraries farther down the list empty handed. Some members complained that it took too long for the lists to circulate because some libraries were not punctual about forwarding them and because it simply takes a while for a list to travel to over 60 participants. So in May 1944, the managing committee adopted a revised plan that accomplished several things. The name was changed to Duplicates Exchange Union (DEU) to allow for the exchange of books and documents as well as periodicals, the budget-based routing sheet was replaced with a simple alphabetical listing of participants, and duplicates lists were to be distributed to all members simultaneously with requests filled on a first-come, first-served basis. And that plan remained nearly unaltered for the next 50 years.

There were, however, a few changes along the way. In 1961 the ACRL decided to discontinue sponsorship of the program, and ALA's Resources and Technical Services Division (now the Association for Library Collections & Technical Services) took it over. ALCTS more clearly defined the mission of the DEU, pointing out that it did not "cover the same field as the U.S. Book Exchange since DEU is geared to the small college and public library which is trying to build up its collection primarily of domestic books and periodicals."[6] This was a wise move, since a study at Northwestern University seemed to indicate that cooperative programs were not suited for research institutions—"the larger the library the less the profit in this method of exchange."[7] And the formula seemed to work, for membership gradually increased over the years and reached a total of 372 members by 1995.

DUPLICATE DRUDGERY?

The Purdue University Calumet Library, serving a commuter campus of nearly 10,000 students (6,400 FTE) with 225,000 volumes, joined the Duplicates Exchange Union in the late 1970s. We are one of the larger current members of the exchange. During any given week we receive 12-15 lists of "duplicates available" from other members, and in an informal study conducted during the second quarter of 1994 we found that it took staff (usually students) approximately 15 minutes to check through each list. We have always constantly updated our "available" list and distributed it twice each year—which generates an average of about five requests per week. In FY 1994-1995 we filled over 200 requests. Clerical staff time spent on these tasks added up to approximately three hours per week. Thus, combined clerical and student staff time spent on duplicates exchange amounted to about six hours per week during the academic year.

Undoubtedly the most tedious part of the entire process is the job that student assistants and other exchange staff most often dread—checking incoming "available" lists against our "needed" file. Going through a lot of lists takes a lot of time and becomes mind-numbing rather quickly. However, there is finally a better way.

DUPLICATES ON-LINE

At its February 1994 meeting during the American Library Association's Midwinter Meeting, the DEU Committee authorized a pilot project to determine the feasibility of electronic exchange of information between DEU members.[8] Ten members participated with such success that the project was opened to all DEU libraries in late summer 1994. This "electronic exchange of information" is accomplished in two ways, through an on-line Internet discussion group and via a DEU gopher site. Both of these projects are housed and managed by staff at Sam Houston State University (SHSU) in Huntsville, Texas.

The on-line discussion group is one of the many Internet "lists" which serve as interactive bulletin boards to allow the exchange of information and which are accessed through e-mail. These lists are given names that are indicative of the area of interest such as Autocat (library cataloging), Travel-L (travel), and Gardens (guess what). The Duplicates Exchange Union's list is called, appropriately enough, DEU-L and is managed by Janice Lange from the libraries at SHSU. To subscribe to DEU-L, send an e-mail message addressed to LISTSERV@SHSU.EDU, leaving the subject line blank. The body of the message should simply say subscribe DEU-L, your first name, your last name, for example:

subscribe DEU-L Bill Gates

You will then be added to the mailing list, and you will receive copies of all messages posted to the list. It iss not a chatty list; most of the traffic is composed of notices about new lists, some procedural information, and the occasional question. The real heart of the on-line DEU project is in the DEU gopher.

The DEU gopher is also housed at SHSU. Like other gopher sites, the SHSU gopher is a collection of databases that are linked together through a main menu that leads to various sub-menus and choices, and the DEU Project is one of the options. One can access the SHSU gopher in several ways. One route is to access your favorite gopher site and choose

All the Gopher Servers in the World
  North America
    USA
      Texas
        Sam Houston State University

If you have a World Wide Web browser such as Mosaic or Netscape, use the Uniform Resource Locator (URL) gopher://niord.shsu.edu to arrive at the same destination. Once you have accessed the SHSU gopher, choose the DEU Library Prototype Demonstration Area. Here you will find several options—names and addresses of participants, individual lists to scan, and the real beauty of this project, a searchable index which allows you to search all of the available lists AT THE SAME TIME.

CHANGES FOR THE ELECTRONIC AGE

For the first time in nearly 50 years, the DEU Project has changed the basic distribution method that Van Deusen and the ACRL Committee devised in the 1940s. A fully participating member has no need for list duplication, no need for mailing labels, no need for postage. Instead, a library uses a word processing program to prepare its "available" list following a set of formatting rules. This list is forwarded in electronic format—either via e-mail or on a disk—to the project manager, currently Janice Lange at SHSU. The manager then adds the new list to the others on the gopher and announces it on DEU-L.

Then what happens? Since all of the lists are in one index, users have to enter only one search for each title needed, and even Boolean searching is supported. That one search will retrieve all instances of the title in ALL lists posted to the gopher. Gone are the days of flipping through pages and pages of list after list looking for that one issue of *Social Science Quarterly*. So all one needs to do is sit down at the PC, connect to the SHSU gopher, and then enter each title being sought—only once—and see if you get any matches. If matches to searches are found, then just send an e-mail request to the originating library without even leaving the PC. The only costs involved are postage reimbursement of anything over $3.

Obviously there are many advantages to this system, the main one being time savings. Instead of spending three to four hours a week combing through incoming lists, a staff member can check our entire want list against the gopher in an hour or less. Once the first "available" list is generated, it is a simple matter to add or delete titles as necessary, and my staff have found that it only takes 20 to 30 minutes per week to maintain the list. And they are also relieved of the duties involved in duplicating the list, printing mailing labels, and preparing it for mass mailing two or three times each year. Instead, it takes one staff member two minutes (literally) to send the list to the DEU project manager via e-mail. So total staff time falls from six hours per week to less than two.

But time savings are not the only benefit. Since newly edited lists do not have to be duplicated or mailed, they can be posted to the gopher at frequent intervals, thus making them more current, correct, and useful. And because the lists are initially sent electronically and then requests for materials from those lists can be made via e-mail, both turnaround time and postage costs decrease dramatically.

ARE THE BENEFITS WORTH THE EFFORT?

Participation in the on-line DEU project *is* a little labor-intensive in the initial stages. In order to participate, an institution must have access to the Internet and a basic understanding of its features. For accurate indexing in the SHSU gopher, each list must be formatted according to explicit instructions, and for proper search retrieval each title on the list must be listed in the same manner.[9] This is initially more time consuming than simply listing the titles according to whim, but it makes things much more efficient in the long run. Mary Gocher, Swarthmore College librarian, understood the need for this almost 60 years ago. As she said at the 1937 American Library Association Conference in New York, "Lists of duplicates for sale or exchange from other libraries present particular difficulties because of lack of uniformity and clarity in method of listing.... My plea is for the adoption of a fairly uniform method of listing duplicates which will make for clarity and uniformity throughout the list. I see the necessity for a clear, concise form, giving all the necessary information, which can be easily and quickly read."[10] Obviously, Gocher would have been an advocate of the Duplicates Exchange Union's on-line project. However, following the formatting guidelines does not need to create additional work for duplicates staff—any added effort here should be more than offset by the relief from mailing label production and mass mailings.

Is participation in the Duplicates Exchange Union worth it? Using the manual system, we spend an average of six hours per week during the academic year (30 weeks) for a total of 180 clerical and student wage hours. During FY 1994-1995 we received 70 items and distributed slightly more than 200. Using $7 per hour as an average of clerical and student wages, each item cost us about $18, which given the nature of our collection is less than we would have paid a vendor. However, by using the on-line system the staff time drops by two-thirds, thus lowering the cost of each item to $6—a real bargain, especially considering that many of the items obtained through the DEU are out-of-print and unavailable elsewhere at any price. And these calculations disregard the benefits we enjoy from clearing out our duplicates and freeing much needed space.

THE MORE THE MERRIER

It would be misleading to imply that the Duplicates Exchange Union is operating in a total on-line environment. The on-line project is very young, and in actuality the DEU is still very much a manual system, operating for the most part under the Van Deusen/ACRL scheme. Participation in the DEU on-line project is by no means mandatory, and currently only a small percentage of the DEU membership participates in the on-line project by subscribing to DEU-L or sending duplicates lists to be posted to the DEU gopher. Of course, it should be understood that many small libraries have only limited access to the Internet or are without it completely, and others are novices with little experience with the World Wide Web. If recent history is any indication, this situation will change very quickly during the next few years as more and more people and institutions become connected to the "information superhighway." As this happens, on-line participation will naturally increase.

Here at Purdue Calumet we recognize these current limitations, and in order to reach all DEU members we still participate in a manual mass mailing, although we now distribute only one paper list per year via U.S. mail. We update our online list every three months. As mentioned above, there are still a relatively small number of lists currently indexed on the DEU gopher, thereby limiting the efficacy of the project, but as more institutions begin to participate, the hit rate will increase dramatically.[11]

This is an exciting new program that demonstrates once again how the capabilities of modern technology can be harnessed to make even the most routine tasks faster, easier, and more efficient. The exchange of duplicate material has always been a necessity for many libraries; now it can be an enjoyable pursuit, too. I believe that Van Deusen would have approved.

NOTES AND REFERENCES

1. Tim J. Watts, "A Preliminary Examination of the AALL Exchange of Duplicates Program," *Law Library Journal* 81 (Spring 1989): 293.

2. Lynn Branch Brown, "Serials Duplicates Exchange Programs: Costs and Benefits," *The Bottom Line* 6 (2,1992): 28.

3. A list of participants in this program can be found in "Periodicals Exchange," *The Christian Librarian* 36(2,1993): 64-66.

4. All details of the initial formation of the Duplicates Exchange Union are contained in an article by Committee Chair Donald E. Thompson, "Duplicate Exchange Union," *College and Research Libraries* 6 (March 1945): 158-160. Thompson is the former college librarian of Wabash College, Wabash, Indiana.

5. Details of ALA's initial sponsorship of the DEU were provided by Karen Whittlesey, ALA/ALCTS.

6. This statement is included in a call for members, *Library Resources and Technical Services* 8(3,1964): 333.

7. Ian W. Thom, "Duplicates Exchange: A Cost Analysis," *Library Resources and Technical Services* 1(2,1957): 81.

8. For further details of the electronic pilot project, see the *DEU Newsletter*, July 1994 update, available from ALCTS.

9. Complete instructions on list formatting, address creation, and other procedural matters are available in the archives located on the DEU gopher and are also distributed upon joining the Duplicates Exchange Union.

10. Mary Gocher, "The Listing of Periodical Duplicates for Sale or Exchange," *Bulletin of the American Library Association* 31 (October 1937): 826.

11. Information about joining DEU may be obtained from Duplicates Exchange Union, Association for Library Collections & Technical Services, American Library Association, 50 E. Huron Street, Chicago, IL, 60611. The chair of the DEU Committee for 1995-96 is Janice Lange, Sam Houston State University, Internet address LIB—JPL@SHSU.EDU. There is no fee to join, and member libraries do not have to be members of ALA.

NATIVE AMERICAN AND CHICANO VIDEO AND FILM:
TOWARD A NEW MODEL FOR COLLECTION DEVELOPMENT IN ACADEMIC LIBRARIES

Ann M. Massmann

ABSTRACT

The number of videos and films relating to Native Americans and Chicanos[1] is rapidly increasing. Significantly, this includes a growing number of films and videos produced by individuals who are themselves Native American, Chicano or Chicana. These visual resources are not only important in and of themselves as creative works of art, but also for what they say and the issues that they address. Video and film make important contributions to people's ability to portray and document their own culture, their own perspective. And in a visual age where television, movies, and music video play a significant role in people's everyday lives, film and video should not be overlooked as teaching and research tools. Native American and Chicano studies classes, as well as many others which may touch on Native American and Chicano issues, can benefit from the use of the visual format as part of the curriculum. Film and video makers tell stories; they bring issues, traditions, histories, and individuals to life. Video and film are valuable as educational tools, as resources to be more fully integrated into instruction and research and into library collections.

The value of video and film in instruction and research cannot simply be taken as a given; if that were so, video and film would be far better represented in our current collections and considered less of a "problematic" collection development issue. The intent of this paper is to explore reasons for focusing additional attention on collecting video and film in the context of Native American and Chicano video and film and to re-examine the biases against video in the textually (and now electronically) oriented academic library.

THE ROLE OF VIDEO AND FILM IN INSTRUCTION AND RESEARCH

The argument for increased attention to video as a teaching and research tool can be tied to three very different developments of recent times. Major changes have been occurring in the media art with the widespread availability and use of the video format, in educational methodology, and in changing concepts of history and how that affects historical research methodology and resources.

First, the video "explosion" that has affected entertainment is also revolutionizing the motion picture field. Video, in essence, has begun the democratization of moving images, much the same as happened with still photography in the twentieth century. Video is easier and cheaper to produce than film, which is meaningful to those who would produce motion pictures but have limited funding and training for film. This increased accessibility to the creation of visual media is of no small importance to Native Americans and Chicanos, as people whose cultures have traditionally been exploited, misrepresented, and/or ignored by the dominant American filmmaking industry. Video is also serving as a door for many Native Americans and Chicanos to get into filmwork, providing experience, recognition, and even funding leading to film school. Of equal importance to increased accessibility for video and filmmakers, is its increased accessibility for viewers. Videos are easier to use and can be cheaper to purchase than films, and thus are capable of achieving a wider audience in classrooms, libraries, and homes, than has been possible for film. These factors, in turn, contribute to increased demand for works on video, theoretically allowing more voices to be heard.

Second, a shift in the educational methodology used in adult education (that is in colleges/universities, continuing education, and professional development) is taking place and challenging traditional forms of teaching (lecture method) and traditional instructional tools (texts). Much of the educational research of the last few decades has shown that "lecture is of little use if the educator or trainer is seeking to promote critical thinking or to encourage adults to be more flexible in their attitudes."[2] More participatory methods of instruction are recommended instead, combining lecture (when appropriate) with techniques such as small and large group discussions, and exercises to stimulate thinking and to bring students' own life experiences into the learning process. Many teaching centers, such as the Center for Teaching and Learning at Stanford University, are actively promoting new methods of participatory, active learning and assessment. Further, the changing demographics of students in higher education is sparking change in instructional methods. Since the 1970s, larger numbers of women, non-traditional aged, physically challenged, and culturally-diverse students have been entering colleges and universities, "bringing with them differing ideas and needs for their education that challenge old ways of thinking."[3] In *Promoting Active Learning*, Meyers and Jones maintain that "When the assertive posture of adults is combined with the expectations of women, African Americans, Latinos, American Indians, Asian Americans, and other student groups that their concerns and experiences be included in higher education, powerful incentives for change result."[4]

Video and film can be an excellent teaching tools when used in combination with discussions and other active teaching methods. The very nature of these media lend themselves to the presentation of complex issues and multiple voices or viewpoints—something a single lecturer is limited in doing. In this media age, where most students have grown up with television and movies, an instructor is more likely to find students watching a video or film to be "engaged with the ideas, skills and knowledge being presented"[5]—a central goal of participatory learning. This visual "spark" can be a powerful springboard for discussion in the classroom, to actively engage students through facilitation from the instructor, and through the validation of diverse cultural and gender-specific experiences.

Third, there has been a major shift in historical research methodology since the 1970s corresponding to the broader-based, more egalitarian form of history, known as the "new" public history. Public history seeks to recognize and document the people and events that have been largely ignored by society and by the historical establishment. Traditionally (with the exception of a period of public history in the 1930s), history in this country has been concerned rather strictly with the top of the economic and social "pyramid." Native American and Chicano histories have particularly suffered in this repressive structure. Public history, conversely, is often described as "history from the bottom up" because it seeks to reverse the focus on stories of the wealthy and "heroic." In it, the common and the everyday is as important to document as is the notable. In fact, through this new lens of history, the powerless, the everyman or everywoman can at last be properly seen as a hero or heroine through their actions, or through their very way of life. This can be seen in films, such as "The Ballad of Gregorio Cortez," in "Agueda Martinez: Our People, Our Country," or in "Navajo Talking Picture." Public history, in combination with the Chicano Movimiento and the American Indian movement of the 1960s and 1970s, has laid the groundwork for the types of Native American and Chicano films and videos so important to the body of work of the last decades.

There has also been a shift in historical methodology that has occurred in connection with public history that has included a democratization and expansion of documentary resources. In order to truly represent traditionally-absent groups and individuals in our history, we need to turn to new arenas of inquiry. Information and documentation on many people, cultures, and events is often not found in the standard textual forms. Traditionally, written primary sources have reigned supreme as the respected materials from which one learned about and documented history, that is, government and other official documents, business records, memoirs, personal papers, and published accounts of events. The pieces of most people's lives, however, especially those emphasizing oral traditions, and those people from lower socioeconomic groups and marginalized cultures, cannot be found in written documents and papers in a library or archives. Instead, historians have turned in part to oral interviews and community-based forms of information. Oral history projects have sprung up everywhere in the last 25 years. There is, however, a continuing struggle to defend the legitimacy of these forms of inquiry against those who would marginalize them. Video and audio taped oral history interviews, as well as taped performances, events, and lectures have become enormously valuable to those working to document and preserve their Native American and Chicano communities. Thus, the role of documentary, non-commercial video must also be recognized and discussed in any Native American and Chicano video collection program.

VIDEO AND FILM IN ACADEMIC LIBRARY COLLECTIONS: TOWARD A NEW MODEL

Arising out of the increased value of video and film in instruction and research is the slowly-developing view of video and film's value in the academic library. Native American and Chicano research collections in many academic libraries were built around books and are only just beginning to look at video and film, often as special funding becomes available. Whereas public and school libraries have long-ago validated audio-visual resources as part of their collections, academic libraries still often marginalize resources such as video. They are somehow relegated to a lower stature in terms of the knowledge they purvey, perhaps being seen as a format primarily for entertainment. Another more concrete factor contributing to this marginalization has to do with the physical access requirements of video, being a machine-readable format. Library media centers are often set up to handle these requirements or else circulation privileges may be granted. Circulation outside of the building can lead, of course, to increased damage or loss of items. If a library media center approach is taken, then care should be taken to keep these collections tied into collecting decisions by subject selectors (such as Chicano and Native American studies librarians) so as not to further alienate these formats from the other research collections.

In libraries then, there is not only the need to change paradigms to fit with the revaluation of video and film for instruction and research purposes, but also to reverse the marginalization that has occurred due to its physical format. Changing technology requires changing perspectives about what is involved in caring for materials and making them available to users. Magnetic media (video and audio tapes) and film do not fall into the longstanding library textual model: "Put it on the shelf"—end of storage issues; "Let users check it out"—end of access issues. Librarians are often wary when it comes to investing in audio, video, and film (unless they are part of a media department) for a variety of reasons that must be addressed. In contrast to books, audio-visual materials require specific playback equipment. This is often complicated by non-identical formats—audio cassettes, open reel tapes, CDs, LPs, 1/2" VHS, 3/4" U-Matic, 16mm film, to name a few. Audio-visual materials are also fragile and impermanent in nature due to chemical instability, handling (playback), and obsolescence of technology (e.g., Beta video tapes, 8-track audio tapes, and vinyl records).

These last three issues are at the core of what makes magnetic media and film "difficult." They are also unalterable facts that libraries must adjust to if they are to accept non-textual media as increasingly important sources of information in our late twentieth century world. With the proliferation of these media and the enormous changes based on electronic resources, non-paper-based media now play an enormous role in how we keep and transfer knowledge.

Most academic libraries have already made a smooth transition to electronic resources for reference, such as CD-ROMS and online databases. Expensive equipment and software were quickly purchased, librarians and staff were trained, and basic access issues were addressed. Of course, this is a simplification; but compare the transition to that of the inclusion of audio and video tapes in a library's research collections. In both general libraries and special collections, audio and video acquisition, accessibility, and promotion are often lacking. Audio and video tend to lag far behind CD-ROMs and online resources, although these formats involve many of the same issues as electronic resources. In order for these media to fulfill their potential role as resources in the academic sphere, libraries will need to recognize the barriers and even prejudices present in the current structure and decide how to best make the shift. This shift cannot be delayed any further with the advent of so many new technologies and the proliferation of video in particular as a cultural resource.

The following points are to be considered in a new video and film library "paradigm."

- Equipment on which to play video and film is required. Like supplying computers and CD-ROM drives in reference, there is just no getting around this issue. In the old model centered on books, equipment like this is a luxury, but in the new model it is a simple necessity, like furniture or lighting for readers.
- Video tape and film are fragile. Like twentieth century books with acidic pages, video is prone to deterioration simply because of its chemical nature. This deterioration happens much more rapidly than paper's, however.[5] Significantly, video tape's nature as machine readable media also leaves it open to extensive damage in the form of information loss, through scratches, dust particles, oils, and liquids that would only cause superficial damage to books. The same is true for film as well. For reasons of both manufacture and use then, magnetic media and film need to be cared for in ways different from non-audiovisual materials.
- Video and film must be housed protectively. Environmental conditions such as temperature, humidity, light, and particulates in the air (such as dust, smoke, and chemicals) can damage magnetic media, which is quite sensitive to these factors. Magnetic fields may damage tapes as well.[7]
- Playback or use policy decisions must be made to balance access needs with the fragile nature of the materials. Do you provide playback equipment in a supervised area? Or do you allow tapes to circulate, increasing the risk of damage? The difference in use policies is central to their longevity, which is then connected to allocating library funds for replacement copies. The regulating of the use of video and film is not necessarily an act of restriction (old model). Rather it is a proactive step to insure that these items will be available to the greatest number of people for the longest period possible. It is a responsible and efficient use of acquisition dollars.
- Many videos and films do cost more than many books. So do many periodical subscriptions, CD-ROMs, and online services. If the value of the information is considered to be significant and appropriate to collection guidelines, then money is usually found to support these other formats. Yet this is often not the case for video and film. In these formats' standard paradigm in libraries, their selection has often been eliminated based primarily on price instead of how they fit

into a collection context. Though the original purchase price can be substantial for some videos ($200-$350 and more) and certainly for films, it is important to compare this with costs over time if professors and groups are forced to continually rent particular titles at, say, $50 per rental. A shift in thinking should occur to allow for purchasing of at least the most significant titles. We have entered a new era in libraries in which we are faced with acquisition decisions regarding quite expensive materials: periodicals, electronic resources, and audio-visual resources. Skyrocketing costs and new media are forcing libraries to "redistribute the wealth" and to look for additional sources of funding. Video and film should not be forgotten in this process; their value must be recognized and advocated.

ISSUES FOR COLLECTING NATIVE AMERICAN AND CHICANO VIDEO AND FILM

Two excellent resources on Native American and Chicano film and video have been published in the last three years which can help librarians and others who wish to learn about specific titles and understand the larger issues involved. These resources are *Videoforum: A Videography for Libraries*[8] and *Mediating History: The MAP Guide to Independent Video.*[9]

Videoforum is a project of National Video Resources (of the Rockefeller Foundation) and the John D. and Catherine T. MacArthur Foundation Library Video Project and includes both Native American (1993) and Latino (1994) issues. These two issues were designed "to assist in building and maintaining a collection of high quality, non-fiction video," and each includes useful essays, a videography, and distributor information. The MacArthur Foundation Project recently concluded a special distribution program for public libraries which reduced the prices for videos Native American and Latino videos significantly.

The Media Alternatives Project (MAP), which produced *Mediating History*, is also funded by the Library Video Project. Like *Videoforum*, this *MAP Guide to Independent Video* features critical essays, videographies, and distributor information, but includes African-American and Asian-American videos in addition to Latino

(Chicano, Puerto Rican, and Cuban) and Native American resources. The intended audience of this volume is history teachers and professors, though the essays and video reviews are highly appropriate for librarians as well.

There is a section of Maria Nesthus' overview essay in *Videoforum* which is particularly useful as a framework for discussing video and film selection issues. In her essay in *Videoforum's* Native American issue, she states criteria which she sees as "fundamental to a well-developed media collection on Native Americans."[10] I will expand the four points she presents to both Native American and Chicano video and film issues.

Native American Video and Film

1. *The major tribal cultures must be accurately represented.* Native Americans are not a monolithic culture, and separate tribal cultures need to be represented whenever possible. It is important to distinguish between the many diverse cultures present in an area and to make sure they are represented on video and film: reservation and non-reservation, rural and urban, traditional and non-traditional. Additionally, when Native American studies is a significant program of study at a university or school, consideration should be given to representation of national issues and major tribal groups from other parts of the country.

2. *Consideration must be given to the degree of Native American cooperation in each production.* "Representation of the film and video work of Native American producers must be a priority." Native American film and video in the past has been characterized by the fact that much of it was *about* Native Americans, *by* non-Natives, and *for* non-Native audiences. Though the value of these ethnographic films and videos differs, they are greatly distinguished from today's growing arena of Native American-produced film and video. As Elizabeth Weatherford of the Smithsonian's National Museum of the American Indian states in *Videoforum*, "Productions in which Native Americans express their own thoughts owe their sense of accuracy to the personal, lived experience that the people in them share.... The result can be profound—a heightened and conscious knowledge of America's first people and of their continuing way of life."[11]

3. *The full scope of Native American history must be indicated and the necessity for reconsideration of that history demonstrated.* "Native American history must be understood to extend from its ancient civilizations up to the concerns of contemporary Native Americans." Weatherford comments on the latter portion of this statement by quoting Sandra Osawa, a videomaker, "'The problem is not so much that we are stereotyped, though that is a problem. It is that we are invisible in the present.' I recall Osawa's words whenever I select titles or recommend works for others to use."[12]

The Southwestern United States, for instance, is fortunate to have both the ancient history and the contemporary lives and issues of Native Americans present and visible before us. Though ignorance and exploitation remain, many non-Natives of the Southwest recognize that diverse issues exist for the Southwest's Native Americans, including land and water rights, gaming, tourism, the arts, cultural preservation, economic development, poverty, health, and health issues. Videos can help educate all people more about these issues of today as well as the issues of the past.

4. *A variety of styles, treatments, and topics must be included to ensure the appeal and interest of the collection to the general public.* For a university, this is essential to ensure the interdisciplinary use of the collection(s) for a variety of classes, programs, organizations, and individual researchers. Both documentary and dramatic works should be included with representation of the range of styles or approaches that can be found. There is currently a sizeable body of videos and films on indigenous people. Estimates by programmers in *Videoforum* and the *MAP Guide* are for approximately 1,800 videos and films on Native Americans at the present time. Once again, Weatherford illustrates: "I judge each selection in terms of its beauty and clarity, its unique voice, its accuracy, and its accountability to the native community it portrays." In addition, she often finds herself reviewing and revising her initial opinions through gathering additional notes, including feedback from audiences.[13]

An additional issue for librarians, programmers, and instructors to consider is the issue of exclusion of information. What is private and sacred? What should not be shown to people outside a certain community? One aspect of native people's distrust of mass media is certainly the "tell-all" nature of what has often been produced about them in the past. The dominant Euro-American culture's sensibility, that very little necessarily has to be private or off-limits, clashes directly with Native American thinking and the desire for protection against outside exploitation.

Chicano Video and Film

Nesthus' criteria for Native American video and film collections are appropriate to the collecting of Chicano and Chicana video and film as well. They are repeated here, modified from her Native American essay.

1. *Varying aspects of Chicano culture must be accurately represented.* Like the broader grouping of "Latinos," Chicanos are not a monolithic group, and this diversity must be represented. Urban or rural, Chicano lives range far beyond the stereotypical gang member or the migrant farm worker images so often seen in mass media. La Raza includes many people: they are first-generation immigrants and descendants of those who have lived here for four centuries; they are wealthy, middle class, and poor; they speak Spanish or English or a combination of both. Chicanos are also geographically widespread—from San Antonio to San Francisco, Washington, D.C. to Washington State, rural and urban—all of which is responsible for further aspects of cultural diversity. As the body of Chicano film and video grows, it reflects this diversity.

2. *Consideration must be given to the degree of Chicano cooperation in each production.* Representation is a critical issue. Despite the apparent successes of a number of recent Chicano-produced Hollywood films (i.e., "La Bamba," "Stand and Deliver," "American Me," "Mi Familia"), Chicanos and the broader Latino grouping of filmmakers, writers, and actors still are grossly under-represented in both commercial cinema and television. Latinos represent 40 percent of the population of Los Angeles and 10 percent of the United States as a whole, yet "each year in this country Latinos direct only 1 percent of all film and television programs produced, write less than one-half of 1 percent of all screenplays produced and fill only 3 percent of all acting roles in television and film production."[14] Independent film and video production remains one of the main avenues for Chicano video and filmmakers to produce works.

3. *The full scope of Chicano history must be indicated and the necessity for reconsideration of that history demonstrated.* This broader view of history includes Native American, Spanish, and Mexican history and a contemporary Chicano history since the conquest of lands in the nineteenth century by the Republic of Texas and the United States. Chicanas too must be written back into Chicano history. Video and film have an important role then to play today. Chon Noriega, in his essay for the *MAP Guide*, "Concrete Experiences: Chicano Film and Video and American History" explains:

> These videos raise a central question: How can Chicanos (and other groups) depict history, when historians, journalists, and Hollywood films have either distorted, censored, or repressed the history of the Chicano experience? The answer, more often than not has been to challenge official histories, with their assumption of an objective past and singular point of view. Rather than match tit-for-tat, these works proffer specific stories of the Chicano experience that complicate the accepted versions of U.S. history.[15]

Several films connected with "El Movimiento" in particular have focused on new portrayals of Chicano history. These include "Yo Soy Chicano" (1972) and "Chicana" (1979). Others work on the level that Noriega suggests, offering stories of specific people and events, such as "Ballad of an Unsung Hero" (1983) about Pedro Gonzales, and "The Lemon Grove Incident" (1985) about the United States' first successful desegregation case. These stories are particularly important for rewriting history to gain Chicano perspectives and a more accurate picture of Chicanos and Chicanas oppression in and contributions of Chicanos and Chicanas in the United States.

4. *A variety of styles, treatments, and topics must be included to ensure the appeal and interest of the collection to the general public.* In the 1970s, 1980s, and 1990s, Chicanos have produced an ever-growing body of work on a vast number of issues. The 1980s and 1990s have brought a number of commercial films to mainstream America via Hollywood. Several other films, made by non-Chicano filmmakers, have helped to place Chicano and Chicana images in films, including "Milagro Beanfield War" (directed by Robert Redford) and "Mi Vida Loca" (directed by Allison Anders). At this stage though, Chicano film and video (particularly that in which Chicanos have had a predominant role in the creative direction) still is of a manageable size for library collecting purposes.

RECOMMENDATIONS FOR COLLECTION DEVELOPMENT OF VIDEO AND FILM

An academic library system can support Native American and Chicano topics in numerous ways. This brings up many issues for future development of these collections.

Collecting Issues

It is typical to have various video and film collections grow independently of each other on a campus. Libraries and library units, Native American and Chicano studies programs, film/media arts programs, and media centers all may build their own collections. When this happens, there is often little rhyme or reason as to who collects what and little communication between collections regarding selection. This is not ideal as there can be overlap and duplication of some works and large gaps in other areas. Because the development of a strong video and film collection can be expensive, it would be far more efficient and cost-effective to have these units communicate with one another and to plan strategies for collecting which take the other collections on campus into account.
Issues to address:

- What role should a library play in collecting Native American and Chicano video and film in addition to textual materials? What collecting policies should a media center have? What roles do the Native American and Chicano studies programs play?
- What funding exists, both on and off campus, and to whom is it currently going to? What additional, untapped sources exist?
- When is overlap of titles in different collections appropriate? What type of overlap should be avoided?
- Copyright restrictions and unauthorized duplication of film and video must also be addressed. What is considered fair use? Most copying is not only illegal but undermines the current and future markets for Native American and Chicano titles. Both the filmmakers and the distribution companies need support for these titles.
- How can a library create systematic collection development policies for Native American and Chicano video and film that

reflect the academic and research interests of the institution: as a university in a particular area of the country; as a university with Native American and Chicano populations; as a university with Native American and Chicano studies programs?
- Should a goal (through one or several collections acting in tandem) be to collect comprehensively in the major areas that affect Native Americans and Chicanos in the region? What level of collecting should be done regarding groups and issues beyond the region?
- How do you deal with the special issues of collecting film?—notably, the high price of 16mm film and the special equipment (projector) needed for viewing. Many important works are still only available on film. Though the initial cost of film may look prohibitive, a number of rentals could equal the overall cost of a film. Also, a well-cared for film should last many times longer than a video tape.
- Which units in the library have space for growing collections? A media center? Reserves? Fine arts? Special collections? The main library? The law library? Many units may not be willing to take on the role of a general media center if a library does not have one, and so collections must be spread out.

Access Issues

While a library's video and film collections may often be cataloged and available online, they may not be searchable by format. If this is so, then one is limited to specific title or director/producer searches, or a broad subject search which includes books. Non-library collections around a campus may not be available in any online form. They often rely on printed lists for the collections which have the disadvantage of becoming obsolete as soon as new titles are added. Also, professors and others who wish to use videos in classes or research must inquire in these various locations for their current holdings.

Recommendations for increasing access to video and film collections:

- Add the videorecording and film designations as a fixed field or material type to records on the local online catalog. This allows patrons to search specifically for videos and films and to allow compilation of subject lists for this media.

- Add outside (non-library) collections of video and film to the library's online catalog. This carries with it technical services staffing implications for the library and may be impractical except by tackling one small collection at a time.
- Create online databases or simple lists that would be available via the Internet. These could be updated periodically to avoid becoming out-of-date the way printed, distributed lists do. Also they would allow professors and researchers to check holdings from one site (their office or the library), using the Internet, as opposed to physically going to multiple sites around campus.
- Create a published guide (or separate guides) to Native American and Chicano studies video and film resources on campus. This would help promote video and film as teaching and research tools and would give potential users a knowledge of what separate collections exist around campus and their policies for use. A guide could conceivably include annotated entries, a bibliography, and distributor information.

CONCLUSION

Native American and Chicano videos and films are significant resources for interdisciplinary studies and deserve to be valued in the ways that textual and electronic resources currently are in the academic library. The increasing use of video and film can be traced to changes in instructional methodology, the evolving perceptions of history and diversity, as well as the video "revolution" that has swept the country. Substantial work remains, however, to change outmoded views toward video and to bring library and other collections up to the levels where they can support the many classes and programs that would utilize these resources.

With increased funding opportunities in recent years for collections like Native American and Chicano studies and the ongoing redistribution of acquisitions funds to nontraditional formats and resources, this looks to be the ideal time for moving a library's video and film collections in solid new directions.

NOTES AND REFERENCES

1. "Chicano" is the accepted term in academic as well as other circles representing persons of Mexican descent in the United States. The term Chicano is also used in this paper for brevity, to represent both Chicanas and Chicanos.
2. Stephen D. Brookfield, "Principles of Effective Practice," *Understanding and Facilitating Adult Learning*, (San Francisco: Jossey-Bass Publishers, 1986), p. 23.
3. Chet Meyers and Thomas B. Jones, "The Case for Active Learning," in *Promoting Active Learning: Strategies for the College Classroom* (San Francisco: Jossey-Bass Publishers, 1993), p. 7.
4. Ibid, pp. 6-7.
5. Brookfield, p. 23.
6. In a "paradox of technology" principle, the newer and more technologically-advanced a format is, the more difficult its preservation and the shorter its lifespan. Consider the technological advancement, yet increasing fragility, of this progression: stone tablets, cotton-rag paper, wood pulp paper, motion picture film, microfilm, audio tape reels, audio cassettes, video cassettes, and computer disks. The cotton and linen rag papers of earlier centuries will outlast our late-nineteenth and twentieth centuries' groundwood pulp/acidic papers. Similarly, film (specifically polyester-based film), remains an archival medium whereas its successor, video tape, has a far shorter lifespan and is not archival.
7. De-magnetization of video and audio tape is less of a general hazard than once thought. Research now shows that it takes a strong magnetic field very close to the tapes to erase them. Nevertheless, care should be taken not to store or place tapes near known magnetic fields, such as that emanating from the back of stereo speakers, computers, and similar electronic equipment.
8. Marie Nesthus, ed., *Videoforum: A Videography for Libraries. Native American Issue* 1 (Winter 1993) and *Latino Issue* 2 (Summer 1994).
9. Barbara Abrash and Catherine Egan, *Mediating History: The MAP Guide to Independent Video by and About African American, Asian American, Latino, and Native American People* (New York: New York University Press, 1992).
10. Marie Nesthus, "Overview," *Videoforum* 1: 3.
11. Elizabeth Weatherford, "A Programmer's Perspective," *Videoforum* 1: 6.
12. Ibid., p. 7.
13. Ibid., p. 7.
14. Jesus Salvador Trevino, "A Cinema of Resistance and Affirmation," *Videoforum* 2: 4.
15. Chon Noriega, "Concrete Experiences: Chicano Film and Video and American History," *Mediating History*, pp. 64-65.

PROMPTCAT:
AN EARLY ASSESSMENT

Claire-Lise Bénaud and Sever Bordeianu

ABSTRACT

As libraries continue to experience budget difficulties, the profession is recognizing that outsourcing has become "a standard business practice."[1] At the 1994 American Library Association Midwinter Meeting, one of the Association for Library Colections and Technical Services discussion groups concluded that "shrinking library budgets and advances in technological capabilities make this topic [outsourcing] one of continuing importance."[2] Library budget cutting strategies had generally concentrated in one of three areas: reducing the acquisitions budget for books and serials, implementing hiring freezes, and contracting out, or outsourcing internal library operations. This paper focuses on a specific aspect of contracting out cataloging, namely, PromptCat.

OCLC and its affiliate regional organizations have recently introduced PromptCat, a full level cataloging service designed for all types of libraries. If successful, it will radically change the way cataloging is performed in OCLC member libraries. This paper evaluates every aspect of PromptCat from its implementation stage by the library to its effects on the acquisitions, collection development, cataloging, and public service departments. It is based on the experience of the University of New Mexico General Library and that of other libraries that have chosen to employ the service at this early stage.

OUTSOURCING CATALOGING

Cataloging library materials is a time-consuming and expensive operation. It is also vital for the library because the cataloging record, whether online or in card form, is the only access patrons have to the library's materials. The lack of a good cataloging record, or the absence of one, is equivalent to the library's not owning the item. Thus, the money spent on obtaining the item has, in effect, been wasted. At the same time, cataloging is an invisible operation to patrons and administrators. It is done away from the limelight, quietly, and most other library staff consider it laborious. This aspect, which contrasts with the glamor of reference service, online and Internet searching, and the teaching of bibliographic instruction, when combined with the high cost associated with processing every book and serial, makes cataloging a quick target for budget cuts.

As the process of contracting out gains in scope, companies are beginning to offer full level cataloging for libraries. Library vendors often advertise services that promise quick and accurate cataloging of materials for a price that library cataloging departments cannot possibly match. In theory, this service should save libraries substantial amounts of money by making cataloging departments obsolete. Indeed, there has been at least one celebrated case in which a library's cataloging department was completely closed down and all the library's cataloging was outsourced.[3] However, most agree that "few of the tasks which can be outsourced threaten the job security of professional librarians."[4] Various vendors offer cataloging services for various kinds of libraries. The practice has not been as common in large academic libraries. But this picture is changing.

WHAT IS PROMPTCAT

Introduced in 1995, PromptCat is a joint effort between OCLC and book vendors. It provides non-serial MARC records from OCLC's Online Union Catalog (OLUC) "promptly" to the library. PromptCat delivers cataloging records for current imprints. PromptCat is not a cataloging service: it does not supply records on a project basis and thus cannot be used for cataloging a backlog or a discrete collection. The aim of this service is to minimize processing of new materials by the local library staff. OCLC asserts that PromptCat will save search charges and labor costs by supplying cataloging information that is labor-intensive for library staff to create and maintain.

A library can only implement PromptCat in conjunction with a participating vendor. There are at least four players involved when a library chooses to sign up for PromptCat: OCLC, a participating book vendor, the online catalog vendor, and the library itself. As of November 1995, three vendors were actively participating in PromptCat: Academic Book Center, Blackwell North America, and Yankee Book Peddler. Three other vendors—Ambassador Book Service, Baker & Taylor Books, and Brodart Books and Services—have contracted with OCLC to provide the service in the near future, and another two dozen vendors are either in negotiations or have expressed interest. Vendors are eager to provide this new service for their customers. Vendors we spoke to reported having received numerous inquiries from libraries.

SYSTEM DESCRIPTION

The first step in the process is for the library to fill out a PromptCat profile with the vendor. Based on this profile, the vendor supplies OCLC with an electronic file identifying the books they have shipped to the library that need PromptCat. This file, called the manifest, prompts OCLC to deliver matching bibliographic records to the library's online catalog and to update the library's holdings in OLUC. In addition to the list of materials, the manifest contains the user's name and other relevant information depending on the library's profile. Vendors can supply additional information to the MARC record such as table of contents, approval plan, and invoicing data. OCLC offers several options for PromptCat cataloging such as record selection, record editing, setting holdings, electronic cataloging reports, and distribution of OCLC-MARC records. All these options are explained in the following text.

Records

PromptCat delivers OCLC records in any format with bibliographic level "m" for books, media, archives and manuscripts, maps, scores, sound recordings, and computer files. The records delivered via PromptCat are regular OLUC records. The library selects what kind of PromptCat records it desires through the choices available on the "PromptCat Order and Options" form. The choices can be made according to record type, encoding level, and record source. The encoding level options are All, Full (levels blank, 1, I, L), CIP (level 8), Not Full (levels 7, 5, 2, K, M), and Other (levels E and J). The cataloging source options include all records found, Library of Congress records, National Library of Medicine records, UKM records, or other member-input records. For example, a library may decide to receive only Library of Congress records. An optional MARC record, called PromptCat Data Record, is created by OCLC when there is no matching record or if the library is not profiled to receive a matching record. PromptCat Data Records are brief and only contain title, ISBN, and vendor-supplied data. A library has the option to refuse data records in its profile.

Record Editing

PromptCat supports limited automatic editing, primarily in the call number fields. The library may choose to move the call number to the local free-text 099 call number field, move the Dewey 082 call number field to a locally assigned Dewey 092 call number, add a User-Option Data 910 field, and delete 5XX, 6XX, 7XX, and 8XX fields from cards. It is also possible to have OCLC add a workmark to the call number—a letter placed after the cutter number—to help insure the uniqueness of the call number in the local database. No other customized editing is provided.

Item and Location Information

PromptCat records can provide item information. OCLC can transfer information from the vendor to the library by inserting the data into the bibliographic record. At the time of profiling, the library can assign the MARC field in which OCLC puts the data. This information pertains to the item being delivered by the vendor. The library needs to contact its vendor to find out what item information it can supply. Item location and barcodes are two common examples. A library may have several accounts with a single vendor and each account can receive customized processing. These accounts may correspond to a particular holding library (a branch library for example). In that case, the distinctive OCLC four-character holding code will be inserted in the 049 field reflecting the library's specific location. Libraries can also choose a default holding code—the OCLC three-character symbol—when it is not feasible to have the vendor pre-assign the four-character holding code. In all cases, some database maintenance is still needed for PromptCat records. Volume and copy numbers, local notes, changes in location (i.e., reference), and other specific information that needs to appear in item fields must be created in-house.

Setting Holdings

PromptCat offers two options for updating holdings in OLUC. Holdings can be updated immediately or after a 21-day delay. In either case, the records are archived on the day that the manifest is processed, after any automatic editing is applied. When holdings are set 21 days later, records are archived and delivered to the library immediately, and they are not archived again. In choosing one of the two holding update options, the library needs to consider the pros and cons of each option. Immediate updates would incorrectly indicate that the book is available for lending, when in fact it is still being processed. This creates problems for Interlibrary Loan. The 21-day delay option provides ample time for the book to be processed and cataloged. On the other hand, this latter option has some drawbacks. For example, a library may incur double charges for setting holdings if it goes in and sets holdings prematurely. In the case when books are returned to the vendor, the library has to wait for the 21-day period before being able to delete its holdings. This requires the additional step of keeping track of when items were received and returned. The library will have to weigh these advantages and disadvantages and make its decision according to its needs.

Housekeeping

PromptCat provides cataloging reports for each day of activity. The cataloging report contains a list of titles sent to the library for which there were matching records ("Records Matched, Products Delivered," "Records Matched, No Records Delivered"), titles sent for which there were no OCLC records found ("No OCLC Record Found"), and a list of titles with "Duplicate Vendor Control Numbers" indicating multiple copies of a title. These cataloging reports provide a wealth of information that facilitate the sorting and routing of materials in the general cataloging workflow. For each title listed, it indicates OCLC number, classification number, cataloging source, encoding level, material type, and the availability of series. In addition, the same information is provided in summary form. These vital reports give the library a continuous and complete picture of activities and enhance the library's control over the entire process. The cataloging reports are accessible electronically via Electronic Data Exchange (EDX) or through the OCLC Product Services Menu. The Product Services Menu is accessible via all OCLC telecommunications methods. Users need to log on to the Product Services Menu to perform the transfer of the cataloging report file.

Distribution of PromptCat MARC Records

The cataloging records are delivered through any of the regularly available OCLC methods: cards, tapeloads, EDX, through a PRISM PromptCat save file, or a combination of the above. Cards match the OCLC master records with the addition of PromptCat automatic editing. OCLC tapes of the library's records can be delivered weekly for local tapeloading. Depending on the local online catalog, records may be loaded through EDX to a processing file for editing or loaded directly to the online catalog. However, a library's option may be limited by the local online catalog since not all online catalogs support OCLC's EDX capabilities.

Physical Processing of Books

Vendors can ship books in shelf-ready condition. Several processing options are available: binding of paperbacks, jacketing, ownership stamping, barcoding, and security stripping. For example, Yankee charges a minimum of $1 for processing. This base price covers several services. Depending on the extent of the processing as well as special treatment, the price will increase accordingly. The type of binding will greatly affect the overall processing fee (Yankee charges between $4-$9 for binding each volume). Depending on the library's requirements, the vendor may not be able to do all the processing. For example, a vendor may only have one type of scanner. It is usually able to add barcodes but may not be able to add OCR numbers. When a library chooses to have its books shelf-ready, it is essential for the library to have a flawless profile. Processed books are non-returnable unless the book is defective.

Cost

The cost of PromptCat consists of a one-time $220 profiling fee, a $1.93 charge for every record processed, and a delivery cost. The cost of delivery varies depending on the option chosen. A library choosing the PRISM PromptCat file is charged the standard export fee of $0.105 per record; EDX costs consist of a $198 annual fee plus a $22 monthly processing charge; magnetic tapes are $33 per tape at 6250 bpi, and $17 per tape at 1600 bpi, delivered weekly. If a library produces cards, OCLC charges the standard fee of 15 cents per card. Notwithstanding the setup fee, the minimum charge is slightly over $2 per record. EDX becomes cheaper as the volume of records received goes up. It is also the most convenient method because it requires the least amount of manipulation. The tapeload delivery method is equally convenient but is considerably more expensive. While EDX and tapeloads are fixed costs, the cost of exporting from the PRISM PromptCat save file—with its per record charge—increases with the number of records exported. Exporting from a save file is also more labor intensive and provides less benefits to the library.

Rick J. Block correctly points out that "outsourcing is not a panacea for the high cost of cataloging."[5] Unfortunately, cost comparisons between in-house cataloging and PromptCat are difficult to establish. Because of the complexity of cataloging, and because PromptCat cuts across many departments as described below, it is difficult to ascertain whether PromptCat delivers true cost savings. For example, Block asserts that "the sum of the salaries of the cataloging staff divided by the number of titles cataloged is not the real cost of cataloging in house."[6] Similarly, when estimating costs for PromptCat, some cataloging tasks are not included (i.e., authority control, item record creation, and database maintenance). An in-depth study of all these costs would provide a better picture for comparison. In addition, the library needs to decide out of which fund to pay for PromptCat (automation, collection development, contingency funds, etc.). It is important to recognize that like other automation functions, PromptCat may not save the library money but will increase the efficiency of library operations. At least initially PromptCat will be an added cost to the library.

IMPACT ON LIBRARY OPERATIONS

Collection Development

While PromptCat is a cataloging service, it is directly influenced by collection development procedures and practices. Therefore, the decision on whether to adopt PromptCat needs to be made jointly between collection development and cataloging: collection development has to determine what vendor to use; cataloging has to decide what records to accept. All subsequent decisions depend on these two initial choices.

Once the library has chosen a participating vendor, there are several collection development issues that have to be addressed. Libraries usually order books in three different ways: on approval, from order slips, and on firm order. It is important for collection development to keep control of what books are bought regardless of the method of ordering. Based on these three methods of acquisition, collection development needs to decide which books should receive PromptCat treatment. The primary concern for collection development is to ensure that no books that should be returned are purchased and cataloged by the library.

Firm orders are the best candidates. Approvals present special difficulties because of the return rate. When the return rate is too high, the vendor and the library need to rework their profile in order to get the return as low as possible. During the research conducted for this paper, we found out that some libraries have decided to accept all books provided on approval and not worry about the few books that might have to be returned. Again, this is an internal library decision, and collection development has to be consulted.

Cataloging

It is evident by now that routines in cataloging will be the most affected by PromptCat. Several policy decisions need to be made by cataloging departments. First, since few departments will use PromptCat for all their records, there will be a need for two workflows. PromptCat records will receive different, and ideally faster, treatment than non-PromptCat records. Second, the department has to determine what type of records to accept.

As mentioned earlier, PromptCat provides a wide choice of OLUC records, ranging from full level to brief records. Libraries can accept any OLUC records, including incomplete records, or restrict themselves to receiving only full level LC records. It is up to each library to decide what category of records to accept. Libraries can also accept different categories of records depending on the vendors' profiles. Regardless of the type of records received, the benefits will occur when libraries accept the classification and call numbers present in the PromptCat record and forego editing. The best case scenario envisions no manipulation of the bibliographic record by catalogers. Catalogers will need to trust member cataloging copy more so than ever. This underlies the importance of high standards in the OCLC database. Projects such as NACO, SACO, BIBCO, and CONSER are essential in this kind of shared environment in order to truly eliminate duplication of effort. As cooperative cataloging projects become more established and as outsourcing services expand, the quality control issue at the national level is becoming more critical.

With the exception of full LC records, some editing of the bibliographic record will still be necessary. This is especially true for CIP records. It is apparent that a large percentage of PromptCat records are CIPs. Some participating libraries put the number at 52 percent.[7] Our vendor, Yankee, expects 45 percent to be CIPs. BNA reports that 60 percent to 70 percent of newly published monographs are CIPs,[8] and other vendors report the number at 60 percent.[9] Libraries need to decide how to check these CIP records and fill in the missing information. At least one library that we contacted accepts the CIPs and retains them in the online catalog until they are upgraded automatically through an OCLC pilot service. Another library receives the updates from its vendor, Academic Book Center. BNA also offers automatic upgrades. Given the high percentage of CIPs, it is logical to expect that more vendors will provide automatic upgrades. This function would increase the functionality of PromptCat dramatically. Aside from CIPs, there will always be peculiarities that will necessitate cataloger intervention. The most obvious cases are local treatment of series and changes in classification based on local needs.

All these factors entail relinquishing a considerable amount of local control over data quality. For most catalogers, this idea goes against the grain because a significant part of their activity consists in editing copy. However, the whole point of PromptCat, like all other cooperative cataloging ventures, is to limit the amount of tweaking done on quality records and to free catalogers for more complex and critical cataloging.

Authority Control

When to perform authority control is a major consideration for a catalog department because of the pivotal role authority control plays in modern online catalogs. It is estimated that as much as 30 percent of all the work performed in cataloging is related to authority control.[10] PromptCat requires post-cataloging authority control. In some systems, post-cataloging authority control is cumbersome and therefore makes PromptCat a less desirable option. When authority control is routinely performed at the time of cataloging, cataloging will need two separate workflows. PromptCat may compel catalog departments to reconsider their entire authority control workflow.

Acquisitions

Besides cataloging, the most directly affected department is acquisitions. In an integrated online environment, it is indispensable to have order information from the very beginning of the ordering process. Acquisitions departments depend on the electronic records generated automatically by the system from the vendors' files. These electronic order records, used for invoicing, are typically linked to temporary or brief bibliographic records. Depending on the capabilities of local systems, PromptCat records may replace the vendor-supplied temporary records. This is the best case scenario. In certain systems however, this will not be feasible. In this case, both a PromptCat record and a temporary bibliographic record will coexist in the system unlinked. These duplicate records will need to be merged, creating confusion and extra work for acquisitions and cataloging staff. Precise workflow procedures need to be devised in order to overcome this problem. It is crucial to keep in mind the needs of the acquisitions department. Otherwise the possible savings achieved in cataloging would be offset—or even negated— by the extra work in acquisitions.

Interlibrary Loan

Concerns were expressed by ILL librarians at the American Library Association 1995 summer conference that the immediate setting of holdings would incorrectly indicate availability and ownership of books. This will slow down and increase the workload in ILL. On one hand, this problem can be overcome by having OCLC update the holdings after a 21-day delay. On the other hand, this would really complicate an already complex workflow in cataloging. Neither solution is fully satisfactory to all parties. The solution to this problem requires more thought, and it will certainly evolve as PromptCat becomes more widely established.

Systems

The systems department involvement depends on the method of record transmission chosen by the library. This department will only be involved in cases when the records are EDXed or tapeloaded. The time commitment is minimal in either case. If a library chooses to receive records via the PromptCat save file, the process bypasses systems altogether.

Public Services

Block states that "good cataloging is fundamental to good reference service since standardization and authority control enable users to find what they need in a timely fashion."[11] Public service librarians should not accept a decrease in the level of access and information provided in the system. Regardless of the way a book is cataloged, it is imperative for the patron that the system indicate the current status of each book: ordered, received, in process, and cataloged. As far as reference is concerned, great care should be taken not to decrease the amount of information currently available in public catalogs.

WHY UNM CONSIDERED PROMPTCAT

At the University of New Mexico, the major impetus for implementing PromptCat is to enable experienced catalogers to concentrate on original and complex cataloging, rare book cataloging, and retrospective conversion. Due to the pattern of the library's book buying, there is a sizable backlog of books that require copy cataloging, especially for current imprints. It was felt that PromptCat could provide the best productivity and results in this area, thus allowing the catalogers to work on the more complex problems. In addition, PromptCat is perceived as a trend for the future of cataloging. The library administration fully encouraged this endeavor. Outsourcing is seen by many administrators as a viable way to save money. Given those circumstances, we found it advisable to try PromptCat at this time.

We started to do our homework. Our overall sense was to start with the straightforward materials in order to get a clear idea of what will work and what will not. We decided to go one step at a time and to fix glitches and expand gradually, rather than to do it all at once. Consequently, we decided to work with a single vendor, Yankee Book Peddler. Our Yankee profile consists exclusively of university presses. We had to decide what Yankee accounts we wanted to catalog through PromptCat. We looked at our rate of returns for approvals and found that for a six-month period, we returned 54 books, or 6 percent. However, a plan with a high return rate would not work well.

After discussions with collection development, we decided to have the approval and firm order accounts go through PromptCat. It is important to note that PromptCat allows a library to put as many or as few accounts on PromptCat as the library finds necessary. This flexibility carries on to future changes in the profile and does not entail additional costs. In our case, the return rate was quite low and the refinements were minimal. Still, we decided not to have our books marked by Yankee because we wanted to be able to keep returning our books (most of them duplicate copies).

Second, we looked at the workflow of the Acquisitions Department. Acquisitions receives brief bibliographic records from Yankee which automatically generate order records. In our local catalog, order records need to be attached to bibliographic records. At this point we ran into our first complication. We found out that PromptCat records could not automatically generate order records, and acquisitions was not willing to give up these brief records because they are essential to the electronic payment of invoices. We agreed that receiving these brief records had to continue.

Initially, we wanted to have our PromptCat records delivered through EDX. We filled out and sent a deceptively simple PromptCat Order and Options form to AMIGOS, our local OCLC network, and were ready to go. After a round of phone calls with Yankee, OCLC, AMIGOS, and Innovative Interfaces Incorporated, which proved to be very time consuming, we found out that more technical problems were looming on the horizon. OCLC informed us that the MARC fixed fields would not load correctly. We decided nonetheless to load a sample of PromptCat records through EDX and confirmed that indeed this was the case. While testing, we also found out that the PromptCat records contained imbedded extraneous characters which interfered with loading. The fact that order records could not be generated and that using EDX for record transmission was not possible at this time were the two determining factors in preventing us from going ahead with our original plan.

We had to rethink our initial strategy. In order to accommodate acquisitions, we would continue to accept brief bibliographic records from Yankee. Because of our system requirements, we had to use the PRISM PromptCat save file as a method of transmission instead of EDX. Catalogers would then have to manually download one PromptCat record at a time and overlay the brief Yankee bibliographic record. This manual merge is required in our local system since it can only overlay on the OCLC number, which is not present in the approval plan brief records. This is true for other libraries using the Innovative catalog.[12] This second scenario is not as attractive because it requires more intervention, but considering the limitations of our local system, we had no other choice. Despite these difficulties, we decided to go ahead with the project because it appears that future software developments by Innovative Interfaces will support EDX transmissions. We think that the full benefits of PromptCat will be realized at that point. But we felt that OCLC underestimated the difficulties we were to encounter.

From the department head's perspective, PromptCat will deter experienced catalogers from working on improving already complete LC bibliographic records. This might solve one of the department's major dilemmas. Catalogers should not be put in the position to wear two hats: a production hat, which encourages high levels of production, and a "purist" hat, which each cataloger more or less wears at all times. The function of deciding quality control should be performed by the department leadership and should not be a burden for each individual cataloger. As Barry Fast points out, "often some of the same people are asked to perform production-oriented work for part of their day (cataloging) and then switch to another position where productivity is far less important (reference services ... or book selection)."[13] For cataloging, non-production activities include authority work, contributions to national projects such as Enhance, and NACO, and recataloging to improve accessibility.[14]

While national contribution is useful to our department, improving quality cataloging is non-productive and useless. On the other hand, when doing copy cataloging, it is unreasonable to request that catalogers not correct mistakes they encounter. We hope that PromptCat will bypass this unnecessary quality control and the records will be added to the system with minimal revision. While this pragmatic view may offend some catalogers, managers have to deal with the much more unacceptable reality of backlogs.

CONCLUSION

Communication is of paramount importance in the implementation of PromptCat. This communication operates on several levels. It is both internal and external. Internally, all technical services units, collection development, interlibrary loan, and reference need to be included in the decision-making process. Even though the literature cautions that "critical outsourcing issues include interfaces between acquisitions and catalog departments,"[15] one of the major problems with PromptCat is that OCLC did not foresee the needs of departments outside of cataloging. It is probable that OCLC did not think about integration of workflow because it remains mostly a cataloging service.

External communication is equally significant. This entire experience proved to be a complex process of communication between the library, the book vendor, OCLC, the regional OCLC network affiliate, and the online catalog vendor. Outsourcing can only be viable as long as there is sound agreement between the vendors and the library defining the extent of the services to be expected and provided from this partnership.[16]

PromptCat is not an off-the-shelf service. In each situation, many variables are at play: different vendors, different OPACs, and different internal workflows. Implementing PromptCat is a lengthy process. As one of the first libraries to sign on to PromptCat, we experienced some of the inevitable frustrations associated with working out the bugs in a new system. This was a learning experience for all the parties involved, and it will provide a much smoother experience for future libraries that sign up for the service. PromptCat is definitely evolving. OCLC has proven again and again that through persistence and vision it is able to devise, and then implement and nurture innovative projects to maturity. FirstSearch is one such example. In this comparison, it is reasonable to expect that PromptCat will be an endeavor that will successfully fulfill expectations. This optimism is shared by at least one other writer, Brian Alley.[17]

PromptCat does not offer a miracle solution. It offers intangible gains—books get faster to the shelves--rather than salary savings. It definitely anticipates the future. PromptCat takes resources, technology, and data that are already in place and connects them in such a way as to create an innovative product. PromptCat proves again that OCLC is a foreword looking organization.

NOTES AND REFERENCES

1. Arnold Hirshon, Barbara A. Winters, and Karen Wilhoit, "A Response to 'Outsourcing Cataloging: The Wright State Experience,'" *ALCTS Newsletter* 6 (1995): 27.

2. Nancy J. Gibbs, "ALCTS/Role of the Professional in Academic Research Technical Services Departments Discussion Group," *ALA Midwinter 1994- Conference Reports*, p. 322.

3. David P. Miller, "Outsourcing Cataloging: The Wright Experience," *ALCTS Newsletter* 6 (1995): 7-8.

4. Janifer Meldrum, "Outsourcing Issues Stir Conference Attendees," *Marcive Newsletter* 23 (September 1995): 1.

5. Rick J. Block, "Cataloging Outsourcing: Issues and Options," *Serials Review* (Fall 1994): 73.

6. Ibid, p. 75.

7. Ibid, p. 76.

8. Blackwell North America, "Development Directions: Shelf and Catalog-Ready Processing Services," *Promotional Flier* (August 1995).

9. Barry Fast, "Outsourcing and PromptCat," *Against the Grain* 7 (2,1995): 50.

10. *OCLS's Automated Authority Control Strategy*, OCLC (July 1995): 1.

11. Block, p. 75.

12. Karen Wilhoit, "Outsourcing Cataloging at Wright State University," *Serials Review* (Fall 1994): 71.

13. Fast, p. 50.

14. William Miller, "Outsourcing: Academic Libraries Pioneer Contracting Out Services," *Library Issues* 16 (2,1995): 3.

15. Gibbs, p. 322.

16. Ibid, p. 321.

17. Brian Alley, "Reengineering, Outsourcing, Downsizing, and Perfect Timing," *Technicalities* 13 (11,1993): 8.

EVALUATING APPROVAL PLAN PROCESSING:
IS PROMPTCAT AN OPTION?

Barbara Albee and Robin Rohrkaste Crumrin

ABSTRACT

Selection of an approval plan requires more than careful evaluation and analysis of a vendor's program. This article explores the impact of an expanded approval plan on the Acquisitions and Cataloging departments at Indiana University-Purdue University Indianapolis University Library as well as looking at the cooperation involved at all levels in implementing such a plan. Comparative information on approval plan vendors and statistics from a sample study used to determine the future utilization of PromptCat at University Library are provided.

INTRODUCTION

On April 8, 1994, University Library held the grand opening of its new, multimillion dollar facility. This impressive five-story structure, considered the crown jewel of the campus of Indiana University-Purdue University Indianapolis (IUPUI), was equipped with state-of-the-art technology and designed to house a collection of approximately 1 million volumes. The print collection at the time of the opening was 432,954 volumes, including both monographs and serials. The new building allowed for collection expansion that previously had been hindered by the much smaller size of the old library. In fact, significant additional monies had already been slated for ongoing support of the development and enrichment of the library collection before the completion of the move to the new facility.

Soon after the grand opening, University Library investigated expanding its approval plan coverage. Our overall objectives were to ensure that materials were processed in a timely manner without an increase in the number of staff. Statistics evaluating type of cataloging record found, the amount of editing required, and the average processing time of approval plan books were gathered with the idea in mind of possibly using services like OCLC's PromptCat in the future. This paper examines the reasons behind IUPUI's decision to implement an expanded approval plan. Discussions of vendor evaluation and selection along with comparative information on approval plan vendors plus approval plan profiling are included. Impact of approval plan implementation on Acquisitions and Cataloging departments and resulting cooperative efforts between the two are explored.

PHASE I: EVALUATION AND SELECTION OF APPROVAL PLAN

In an era of widespread budget cuts elsewhere, University Library was in the fortunate position of realizing an increase in monies allocated for the library materials budget. The impact of an increased budget and implications of current staffing were major factors considered in vendor evaluation and the ultimate selection of an approval plan vendor. The decision to take advantage of an approval plan was not made in a vacuum. Cooperative efforts existed from the beginning. The decision-making process included library administration, subject liaison librarians, technical services staff, and teaching faculty.

As stated above, one major factor in the decision to implement an expanded approval plan was the increase in the library materials budget. The fiscal year budget saw a 22 percent increase from 1992-1993 to 1993-1994. With strong support from administration in its dedication to support the new library, the materials budget was growing, and there were clear indications that the library materials budget would continue to grow. An increase of 15 percent was ultimately realized for 1994-1995. Funds were distributed among 28 disciplines including the professional schools and the more standard liberal arts departments which concentrate on undergraduate programs. This resulted in a reevaluation of collection development guidelines among several disciplines. The increases led to discussion of what an approval plan could do for University Library. An amount of $200,000 was projected for use in an approval plan. Contributions came from the library funds for each of the participating 28 undergraduate programs and professional schools involved.

The library was not entirely new to the concept of an approval plan. A very limited plan based primarily on notification slips was already in place as well as book plans for selected minor areas. Benefits of committing to an expanded approval program would help achieve more effective collection management. For example, recently published scholarly works would be acquired for the collection automatically. Selectors and processing staff would be able to use their time more effectively. The library could also benefit by more efficiently spending the materials budget while taking advantage of higher discounts and customized vendor services.

Another factor playing an important role in the decision to expand the approval plan was the staffing budget. In contrast to the materials budget, the staffing budget was slow to increase. Although not anticipating potential downsizing of staff like other academic institutions, University Library did not expect to increase its staff. Hiring additional full-time staff to handle an increase in orders was not an option. This presented a significant problem since allocations are set at the beginning of the fiscal year and must be encumbered or spent by specific deadlines throughout the year. Monies not encumbered may be lost. With an expanded approval plan in place, the burden of processing an increased number of orders could be diminished. Based on the above analysis, a favorable consensus among librarians and the library administration was reached to proceed with the review and selection of an approval plan vendor.

	A	B	C	D
Publishers Used				
University Presses	North American	US and CA	US and CA	US,CA,UK
Trade	Yes-and other scholarly	Yes	Yes	
Other	Professional Presses Foreign pubs. dist. in US	Blackwell-UK Foreign pubs. dist. in US	Foreign pubs. dist. in US	Foreign pubs. dist. in US Non-Univ. P pubs who join AAUP
Profiling				
Publisher based	Yes	Yes	Yes (& Univ.Press based)	Yes
Subject based	Yes-LC framework	Yes	Yes	Yes-LC framework
Thesaurus		LC or BNA Thesaurus	B&T Thesaurus	
Electronic tape loads				
Cost of tapes		Some cost for tape .25 per record	Tape free	
Electronic Invoice	Yes--tape inc. with shipments		Marc tape has list price only, not invoicing price.	Yes-Info in 900 field of marc rec.
Electronic Ordering	Yes-no interface w/NOTIS	Yes-no interface w/NOTIS	Yes-no interface w/NOTIS	Yes-no interface w/NOTIS
Database of titles	Folio (120,000 titles dbase) View only or View/order Free via Internet Full marc tape or disc LC Records from marcive	NTO marc w/Books: $500 (fee waived if 2500+books) optional TOC $1300 Via internet	BTLink on CDRom title file, (monthly updates) $900 Marc-like records	
CIP		Included-upgrade if request	Yes-no choice on marc tapes; Available: CIP, LC, B&T original	
Reports available				
Title lists	Yes	Yes	Yes	Yes
Management reports	Yes	Yes-customized	Yes-customer reports	Yes

Labels (Spine, pocket, barcodes, tattletapes costs)	Yes-provide and/or process	Spine: .14; no processing Pocket: .11; no processing Barcode: .11 .17 if attached	Spine: .05; no processing Pocket: .15; no processing Barcode: .05; np (we can't use) Tattle: .20 inst; can't return item Custom design label: .05	Yes: processes books; provides label sets (3 labels)
Turnaround Time	5-7 days; orders placed 4 wks in advance w/publisher Pbk w/in 8 wks or hbk sent	Bks received as published; ordered 3 mos in advance	3-4 weeks after book published; ordered 2-3 months in advance	4-5 weeks for O/S titles
Return policy	120 day return deadline	30 days (60 acceptable)	Up to 6 months	45-90 days; will return MW buchram bound pbk returns
Postage		UL covers postage	Allowed except for firm orders; UL covers postage	UL covers postage
% Returns allowed	7% avg.	10%	10% or below	10-11%
Book reviews	NY Times	Info from dust jacket scanned into Dbase	NY Times & Chronicle	no
Binding services	?	?	Contract binding in new books	Yes- 4 types
Discounts	125-199,999 14% 200,000+ 15%	For BNA only; Not BH/Black-Oxford 100-250,000: 15.5% If prepay all, add 3% If prepay half, add 2%	75-100,000: 14% 100-150,000: 15% 150-200,000: 16% Prepay 50,000 add .5% (add .5% per every 50,000 prepay)	$20,000 min. starts at 13% (books) 10% slips Prepay discounts higher per vol.
Duplicates	?	Automatic check against standing orders Manual check against firm orders	Check against standing orders; Do not check against firm orders	?
Internet Access	Yes	Yes	No	?

Figure 1. Approval Plan Summary

Note: Facts and figures as of June, 1996.

Four major vendors (Yankee, Blackwell NA, Baker & Taylor, Midwest) offering approval plan services were invited to give presentations regarding their programs. General guidelines were established to evaluate vendors and programs. Primary considerations and secondary considerations were determined. Primary considerations included publisher coverage, discounts, the availability of electronic tapeloads, the operations of a notification or slip program, and profiling options (including types of subject descriptors). Secondary considerations covered management reports, return policies, and turnaround time. Further criteria developed as vendors were reviewed. Ability to supply book spine labels, binding format, electronic invoicing, Internet access, and electronic reference tools were added to our previous considerations.

Technical Services solicited input from subject liaisons, library administration, faculty, and library staff in evaluating these criteria. Recommendations from these groups played an important role in the evaluation and final selection of a vendor. Data was compiled in a spreadsheet to facilitate vendor comparison. Vendors are referred to as Vendor A, B, C, and D. Based on University Library's needs, Vendor C had the most to offer (see Figure 1).

A proven track record with Vendor C had already been established through our firm order business and a small approval program. A key factor in selecting Vendor C was the high discount rate for the prepaid deposit account level we could invest at that time. Vendor C offered the highest discount rate for prepaid accounts of $150,000 to $200,000.

The next crucial step was profiling. Extensive profiling sessions were conducted between the vendor representative and the subject liaisons. Some sessions included faculty participation. Profiling proved to be a labor-intensive and time-consuming process. Subject areas were defined in terms of the curriculum offered at our campus. Preliminary sessions were held to determine a dollar amount from each subject area to start the approval program. Later, the vendor representative met individually with liaisons to define highly specialized subject areas. Additional profiling sessions became necessary when it was later discovered that some subject areas had been too narrowly defined, or too broad, which caused the final estimated dollar amount to be either too small or too large. Fine tuning the profile proved to be a key element in arriving at a suitable approval plan for University Library.

We found that vendors are flexible in setting up approval plans to meet a library's budget. University Library had a predetermined dollar amount for the approval program based on the increase in the budget and the desire not to reduce the previous discretionary funding. The profile was refined until it matched the money set aside to start the approval program. Vendor C arrived at an initial figure using projections based on their 1993 approval plan figures. Dollar amounts were increased by 4 percent for inflation of book prices in 1994-1995.

Significant savings through approval plan discounts have been disputed in the literature. Barker questioned the value of the approval plan in terms of discounts and staff savings. He asked the question, "should we continue to have approval plans?" University of California-Berkeley at the time of his study had 42 approval plans and blanket orders based on subject profiles and was working in a budgetarily constrained environment putting $500,000 into all approval plans combined. Barker reported only a 1.8 percent to 2.1 percent gained increase in savings over firm orders.[1]

University Library has averaged a 10 percent to 12 percent discount on firm orders. In contrast to Barker's study a 6 percent to 8 percent gained increase would be realized with the implementation of Vendor C's approval plan. We felt this was a significant increase in savings. The discount was even higher when considering scholarly publications alone for which we averaged a 5 percent discount on firm orders. Our overall approval plan profile with Vendor C leaned heavily toward scholarly publications through use of its modification patterns. The profiling sessions and selection of precise modification patterns assured acquisition of publications that met the academic and teaching goals of the university. The plan was scheduled to begin in August 1994 with the initial profile in place.

PHASE II: IMPLEMENTATION OF THE PLAN

It was recognized early on that a special working relationship would need to be established between Acquisitions and Cataloging in order to make the plan work to its best advantage. Acquisitions and Cataloging met to work out a viable plan for processing approval plan books that would get these titles in the hands of our users as quickly as possible. To assist in this effort, a cataloging librarian with a background in acquisitions agreed to act as a liaison between the two departments. Turnaround time, duplication of work, and streamlining of procedures were addressed in these discussions.

Vendor C notified us that the profile could potentially generate shipments of up to 200 books per week. We had considered the impact of the budget increase on the monographic ordering side. Now, we had to address the impact on receiving. This had serious consequences for the receiving staff. University Library uses the NOTIS acquisitions module, which is extremely labor intensive. NOTIS also does not make it easy to track depository accounts. The approval plan was prepaid to ensure the highest discount rate, which in effect was a depository account. Previously, it was the responsibility of the receiving area to select a bibliographic record for entry into the automated system and create a payment statement for every approval book received. The receiving area was staffed by 1.5 FTE plus additional part-time help. In our estimation, these tasks were extremely time consuming and defeated our goal of moving all books through the Technical Services area in a timely manner. We had no plans to increase staff in receiving, nor would we want to. Our goal was to either streamline procedures or shift tasks to reduce the impact of an increased volume of shipments in the receiving area.

A joint decision between Acquisitions and Cataloging was reached. Receiving would no longer select a record and input payment information into the online system. Instead, approval plan books would be routed to Cataloging after a one-week period slotted for review by subject liaisons. At a future date, management reports and a refined profile will eliminate the need for a review period and books will be released directly to Cataloging. In our new workflow, Cataloging would select the appropriate bibliographic record and process approval books as a top priority. We hoped to eliminate potential duplication with firm orders by getting records in as soon as possible and continuing to move the approval plan books through Technical Services in a timely manner. A code using Vendor C's invoice date and number was devised and typed into the NOTIS copy holdings record by cataloging staff. This provided a link to the invoice if books needed to be returned and eliminated the need for a payment statement.

Initially, tapeloaded records were a primary consideration in our review of vendors. After further investigating tapeloaded records, we found them not to be a viable option. We concurred with Grahame that they caused problems on the cataloging end, even though they might be advantageous to processing in Acquisitions. Like the system used at the University of South Florida, University Library would have to overlay records supplied by the vendor with OCLC records and record our holdings in the OCLC system.[2] Vendor C was not then a participant in the PromptCat program and could not put our holdings in the OCLC database at that time. That step would still have to be done by cataloging staff, so little advantage in time or money savings would be gained by tapeloading records supplied by the vendor. Additionally, Vendor C only supplied records on reel-to-reel tape which was not compatible for loading into our system. This particular type of record transfer would have to be done at another campus site and could not always be guaranteed to be done as soon as required.

A review of the literature has shown that other libraries have found it necessary to combine acquisitions and cataloging functions. Some libraries have even created approval plan units, such as the University of South Florida and at University Libraries, State University of New York at Buffalo.[3] Like the University of South Florida, University Library adopted inhouse procedures to accommodate our automated environment.[4] We are not at a staffing level where we can break off a separate unit for the approval plan but rely on the cooperative efforts of both cataloging and acquisitions staff to reduce redundancies and increase turnaround time.

The impact of the increased number of books flowing into the Cataloging Department was also an area of concern. However, it was felt that with streamlined procedures the load could be handled by the existing five full-time copy catalogers. The approval plan profile primarily covered university presses and major commercial publishers. Procedures were established on the assumption that a high percentage of these records would be either full level LC or LC-CIP records in OCLC. These types of records require little editing by the copy catalogers and turnaround time was expected to be minimal. Typing in the abbreviated, inhouse invoice code on the copy holdings record would only add a few extra keystrokes to their routine. Typing in the code has worked well for both Acquisitions and Cataloging. The overall change in procedures was endorsed by the Acquisitions and Cataloging Departments and went into effect with the first shipment of books in August 1994.

PHASE III: APPROVAL PLAN FOLLOW-UP STUDY

An inhouse sample study was conducted for four weeks in January and again for four weeks in March 1995 to determine if some of our original goals were met. We wanted to evaluate our findings to determine the efficiency of our workflow in light of the arrival of OCLC's PromptCat service. Statistics were gathered for approval books received during each four-week sample. Book shipment levels never did reach the level of 200 per week as predicted by Vendor C. This may have been due to internal changes in Vendor C's ordering processes, or the original figure was an overestimation resulting from overlapping of subject areas in our profile. Of the 698 books tracked during those eight weeks, 61 percent had full LC copy and 32 percent were LC-CIP. This confirmed our assumption that a large majority would require minimal handling in the Cataloging Department. Our full LC copy rate was higher than a Michigan State University study reporting a 40 percent LC copy rate for approval plan books. Our LC-CIP rate was lower than their reported 51 percent rate (see Figure 2). The Michigan State University study figures resulted from a test of the PromptCat service on approval books supplied through Yankee Book Peddler.[5] University Library's approval plan is not as extensive in coverage as the Michigan State University Libraries plan, but we found our overall LC copy rate to be comparable. All of the CIP records in our study required updating of 300 fields (addition of pagination, illustration, and size). Other CIP records had incomplete 504 fields (lacking bibliography pagination), and a very few needed dates changed in call numbers and 260 fields. Other types of changes involved editing series to reflect local tracing practices.

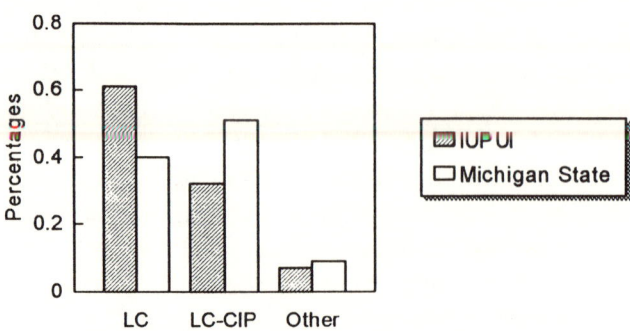

Figure 2. Source of Cataloging Copy

Only 6 percent of the books had member-contributed cataloging records and 1 percent had no records at the initial search. These were routed to a cataloging librarian. Member records required a variety of additional work. The majority (30) had full-level records which only required adjusting the cutter after the call number was verified. Of the member records, four required addition of LC subject headings and 15 required an LC call number to be assigned. Original cataloging was input into OCLC for only one book without copy. All others found not to have records in OCLC during the first search were researched after four weeks. Member-contributed records were found for all of these titles during the later search.

The editing required for approval plan books, including keying in the abbreviated invoice number for acquisitions on copy holdings statements, did not slow the pace of the copy catalogers. We calculated statistics for turnaround time based on actual working days, excluding weekends and holidays. Our statistics showed that approval plan books were cataloged and sent to the book processing area in less than one day. In fact, the March sample indicated that most books were cataloged in less than half a day. It was apparent that the Cataloging Department was meeting its goal of a quick turnaround time for approval plan books.

Final physical processing of approval plan books is handled in the Bindery/Book Prep area. Our statistics showed that it took almost three working days for a hardback book to be prepared for release to the stacks in the January sample. We were clearly not meeting our goal of processing approval plan books quickly. An investigation showed that a drop in the normal part-time help had occurred during the January sample. Bindery/Book Prep staff also prepare for shipment any books which require commercial binding. An increase of bindery shipments may have contributed to the delay in processing of approval plan books in January. When the March sample was taken, staffing was once again at normal levels and Bindery/Book Prep was releasing books to the Circulation Department for shelving in 1.35 working days. This confirmed our initial theory that even with the increased flow of books an acceptable turnaround time could be achieved with a few changes in normal procedures.

OCLC's PromptCat service which supplies cataloging records to participating libraries and adds holdings symbols to the OCLC database is a service we may consider in the future. At present, with book shipments at a workable level, and no threat of reduction of cataloging staff, we do not plan to take advantage of the service. The primary advantage of PromptCat, in our view, would be the receipt of OCLC records for use in our database, and the updating of holdings on OCLC without incurring searching and exporting charges. Presently, we see no real savings in time, since we would continue to review and edit any records submitted by the PromptCat service. CIP records would still be upgraded and access points checked. So far, our copy cataloging staff has not only kept up with the increase in approval plan books, but has undertaken the retrospective conversion of books cataloged prior to 1977 and not currently represented in our online catalog. There has been, however, an increase in non-print material orders. We are seeing a swell in orders for videos, CD-ROMs, and other media that are more complex to catalog and process, and require a higher level of expertise than the processing of approval plan books. If this trend continues, we may need to reevaluate our current stand and take advantage of PromptCat. It could free our copy catalogers from the relatively routine process of searching for and exporting approval plan book records and allow more time to deal with the influx of complex media materials.

CONCLUSION

The expanded approval plan at University Library has been successful so far in expending the budget increase within fiscal year deadlines. Evaluation of the plan is ongoing. Continual monitoring of the plan is necessary to ensure that items received fall within profiling criteria. The plan must continue to provide benefits to the library in terms of costs savings as well as an efficient and timely supply of scholarly publications. It is also crucial to keep abreast of services like PromptCat to determine whether they can provide substantial savings in time and costs. The continued use of internal studies should help us decide which services, if any, may provide the greatest benefits to University Library and the clientele it serves.

NOTES AND REFERENCES

1. Joseph W. Barker, "Vendor Studies Redux: Evaluating the Approval Plan Option from Within," *Library Acquisitions: Practice and Theory* 13 (1989): 134.

2. Vicki Grahame, "Approval Plan Processing: Integrating Acquisitions and Cataloging," *Technical Services Quarterly* 10(1,1992): 35.
3. Susan M. Neumeister and Judith Hopkins, "Copy Cataloging in an Acquisitions Department," *Acquisitions Librarian* 12(1994): 81-94.
4. Grahame, p. 37.
5. Colleen F. Hyslop, "Using PromptCat to Eliminate Work: MSU's Experience," *Library Acquisitions: Practice and Theory* 19(3,1995): 360.

DUE DATE

ILL # 1768707
Due 5/1/98

MAY 1 2 1998

ILL # 320062
Due 7/6/98

JUL 0 8 1998